Protecting Intellectual
Freedom and Privacy
in Your School Library

Protecting Intellectual Freedom and Privacy in Your School Library

Helen R. Adams

SLM Hot Topics

LIBRARIES UNLIMITED

AN IMPRINT OF ABC-CLIO, LLC
Santa Barbara, California • Denver, Colorado • Oxford, England

ALSO BY HELEN R. ADAMS

School Media Policy Development: A Practical Process for Small Districts (Libraries Unlimited, 1986).

Privacy in the 21st Century: Issues for Public School, and Academic Libraries (co-authored with Robert F. Bocher, Carol A. Gordon, and Elizabeth Barry-Kessler, Libraries Unlimited, 2005).

Ensuring Intellectual Freedom and Access to Information in the School Library Media Program (Libraries Unlimited, 2008).

Copyright 2013 by ABC-CLIO, LLC

Library of Congress Cataloging-in-Publication Data

Adams, Helen R., 1943–
    Protecting intellectual freedom and privacy in your school library / Helen R. Adams.
        pages cm. — (SLM hot topics)
    Includes bibliographical references and index.
    ISBN 978-1-61069-138-3 (pbk.) — ISBN 978-1-61069-139-0 (ebook)
    1. School libraries—Censorship—United States.   2. School libraries—Law and legislation—United States.
3. Intellectual freedom—United States.   4. Privacy, Right of—United States.   I. Title.
    Z675.S3A2195 2013
    025.2'13—dc23   2012049687

ISBN: 978-1-61069-138-3
EISBN: 978-1-61069-139-0

17 16 15 14 13   1 2 3 4 5

This book is also available on the World Wide Web as an eBook.
Visit www.abc-clio.com for details.

Libraries Unlimited
An Imprint of ABC-CLIO, LLC

ABC-CLIO, LLC
130 Cremona Drive, P.O. Box 1911
Santa Barbara, California 93116-1911

This book is printed on acid-free paper ∞
Manufactured in the United States of America

Copyright Acknowledgments

Figure 1 (Chapter 9). Originally published: "Solo Librarians and Intellectual Freedom: Perspectives from the Field." *Knowledge Quest,* XXXX (2) (December 2011): 34. Reprinted with permission from the American Association of School Librarians.

To my husband Ed, who has always supported my writing and to Jake, the German shepherd, who faithfully stayed with me throughout long hours of research and writing.

To the Wisconsin and Minnesota Intellectual Freedom leaders who inspired me: Dr. Dianne McAfee Hopkins, Ginny Moore Kruse, Megan Schliesman, and Dr. Frances Beck McDonald.

To all school librarians who protect minors' First Amendment right to receive information in libraries and keep their information-seeking and library records confidential.

Contents

Preface

This book is comprised of a collection of "quick read" essays on intellectual freedom and privacy. They were published, with one exception, as "IF Matters: Intellectual Freedom @ your library®" or "Privacy Matters" columns in *School Library Media Activities Monthly* (renamed *School Library Monthly*) between September 2006 and September/October 2012. The topics concentrate on how intellectual freedom, privacy, and access (the core values of the library profession) translate into everyday practice for school librarians. The content incorporates information on relevant state and federal laws, the impact of the First Amendment on minors' freedom of speech rights, and references to the American Library Association (ALA) intellectual freedom documents such as the *Library Bill of Rights* and its interpretations and the *Code of Ethics*.

The readings are arranged into nine chapters, covering broad topics such as serving students with special needs, privacy and confidentiality in the context of a school library, challenges to school library materials, and intellectual freedom online. Each chapter's brief introduction is followed by the reprinted columns. Sidebars are used liberally throughout the columns to add information and resources acquired since the columns were originally published. For example, the American Association of School Librarians (AASL) used the terms "school library media specialist," "school library media center," and "school library media program" until 2010, when the AASL Board of Directors officially changed the terminology to "school librarian," "school library," and "school library program," respectively. All online reference citations were rechecked before publication in 2013 and the latest date of accessibility noted. The chapters end with a summary of key ideas, annotated resources for the reader's intellectual freedom toolkit, and thought-provoking discussion questions. These special features make it an ideal book for use by pre-service students in graduate and undergraduate library and information studies programs.

Chapter 1 defines intellectual freedom and the role of the school librarian as its guardian through the lens of core American Library Association (ALA) documents: the *Library Bill of Rights* (and its more than twenty interpretations) and the *Code of Ethics of the American Library Association*.

Chapter 2 illustrates the types of issues school librarians face when applying intellectual freedom principles to common situations encountered in daily work. Dilemmas range from access to library resources for students with overdue or lost library materials to the impact of reading management programs on students' reading choices to the confidentiality of students' circulation records.

Chapter 3 explores one of the top fears of school librarians: challenges to school library resources. The information centers on formal challenges to library resources, where to find support when a challenge occurs, and the materials selection policy as a document that provides guidance during selection and/or reconsideration of a library resource. The

"Challenge-Proofing Your School Library Checklist" will assist readers in gauging their library's readiness for a challenge before it occurs.

Chapter 4 focuses on intellectual freedom online. Integral to the discussion is the effect of filters on students' First Amendment right to receive information and to learn to evaluate information from diverse points of view. Banned Websites Awareness Day, AASL's response to overly restrictive filtering in many schools, is spotlighted with ideas for observing the day during Banned Books Week. An argument is made for updating acceptable use policies frequently, and a consultant for a state school board association provides recommendations. Finally, a police officer who specializes in cybersafety for youth contributes examples of how teens jeopardize their privacy in social networking sites.

Chapter 5 defines broadly those students considered to have "special needs" as library users. The definition includes students with physical, cognitive, and learning disabilities; those with chronic illnesses and disorders; English language learners; homeless students; and incarcerated and detained youth. All students (regardless of personal handicaps) have the right to access information and use services in a school library, and the readings provide resources and strategies for serving those student populations.

Chapter 6 covers multiple aspects of privacy in a school library from discussing whether age makes a difference in extending privacy to creating a privacy policy to evaluating a library's privacy level by completing the "School Library Program Privacy Checklist."

Chapter 7 highlights the "intellectual freedom community," comprised of informal and formal groups or organizations that advocate for intellectual freedom, free expression, and privacy for library users of all ages, while resisting censorship. The organizations include, but are not limited to, state library associations; national American professional, trade, and advocacy organizations represented by the American Library Association, the Freedom to Read Foundation, the Association of American Publishers, and the American Civil Liberties Union (to name a few); and international organizations such as the International Federation of Library Associations and Institutions.

Chapter 8 redirects the traditional advocacy campaign for the school library program into an advocacy plan to promote and protect students' intellectual freedom. The columns provide specific strategies for reaching out to and educating principals, teachers, students, and parents about students' First Amendment rights to receive information as well as school library and state and federal privacy laws. The chapter culminates in a school-year intellectual freedom advocacy calendar, celebrating such national events as Banned Books Week, Banned Websites Awareness Day, Constitution Day and Citizenship Day, Bill of Rights Day, School Library Month, and Choose Privacy Week.

Chapter 9 considers the future of intellectual freedom in school libraries, with special concern for the nationwide loss of full-time school library professional positions. It also reflects on whether a "solo librarian," responsible for the entire K–12 school library program in multiple schools, can effectively advocate for and defend the intellectual freedom and privacy principles of the profession. How much can one person accomplish?

The Appendices include the text of the *Library Bill of Rights* and the *Code of Ethics of the American Library Association* (Appendix A) and an annotated list of sixteen pro–First Amendment and privacy organizations with contact information (Appendix B).

Although state and federal laws are referenced throughout, the book does not provide legal advice. Instead, its purpose is to educate and raise the consciousness of school librarians and other educators about the impact of the First Amendment and federal and state laws on minors using school libraries. Readers with specific legal questions about local situations should consult their institution's legal counsel.

Helen R. Adams
Readfield, Wisconsin

Acknowledgments

Undertaking to write a book is a lengthy and thought-intensive process that includes support from many persons and organizations. For their expertise and assistance, I acknowledge the following for their contributions to this book:

- School librarians and technology directors who shared their stories, experiences, and ideas for ensuring intellectual freedom and protecting privacy of their students

- Barbara Jones, director of the American Library Association Office for Intellectual Freedom, and OIF staff: Deborah Caldwell-Stone, Angela Maycock, Nanette Perez, and Jonathan Kelley who keep the "intellectual freedom lights on" across the United States

- The ALA Office for Intellectual Freedom and the American Association of School Librarians for granting permission to quote from intellectual freedom and privacy policy statements and "Standards for the 21st-Century Learners"

- Deborah Levitov, *School Library Monthly* managing editor

- Sharon Coatney, Libraries Unlimited acquisitions editor

- Emma Bailey, Senior Production Coordinator at ABC-CLIO

- Carol Bifulco and team at BookComp, Inc.

- Erin Larson, Landmark Editorial Services

Chapter 1

What is Intellectual Freedom?

Including the Columns

"What is Intellectual Freedom?"

"The *Library Bill of Rights* and Intellectual Freedom"

"The 'Ever Green' Interpretations of the *Library Bill of Rights*"

"The *Code of Ethics* and Intellectual Freedom"

"*The Intellectual Freedom Manual*: A Guide to Protecting Minors' Rights in a School Library"

Chapter 1

What is Intellectual Freedom?

INTRODUCTION

Intellectual freedom is one of the basic tenets of the library profession, but the term is not common in everyday conversation, nor is it easy to explain. This chapter is devoted to defining intellectual freedom and highlighting some of the foundational documents set forth by the American Library Association (ALA) to support this core value—the *Code of Ethics of the American Library Association*, the *Library Bill of Rights*, and the over twenty interpretations of the *Library Bill of Rights*. This chapter includes five previously published columns from *School Library Media Activities Monthly* (later renamed *School Library Monthly*), all focused on intellectual freedom and including examples of how this concept is demonstrated in a school library. For a unique introduction to the topic, consider the concept of intellectual freedom from another perspective: a recipe.

A Recipe for Intellectual Freedom

The recipe for intellectual freedom in a school library appears deceptively simple. While lengthy, the list of ingredients is straightforward, and the instructions are similar to those offered by an experienced cook or baker—add "a pinch of this" and "stir until the mixture reaches the right consistency." As the experienced librarian knows, however, simply having the proper ingredients is not enough: creating intellectual freedom requires just the right mysterious interaction among the elements. The resulting product—students' free access to library resources and services—is a highly variable commodity that can take from days to months to years to be completed and enjoyed.

Perhaps surprisingly, the concept of intellectual freedom and its guiding principles evolved over time. To investigate the fascinating history of how intellectual freedom became one of the library profession's core values, read "ALA and Intellectual Freedom: A Historical Overview" in the eighth edition of the *Intellectual Freedom Manual* published by ALA Editions in 2010.

Intellectual Freedom

Ingredients:

- School librarian
- Library support staff and volunteers
- Students
- Teachers
- Principal
- Parents
- Community members
- School library
- Diverse collection of resources in all formats
- Access to online resources
- Library policies
- Staff development
- Integrated information and digital literacy instruction
- First Amendment free speech right
- First Amendment case law
- The American Library Association
- *The Library Bill of Rights*
- *The Code of Ethics of the ALA*
- *The Freedom to Read* statement
- Student library privacy
- State confidentiality of library records laws
- Family Educational Rights & Privacy Act (FERPA)
- AASL's "Position Statement on the Confidentiality of Library Records"

Instructions:

1. Assemble the following in a school: knowledgeable school librarian, eager students, helpful teachers, and proactive principal.
2. Add the First Amendment free speech right and case law supporting minors' right to receive information in a school library.
3. Fold in the ALA's *Library Bill of Rights* and its interpretations, the *Code of Ethics*, and the *Freedom to Read* statement.
4. Combine state confidentiality of library records laws, FERPA, and AASL's "Position Statement on the Confidentiality of Library Records" to protect student privacy.
5. Create and blend in library policies.
6. Add a diverse collection of resources in all formats to the school library.
7. Stir in Internet access to online resources.
8. Add bite-sized pieces of staff development as needed.
9. Blend student instruction about censorship and First Amendment free speech rights.
10. Mix in parents and community members. Stir to desired positive climate.
11. Pour into the school community, and sprinkle with enthusiasm.
12. Cut into individual servings.

Note: Recipe makes unlimited servings of freedom to read for minors using school libraries.

IF Matters: Intellectual Freedom @ your library®

What is Intellectual Freedom?

By Helen R. Adams

Originally published in the IF Matters: Intellectual Freedom @ your library® column, *School Library Media Activities Monthly*, XXIV (1) (September 2007): 32.

According to the American Library Association (ALA), "Intellectual freedom is the right of every individual to both seek and receive information from all points of view without restriction" (ALA http://www.ala.org/Template.cfm?Section=basics&Template=/ContentManagement/Content Display.cfm&ContentID=164089). Intellectual freedom is one of the core beliefs of librarians and includes access to information, First Amendment liberties, and the right to privacy when using library facilities, resources, and services.

> **Changing School Library Terms**
>
> In 2010, the American Association of School Librarians (AASL) Board of Directors voted to change its official terminology from "school library media specialist," "school library media center," and "school library media program" to "school librarian," "school library," and "school library program" respectively. The change has not been universally accepted by practitioners, however, who continue to refer to themselves with a range of terms, including the title "teacher librarian." "Learning commons" is also a recent term for describing a school library (American Association of School Librarians. 2010. "AASL votes to adopt the professional title school librarian." January 16, 2010. http://www.ala.org/news/news/pressreleases2010/january 2010/adopt_aasl [accessed January 15, 2013]).

School library media specialists take responsibility for promoting and maintaining students' intellectual freedom seriously. They are the schools' resident intellectual freedom experts—the persons with the most knowledge about the strong link between students' free speech rights under the First Amendment and unrestricted patron use of the school library's print collection, electronic resources, and the Internet.

Intellectual freedom is not a fuzzy concept but rather has its basis in the First Amendment. The First Amendment states that "Congress shall make no law respecting an establishment of religion, or prohibiting the free exercise thereof, or *abridging the freedom of speech*, or of the press, or the right of the people peaceably to assemble, and to petition the government for a redress of grievances" (U.S. Bill of Rights). In the First Amendment, freedom of speech refers to more than oral communication and has been interpreted as including a minor's right to read and receive information and ideas.

In addition to First Amendment protections, the concept of intellectual freedom has been strengthened through *case law* or "law based on judicial decision and precedent rather than on statutes" (Answers.com). The lawsuit *Counts v. Cedarville School District* (2003) is an example of a legal battle that resulted in case law. In this lawsuit, the school board voted to limit access to the *Harry Potter* books in the school library collection because it perceived that the books encouraged disobedience and included characters engaging in witchcraft and the occult. The board required students to have signed permission slips from their parents or guardians before checking out the books. The Court reversed the board's decision, ruling that the written permission requirement infringed upon students' First Amendment right to receive information (ALA http://www.ala.org/offices/oif/firstamendment/courtcases/courtcases). As a result, the *Harry Potter* books were returned to unrestricted circulation in the school library. The American Library Association Office for Intellectual Freedom website has detailed information on other First Amendment–related court cases involving the right to read and minors' First Amendment rights (http://www.ala.org/offices/oif/firstamendment/courtcases/courtcases).

Knowing the legal basis for intellectual freedom and its definition are not enough. What does intellectual freedom *really mean* in a school library? The spirit of intellectual freedom is present when students may:

- exercise their First Amendment right to receive ideas and information without restriction,
- use resources freely without undue scrutiny,
- ask reference questions without being questioned as to why the information is needed,
- select books to read without being forced to choose only those titles that match their reading levels,
- borrow materials without having their use of library resources divulged,
- request interlibrary loan services to obtain information not available within the local collection, and
- seek information using the Internet without filtering software blocking educationally useful websites.

Students' intellectual freedom is also greatly affected by the practice of school library media specialists. Intellectual freedom exists when school library media specialists:

- select materials based on their district's collection development policy and do not allow their own personal biases, beliefs, or fears to restrict material selection,
- encourage students to read books of interest to them and provide reader guidance as needed,
- refrain from shelving controversial titles separately from the rest of the collection,
- defend student and staff access to Internet information by advocating for the least restrictive level of filtering,
- collaborate with teachers to instruct students about evaluation of information on websites and how to be responsible searchers,
- ensure materials, services, and facilities are accessible for students with special needs,
- treat those who question the appropriateness of library materials respectfully and assist with the reconsideration process,
- serve as an advisor to the principal during a challenge,
- provide information to the Reconsideration Committee about the challenged resource,
- protect the confidentiality of student library records,
- refrain from imposing economic barriers such as fines and lost/damaged book fees,
- inform the entire school community proactively about minors' rights under the law and the importance of having a wide range of materials on various topics with varied points of view represented in the collection, and
- demonstrate support for intellectual freedom in schools and school libraries daily.

The Freedom to Read, a joint statement by the ALA and the Association of American Publishers proclaims, "The freedom to read is essential to our democracy" (ALA 2004). While library media specialists may not consider themselves "defenders of democracy," they frequently act in that capacity when they protect minors' rights to read and receive information under the First Amendment and case law. Daily actions and advocacy by library media specialists affect youthful patrons' intellectual freedom and have far-reaching implications in their lives. School librarians must speak up—and speak out—for intellectual freedom!

REFERENCES

American Library Association. 2004. *The Freedom to Read Statement.* http://www.ala.org/advocacy/ intfreedom/statementspols/freedomreadstatement (accessed January 15, 2013).

American Library Association. Office for Intellectual Freedom. "Intellectual Freedom and Censorship Q & A." http://www.ala.org/Template.cfm?Section=basics&Template=/Content Management/ContentDisplay.cfm&ContentID=164089 (accessed January 15, 2013).

American Library Association. Office for Intellectual Freedom. "Notable First Amendment Court Cases." http://www.ala.org/offices/oif/firstamendment/courtcases/courtcases (accessed January 15, 2013).

Answers.com. http://www.answers.com/topic/case-law (accessed January 15, 2013).

U.S. Bill of Rights. 1791. http://www.law.cornell.edu/constitution/billofrights (accessed January 15, 2013).

IF Matters: Intellectual Freedom @ your library®

The *Library Bill of Rights* and Intellectual Freedom

By Helen R. Adams

Originally published in the IF Matters: Intellectual Freedom @ your library® column, *School Library Media Activities Monthly*, XXIV (5) (January 2008): 32.

Most professional organizations have significant documents that frame the guiding principles for members. For example, the American Library Association (ALA) has three such documents: the *Library Bill of Rights*, the *Code of Ethics*, and the *Freedom to Read*. This column will focus on the *Library Bill of Rights*.

Next to the First Amendment, the most important document for school library media specialists is ALA's *Library Bill of Rights*. It was originally written by a public librarian from Iowa in 1938 and was adopted by ALA's Council (its elected governing body) in 1939. Its seven articles make a strong case for intellectual freedom in *all* libraries (ALA *Intellectual Freedom Manual* 2006, 57). It offers special protections to minors using libraries when it affirms in Article V, "A person's right to use a library should not be denied or abridged because of origin, *age*, background, or views" (ALA *Intellectual Freedom Manual* 2006, 55). The word "age" was added in 1967 and reaffirmed in 1996 to ensure the rights of children and young adults while using libraries and their collections (ALA Intellectual Freedom Manual 2006, 65).

> **The *Library Bill of Rights***
>
> A copy of the *Library Bill of Rights* is reprinted in Appendix A.

The *Library Bill of Rights* offers much guidance to school library professionals. For example, Article II directs library staff to provide resources and access to information representing diverse points of view (ALA *Intellectual Freedom Manual* 2006, 55). For school library professionals this means selecting materials not only to support the curriculum but also to meet the recreational interests of student patrons. Article III directs librarians to resist censorship (ALA *Intellectual Freedom Manual* 2006, 55). This statement is particularly relevant to school library media specialists since the majority of challenges reported to the ALA Office for Intellectual Freedom occur in schools and school libraries.

Beyond the original document, there are currently eighteen interpretations attached to the *Library Bill of Rights*, most of which hold concepts related to school libraries. Two of the interpretations, "Access to Resources and Services in the School Library Media Program: An Interpretation of the Library Bill of Rights" and "Free Access to Libraries for Minors: An Interpretation of the Library Bill of Rights," express clearly the responsibilities of school library media specialists in guarding and maintaining students' intellectual freedom. For example, in "Free Access . . . ," the interpretation lists examples of age-based access limitations frequently imposed in school libraries. These include:

- restricting access to selected content based on the age or grade level of the student,
- requiring written permission from a parent to use certain resources because of a student's age or grade level, and
- refusing to grant interlibrary loan services based on age or grade level (ALA *Intellectual Freedom Manual* 2006, 162–163).

The School Library Bill of Rights

Occasionally, a school librarian will find reference to the *School Library Bill of Rights*. This statement was approved by AASL in 1955 but was withdrawn in 1976. The similarity of the title and the redundancy of content with the ALA *Library Bill of Rights* was the rationale for retiring the AASL document. Because of the increasing number of challenges to materials in school libraries in the 1980s, AASL and the ALA Intellectual Freedom Committee created "Access to Resources and Services in the School Library Media Program: An Interpretation of the Library Bill of Rights" (http://ifmanual.org/accesslmp), and it was approved by the ALA Council in 1986. There have been several revisions, the latest in 2008. The interpretation focuses on the responsibility of the school librarian to ensure that collections reflect a pluralistic society with diverse points of view represented (American Library Association. 2008. Office for Intellectual Freedom. *Intellectual Freedom Manual*. 8th ed. Chicago, Illinois: American Library Association: 94–96).

The *Library Bill of Rights* as a Living Document

Since this column was published, new interpretations of the *Library Bill of Rights* have been created. There are now twenty-two interpretations, with the most recent additions being "Services to Persons with Disabilities" (January 2009), "Minors and Internet Interactivity" (July 2009), "Importance of Intellectual Freedom to Education" (July 2009), and "Prisoners' Right to Read" (June 2010).

These practices are in direct conflict with Article V of the *Library Bill of Right*'s assertion that library users' rights should not be abridged based on *age*.

Another interpretation, "Economic Barriers to Information Access: An Interpretation of the Library Bill of Rights," is also particularly pertinent because it cautions school library media specialists against placing economic barriers such as fines and fees between school library users and access to information (ALA *Intellectual Freedom Manual* 2006, 128). Overdue and lost books are a fact of life in school libraries, and there are children from low-income families who *cannot* pay fines or replacement costs for lost items. School library professionals must be creative in finding ways to instill responsibility while at the same time not barring access to books and other materials for their users. These strategies could include:

- Arranging for a child to pay for a lost item on the "installment" plan, paying a little bit each week or month.
- Checking if a family can donate another paperback or hardcover book in reasonable condition if they are unable to reimburse for a lost item.
- Asking the child to help in the library during recess if donating a replacement item is not an option. There are always tasks to be done such as dusting shelves, straightening books, and cleaning library tables.

While there are currently eighteen interpretations, new ones are added as the need arises. For example, "Privacy: An Interpretation of the Library Bill of Rights," was added in 2002. Although the topic had been under discussion for some time, the passage of the USA PATRIOT Act and concerns for privacy of library records spurred its completion (ALA *Intellectual Freedom Manual* 2006, 196).

The ALA Intellectual Freedom Committee is currently beginning a review of all ALA documents related to intellectual freedom in anticipation of the publication of the eighth edition of the *Intellectual Freedom Manual* in two years. At its most recent meetings, the committee discussed possible topics for additional interpretations including statements relating to minors' social networking and the impact of computerized reading programs on students' reading choices. Because of their importance, these interpretations take much thought, many drafts, and the input of numerous individuals and groups before they are adopted.

> **Update on the *Intellectual Freedom Manual***
>
> The eighth edition of the *Intellectual Freedom Manual* was published in 2010. In January 2012, the ALA Intellectual Freedom Committee began discussing the lengthy process of reviewing all policies, *Library Bill of Rights* interpretations, and all statements relating to intellectual freedom in anticipation of the next edition of the manual due in 2014.

The full text of the *Library Bill of Rights* and its current eighteen interpretations can be found on the ALA Office for Intellectual Freedom website (http://www.ala.org/advocacy/intfreedom/librarybill). These statements are crucial for protecting students' intellectual freedom and access to information.

REFERENCE

American Library Association. 2006. Office for Intellectual Freedom. *Intellectual Freedom Manual.* 7th ed. Chicago, Illinois: American Library Association.

IF Matters: Intellectual Freedom @ your library®

The "Ever Green" Interpretations of the *Library Bill of Rights*

By Helen R. Adams

Originally published in the IF Matters: Intellectual Freedom @ your library® column, *School Library Monthly*, XXVI (6) (February 2010): 48–49.

The American Library Association's (ALA) *Library Bill of Rights* is important to school librarians because it provides the philosophical structure for intellectual freedom in school libraries and asserts the rights of minors. Article V emphatically states that the right of an individual cannot be abridged because of *age*. A child's or young adult's age should not affect his or her right to use library materials (ALA 1996).

The *Library Bill of Rights* and Its Interpretations

> **Prisoners' Right to Read: A New Interpretation**
>
> The "Prisoners' Right to Read: An Interpretation of the Library Bill of Rights," approved by the ALA Council in July 2010, is the *twenty-second* interpretation. It lays out the principles of library services to those in prisons, juvenile facilities, immigration detention centers, and other places of confinement (American Library Association. 2010. "Prisoner's Right to Read: An Interpretation of the Library Bill of Rights." http://www.ifmanual.org/prisoners [accessed January 15, 2013]).

There are currently twenty-one "interpretations" of the *Library Bill of Rights,* and they provide direction to school librarians while protecting minors' First Amendment rights in day-to-day practice. Periodically interpretations have been added or revised to satisfy emerging needs and to keep all current statements fresh and green. Anticipating the publication of the next edition of the *Intellectual Freedom Manual* in spring 2010, the ALA Intellectual Freedom Committee reviewed all of the association's intellectual freedom policies and documents including the *Library Bill of Rights* and its interpretations. The interpretations are listed alphabetically on the ALA Office for Intellectual Freedom website (http://www.ala.org/advocacy/intfreedom/librarybill/interpretations).

Nearly every interpretation of the *Library Bill of Rights* is relevant to school libraries. A sampling of the recently revised or newly created interpretations includes:

- "Access to Resources and Services in the School Library Media Program: An Interpretation of the Library Bill of Rights" (revised July 2, 2008)
- "Free Access to Libraries for Minors: An Interpretation of the Library Bill of Rights" (revised July 2, 2008)
- "Access to Library Resources and Services Regardless of Sex, Gender Identity, or Sexual Orientation: An Interpretation of the Library Bill of Rights" (revised July 2, 2008)

- "Diversity in Collection Development: An Interpretation of the Library Bill of Rights" (revised July 2, 2008)
- "Restricted Access to Library Materials: An Interpretation of the Library Bill of Rights" (revised January 28, 2009)
- "Minors and Internet Interactivity: An Interpretation of the Library Bill of Rights" (new, July 15, 2009)
- "Services to Persons with Disabilities: An Interpretation of the Library Bill of Rights" (new, January 28, 2009)

Minors and Internet Interactivity: An Interpretation of the Library Bill of Rights

The new "Minors and Internet Interactivity: An Interpretation of the Library Bill of Rights" will support school librarians who are encouraging the use of Web 2.0 tools in their schools. The first paragraph emphasizes that minors have First Amendment rights online:

> The rights of minors to retrieve, interact with, and create information posted on the Internet in schools and libraries are extensions of their First Amendment rights. (ALA 2009a)

With carefully crafted rationale, the interpretation acknowledges that students will use interactive Web tools for academic purposes, as well as for personal creative expression and social interaction. It acknowledges that there are two competing issues when minors use social technologies: the right to free expression and the concern for students' privacy. The interpretation speaks to the fact that filtering social network sites is not a solution; instead, it is more effective when teachers and librarians educate students to be safe and ethical online. The interpretation further emphasizes that parents have a responsibility to monitor their children's activities online as they do in the physical world (ALA 2009a).

Services to Persons with Disabilities: An Interpretation of the Library Bill of Rights

Although "Services to Persons with Disabilities: An Interpretation of the Library Bill of Rights" does not single out school libraries by name, school library professionals have both a legal and an ethical responsibility to provide access to the facilities, resources, and services in the library media program for students with physical, cognitive, and learning disabilities, as well as chronic illnesses and disorders. The new interpretation states:

> The First Amendment to the U.S. Constitution mandates the right of all persons to free expression and the corollary right to receive the constitutionally protected expression of others. A person's right to use the library should not be denied or abridged because of *disabilities* [emphasis added]. The library has the responsibility to provide materials "for the interest, information, and enlightenment of *all people of the community the library serves*" [emphasis added]. (ALA 2009c)

Ideas on how to serve students with disabilities can be found in Chapter 5 of this book in the column titled, "Access for Students with Disabilities."

Restricted Access to Library Materials:
An Interpretation of the Library Bill of Rights

Although not new, this interpretation was revised substantially to include support for school librarians facing pressure to restrict students' free access to library materials and reorganization of their collections in a non-standard manner due to the implementation of reading management programs. The modified text states:

> In some libraries, access is restricted based on computerized reading management programs that assign reading levels to books and/or users and limit choice to those materials on the program's reading list. . . . Organizing collections by reading management program level, ability, grade, or age level is another example of restricted access. (2009b)

"AASL Position Statement on Labeling Books by Reading Levels"

In 2011, the AASL Board of Directors approved a position statement related to the practice of labeling spines of books with "book levels" corresponding to reading management programs. The statement focuses on three issues: how using spine labels that reveal book levels influences students browsing behavior, how visible book levels on spines threaten students' privacy, and how non-standard shelving practices confuse students' learning to locate items in other libraries, such as a public library. The document is located with other AASL position statements on the AASL website (American Association of School Librarians. 2011. "AASL Position Statement on Labeling Books by Reading Levels." http://www.ala.org/aasl/aaslissues/positionstatements/labeling/ [accessed January 15, 2013]).

The improper implementation of computerized reading programs can seriously impede students' First Amendment right to read freely in a school library and should be resisted vigorously. The interpretation also addresses overly restrictive filtering and its potential for limiting students' access to constitutionally protected information.

How Can School Librarians Use the *Library Bill of Rights* Interpretations?

To protect students' access to information and privacy in a school library, school librarians can use the *Library Bill of Rights* interpretations to:

- Clarify and develop a deeper understanding of intellectual freedom principles for themselves,
- Provide support in written board approved library policies, and
- Explain rationale for library policies to administrators, colleagues, students, and parents.

By using and referring to the *Library Bill of Rights* and its interpretations, the principles of intellectual freedom remain ever green and relevant, positively affecting the lives of students using school libraries.

REFERENCES

American Library Association. 1996. *Library Bill of Rights*, Article V. http://www.ala.org/ala/issuesadvocacy/intfreedom/librarybill/index.cfm (accessed January 15, 2013).

American Library Association. 2009a. "Minors and Internet Interactivity: An Interpretation of the Library Bill of Rights." http://www.ala.org/advocacy/intfreedom/librarybill/interpretations/minorsinternetinteractivity (accessed January 15, 2013).

American Library Association. 2009b. "Restricted Access to Library Materials: An Interpretation of the Library Bill of Rights." http://www.ala.org/advocacy/intfreedom/librarybill/interpretations/restrictedaccess (accessed January 15, 2013).

American Library Association. 2009c. "Services to Persons with Disabilities: An Interpretation of the Library Bill of Rights." http://www.ala.org/advocacy/intfreedom/librarybill/interpretations/servicespeopledisabilities (accessed January 15, 2013).

IF Matters: Intellectual Freedom @ your library®

The *Code of Ethics* and Intellectual Freedom

By Helen R. Adams

Originally published in the IF Matters: Intellectual Freedom @ your library® column, *School Library Media Activities Monthly*, XXIV (9) (May 2008): 31.

Three powerful documents from the American Library Association (ALA)—the *Library Bill of Rights*, the *Code of Ethics for the American Library Association*, and the *Freedom to Read* statement—are important to school library media specialists. This column will focus on the *Code of Ethics* which will be 70 years old in 2009. "Ethics" are defined as "a system of principles governing morality and acceptable conduct" (The Free Dictionary). They may be personal to an individual or may be standards governing the behavior of an entire group or profession.

The *Code of Ethics of the American Library Association* provides guidance to clarify decision-making, especially in situations that are complex or uncomfortable. For example, perhaps a principal or school administrator is pressuring to have a book removed without using the district's reconsideration process. Maybe a teacher is asking for a list of books checked out by a specific student. Or a library media specialist may be struggling with his or her own biases when it comes to collecting books on a certain subject such as homosexuality and is tempted with self-censorship. In the *Code of Ethics*, articles such as: "We uphold the principles of intellectual freedom and resist all efforts to censor library resources" (Article II), "We protect each library user's right to privacy and confidentiality with respect to information sought or received and resources consulted, borrowed, acquired or transmitted" (Article III), and "We distinguish between our personal convictions and professional duties and do not allow our personal beliefs to interfere. . . ." (Article VII) offer direction and provide a moral framework that school library media specialists may use in their daily practice (http://www.ala.org/advocacy/proethics/codeofethics/code ethics). Refer to Appendix A for the full text of the *Code of Ethics of the American Library Association*.

In another ethics-related situation, school library professionals may find themselves facing a dilemma when compelled to work with filters required by law, while at the same time wanting to protect students' First Amendment right to receive information via the Internet. Whether the decisions to filter more heavily are made out of fear of online predators, parent complaints, the threat of legal action, or the response to student actions, filtering is an ethical issue for library media specialists when the *Code* emphasizes that all librarians have a responsibility to assure access to information from many perspectives is available to library users (ALA 2008).

Another ethics consideration for school library professionals can be found in Article I of ALA's *Code of Ethics*. This article directs school library professionals to provide the highest level of service and equitable access to *all* patrons; however, at times library media specialists' practice or district policy may be in direct conflict with the *Code* when:

- kindergarten students are not permitted to borrow books for fear they will lose or damage the library materials,

- students are restricted in the number of books that can be borrowed at one time or in their frequency of visits to the library media center,
- students with overdue book fines and outstanding replacement book fees are barred from borrowing library resources, and
- a segregated collection for works considered controversial is maintained, and written permission is required from a parent or guardian to check out those books.

Every one of the above practices threatens students' access to library resources. Articles I, II, III, and VII of the *Code of Ethics* protect library users *access* to resources in a school library media center (ALA 2008). In this case, the term "access" is synonymous with intellectual freedom.

The *Code of Ethics* is crucial for protecting students' intellectual freedom, and library media specialists should be aware of the many ways in which it may be applied in their practice. The actions of *every* school library media specialist have far-reaching effects on students' lives, and the *Code of Ethics* helps library professionals know where to "draw the line."

Other useful resources in the area of ethics include the following:

- Johnson, Doug. December 2004. "Lessons School Librarians Teach Others: Class the Subject is Integrity." *American Libraries*. http://www.ala.org/advocacy/sites/ala.org.advocacy/files/content/intfreedom/iftoolkits/ifmanual/lessonsschoollibrariansteachothers.pdf.
- Kidder, Rushworth M. 1995. *How Good People Make Tough Choices: Resolving the Dilemmas of Ethical Living*. Fireside (Simon & Schuster).
- Simpson, Carol, ed. 2003. *Ethics in School Librarianship: A Reader*. Linworth Publishing.

> **Additional Resources on Ethics in the Library Profession**
>
> - American Association of School Librarians. 2009. *School Library Media Programs in Action: Civic Engagement, Social Justice, and Equity*. Chicago: AASL.
>
>   Compiled from articles first published in AASL's journal *Knowledge Quest*, an underlying theme of ethics and librarians' impact on their students' educational experiences runs throughout the volume.
>
> - Elizabeth A. Buchanan and Kathrine A. Henderson. 2008. *Case Studies in Library and Information Science Ethics*. Jefferson, North Carolina: McFarland.
>
>   This book includes 125 case studies that take ethical principles and combine them with real-life library scenarios to explore ethical issues involving intellectual freedom, privacy, intellectual property, and professional ethics.

REFERENCES

American Library Association. 2008. *Code of Ethics of the American Library Association*. http://www.ala.org/advocacy/proethics/codeofethics/codeethics (accessed January 15, 2013).

The Free Dictionary. http://www.thefreedictionary.com/ethics/ (accessed January 15, 2013).

IF Matters: Intellectual Freedom @ your library®

The Intellectual Freedom Manual: A Guide to Protecting Minors' Rights in a School Library

By Helen R. Adams

Originally published in the IF Matters: Intellectual Freedom @ your library® column, *School Library Monthly*, XXVII (5) (February 2011): 52–53.

> *The Intellectual Freedom Manual*, 8th edition, is dedicated to Judith Krug (1940–2009), the first Director of the ALA Office for Intellectual Freedom and the creator of the original *Intellectual Freedom Manual*.

Where do librarians turn when they need in-depth information about intellectual freedom? For more than thirty-five years, the answer has been the American Library Association's *Intellectual Freedom Manual*. The eighth edition, published in 2010, is, however, quite a contrast to the first edition of the manual which was published in a loose-leaf format in 1974. Within four years, a bound version was published with revised editions occurring thereafter (ALA 2010, xii).

What's in the New Manual?

For many in the profession, *The Intellectual Freedom Manual* is a "bible" that combines a strong defense of library users' rights with philosophical and ethical guidelines for school, academic, and public librarians. Through successive editions, it has reflected the changing issues in the intellectual freedom spectrum, and the eighth edition continues that tradition. Candace Morgan, editor, views four of the current top issues as: 1) the specific right of minors to access library resources in all formats including print, digital, and online information, 2) Internet access with the accompanying problem of overly restrictive filtering in schools, 3) ensuring the privacy of patrons and protecting the confidentiality of their library use records, and 4) meeting the needs of a broad spectrum of users (ALA 2010, 37). Each of these issues is connected to the mission of school libraries, and the Manual provides relevant information for school library professionals.

The eighth edition is a mix of essays intermingled with an extensive set of ALA intellectual freedom statements and policies. It is divided into the following six broad areas:

- An overview of intellectual freedom and libraries,
- The *Library Bill of Rights* and its interpretations,
- A collection of ALA policy statements including the *Freedom to Read,*
- The *Code of Ethics of the ALA* and explanatory information,
- The impact of state and federal legislation as well as case law on intellectual freedom, and
- Strategies for advocating for and protecting intellectual freedom (ALA 2010, v–ix).

This edition has significant new and updated information of interest to school librarians. In preparation for the book, the ALA Intellectual Freedom Committee (comprised of school, public, and academic librarians) reviewed *every* interpretation of the *Library Bill of Rights* and *all* other ALA policy statements related to intellectual freedom. Extensive input was received from many of ALA's divisions and other units. As a result, ten interpretations were revised and reaffirmed by the ALA Council (ALA 2010, xii). Additionally, three new interpretations of the *Library Bill of Rights* were created and added to the Manual:

- "The Importance of Education to Intellectual Freedom: An Interpretation of the Library Bill of Rights"
- "Minors and Internet Interactivity: An Interpretation of the Library Bill of Rights"
- "Service to Persons with Disabilities: An Interpretation of the Library Bill of Rights" (ALA 2010, xii). Note: Additional information on the revised and new interpretations can be found in the article, "The 'Ever Green' Interpretations of the *Library Bill of Rights*" in *School Library Monthly* (Adams 2010) and the third reading in this chapter.

How Can the Manual Help You?

Applying intellectual freedom concepts to real-life situations is not easy, and support for intellectual freedom is seldom black and white but rather nuanced in shades of gray. When confronting dilemmas of materials selection, access to library resources, patron privacy, filtering, censorship, services to English language learners, and other issues, a school librarian may need to review the intellectual freedom principles defined and analyzed in the Manual's essays and policy statements. Two examples follow:

Because school librarians work with minors, protecting the confidentiality of minors' library records can be a thorny legal and ethical topic. The Manual provides guidance on a range of privacy issues through attorney Deborah Caldwell-Stone's essay, "Privacy and Confidentiality in Libraries." In it she counsels librarians that only when library users feel free from scrutiny and have an expectation of some level of privacy will they seek out their true information needs (ALA 2010, 361). "Privacy: An Interpretation of the Library Bill of Rights" and Article III of the ALA *Code of Ethics* provide additional direction.

Many persons find it difficult to accept that minors have First Amendment rights in school libraries. It is critical for school library professionals to possess knowledge in this area if they are to protect students' rights to seek information. In the essay, "Minors' First Amendment Rights to Access Information," Freedom to Read Foundation legal counsel Theresa Chmara uses landmark court cases to lay out how minors have been accorded the *legal right to receive information* in school libraries in *any* format, including Internet resources (ALA 2010). With the Manual at hand, school librarians have their rationale ready for conversations with parents, administrators, teachers, and students.

The Manual Is Online

For the eighth edition, ALA created a new website (http://www.ifmanual.org) to serve as a central presence for the manual online (ALA 2010, xii). Although not well developed at this time, the companion website holds much promise. The site will supplement content

Libraries and the Internet Toolkit

Office for Intellectual Freedom staff continue to add content to the website associated with the eighth edition of the

Intellectual Freedom Manual, and it is becoming more robust and useful. In 2012 the revised "Libraries and the Internet Toolkit" was added in PDF format to the companion website at http://www .ifmanual.org/litoolkit/.

in the print Manual and allow for posting of new *Library Bill of Rights* interpretations or revisions of current documents between editions. For instance, the "Prisoner's Right to Read: An Interpretation of the Library Bill of Rights" was approved by the ALA Council in June 2010, too late to be included in this Manual; however, it is available on the new website (http://ifmanual .org/prisoners). Looking ahead, a revised version of the "Internet Toolkit" is forthcoming.

Unique to the website is an essay, "School Library Media Centers and Intellectual Freedom," written by retired school librarian Pat Scales (http://www.ifmanual.org/slmcif). In it she voices a rationale for why school library professionals must be knowledgeable about intellectual freedom. She explains that all communities have members who wish to "protect" children and young adults from ideas—in books and online—considered to be too controversial or that would corrupt youth. Like Candace Morgan earlier in this column, Pat sees many of the same issues facing school librarians who are protecting students' intellectual freedom: access to information for minors based solely on their age, challenges to library resources, privacy for student library users and confidentiality of their library records, and Internet use limited by filtering (Scales 2010). Pat's essay reminds school librarians of their ethical responsibility under Article II of the *Code of Ethics* to protect intellectual freedom and resist censorship (ALA 2008).

The Final Word

By using the *Intellectual Freedom Manual* and its accompanying website, school librarians will have the information needed to protect minors' First Amendment and privacy rights. The latest manual can be purchased in both a print and e-book format from the ALA Store (http://www .alastore.ala.org/), and the print version is also available from the usual online book sources such as Amazon.com.

REFERENCES

Adams, Helen R. 2010. "The 'Ever Green' Interpretations of the *Library Bill of Rights.*" *School Library Monthly* XXVI, no. 6 (December 2010): 48–49.

American Librarian Association. 2010. *Intellectual Freedom Manual.* 8th ed. Chicago, Illinois: ALA Editions.

Scales, Pat. 2010. "School Library Media Centers and Intellectual Freedom." http://www.if manual.org/slmcif (accessed January 15, 2013).

Key Ideas Summary

Readings in this chapter define intellectual freedom, discuss ALA core documents, and examine the role of the school librarian in preserving students' intellectual freedom. Major ideas include:

- Intellectual freedom has its basis in the First Amendment of the U.S. Constitution. The First Amendment right of freedom of speech refers to more than oral communication and has been interpreted by courts of law as including a minor's right to read and receive information and ideas.

- School librarians are key defenders of students' intellectual freedom and ensure minors' unrestricted use of the school library's print collection, electronic resources, and the Internet.

- The guiding principles of intellectual freedom are found in the ALA's three core documents: the *Library Bill of Rights*, the *Code of Ethics of the American Library Association*, and the *Freedom to Read* statement.

- Article V of the *Library Bill of Rights* affirms the rights of library users regardless of age and ensures the rights of children and young adults to use library materials and services.

- The *Library Bill of Rights* has "interpretations" that set forth more specifically the rights of library patrons and the responsibilities of librarians in specific areas such as privacy, services to persons with disabilities, and access to resources and services in school libraries.

- Current *Library Bill of Rights'* interpretations are periodically reviewed for revision based on current societal conditions and new interpretations added to satisfy emerging needs. The most recent interpretation is the "Prisoner's Right to Read: An Interpretation of the Library Bill of Rights" approved by the American Library Association in 2010.

- *The Code of Ethics of the American Library Association* is a set of ethical principles that provide guidance for acceptable library practice by all types of librarians facing complex dilemmas.

- *The Code of Ethics* embodies a framework for decision-making in the areas of service, intellectual freedom, censorship, privacy and confidentiality, intellectual property, personal beliefs versus professional responsibilities, promotion of personal interests over needs of library users, the maintenance of positive relationships with co-workers, and professional development for all librarians.

- The ALA's *Intellectual Freedom Manual* is a comprehensive volume that includes a history of intellectual freedom within the ALA, essays discussing the legal, philosophical, and practical concepts of intellectual freedom, and copies of all the current core documents supporting intellectual freedom.

- The 2008 edition of the *Intellectual Freedom Manual* has a companion website (http://ifmanual.org) that includes all the ALA intellectual freedom statements and policies plus additional content that highlights the evolving nature of intellectual freedom.

Resource Roundup:
Core Intellectual Freedom Resources

- **American Library Association. Office for Intellectual Freedom website.
  http://www.ala.org/oif**

  This extensive (although sometimes difficult to navigate) website contains a wealth of resources ranging from summaries of landmark First Amendment cases relating to libraries and their patrons to advice on fighting censorship to ALA's key intellectual freedom statements and policies.

- **American Library Association. Office for Intellectual Freedom.** *Intellectual Freedom Manual.* **Chicago: American Library Association**

  Considered by many to be *the authoritative work on intellectual freedom,* the manual includes all of ALA's documents related to intellectual freedom as well as chapters by experts on the intellectual freedom issues related to all types of libraries. The manual is updated regularly with the next edition expected in 2014.

- **American Library Association. Office for Intellectual Freedom.** *Intellectual Freedom Manual.* **8th ed. Online Companion http://ifmanual.org**

  Beginning with the 8th edition of the *Manual,* a website was created to complement the print version. It includes all of ALA's intellectual freedom statements and policies, as well as extra content of interest to school libraries such as Pat Scales' "School Library Media Centers and Intellectual Freedom."

- **First Amendment, Bill of Rights of the Constitution of the United States. 1791.
  http://www.law.cornell.edu/constitution/first_amendment/**

  The constitutional right of free speech is the underlying legal principle of intellectual freedom in libraries.

Discussion Questions

- What is your recipe for intellectual freedom? How does it differ from the one proposed by the author in the chapter introduction?

- Maintaining intellectual freedom is crucial to students in school libraries. Enumerate the ways in which school librarians can use the ALA intellectual freedom statements and policies to protect students' right to receive information in school libraries.

- School librarians can seek guidance from a *Library Bill of Rights* interpretation that pertains directly to school libraries. List and evaluate the importance of the varying aspects of intellectual freedom found within "Access to Resources and Services in the School Library Media Program: An Interpretation of the Library Bill of Rights."

- *Library Bill of Rights* interpretations are added as a need is perceived by the library community. Reflect on whether there is a "missing" interpretation and what you would add.

- The ALA has codified ethical principles to guide the decision-making of all types of librarians. In what ways does the *Code of Ethics of the American Library Association* speak to *you*?

- Relate two examples of how the *Code of Ethics of the American Library Association* applies to, or will apply to, your work as a school librarian. If you are not yet a school librarian, seek insights into this question from a local school library professional.

Chapter 2

Intellectual Freedom:
From Principles to Practice

Including the Columns

"The 'Overdue' Blues: A Dilemma for School Librarians"

"Principals and Confidentiality of Library Records"

"Computerized Reading Programs and Intellectual Freedom"

"How School Budgets Affect Students' Intellectual Freedom"

"Bring Your Own Device (BYOD) and Equitable Access to Technology"

Chapter 2

Intellectual Freedom: From Principles to Practice

INTRODUCTION

To be effective *intellectual freedom* must be translated from guiding principles into common practice. The five reprinted columns in this chapter are a sampler of intellectual freedom issues covering handling overdue materials, responding to a principal's request for a students' library reading records, the troublesome consequences of reading management programs on student reading choices, the hidden impact of schools' financial distress upon school libraries, and the effects of the "bring your own device" (BYOD) trend in schools. In coming chapters, additional intellectual freedom–related concerns will be explored including challenges to library resources and filtering of Internet resources.

A Dilemma for School Librarians

The first column, "The 'Overdue' Blues," is an example of an intellectual freedom dilemma that plagues school librarians every year. They engage in a balancing act: continuing to offer access to library materials for students who have overdue materials or outstanding fees for lost or damaged items, while at the same time carrying out their fiduciary responsibility to maintain the collection. As you read the column, consider how you will manage overdue books and unpaid fees. Options range from cutting off students' checkout privileges to teaching students about responsibility by using one of the strategies recommended in the reading.

Confidentiality of Student Library Records

Privacy and confidentiality are also core values for librarians, but the state and federal laws that protect the confidentiality of library records for minors are difficult to interpret. The second column, "Principals and Confidentiality of Library Records," demonstrates the need for an established library privacy policy. Without one, a school librarian can be hard-pressed to explain to an administrator why minors' library reading records cannot be relinquished without question. For any request to view students' library records, both the state confidentiality of library records laws and the federal Family Educational Rights and Privacy Act (FERPA) may be involved. In addition, Article III of the *Code of Ethics of the American Library Association* instructs librarians to protect the privacy of library users and the confidentiality of their library use records (ALA 2008). Although not a legal defense, the American Association of School Librarians' "Position Statement on the Confidentiality of Library Records" further states, "The library community recognizes that children and youth have the same rights to privacy as adults" (AASL 2012). Without a board approved privacy policy, school librarians are left in a vulnerable position, uncertain of the correct legal action when asked to divulge students' library use records. Having a library privacy policy approved by the school board is crucial to protecting minors' privacy.

Reading Management Programs and the School Library

"Computerized Reading Programs and Intellectual Freedom," the third reading, highlights a major conflict in schools over the implementation of reading management programs and their effect on school libraries and their users. Principals and teachers are urging school librarians to label the spines of books with a "book level" as determined by the school's reading management program (such as "Accelerated Reader"). Some teachers then restrict students' reading choices to their tested reading level, disallowing students' usual unrestricted free browsing and personal reading preferences. The labeling of book spines with book levels also affects the privacy of students during their book selection.

Budgets and the School Library

The fourth reading in this chapter, "How School Budgets Affect Students' Intellectual Freedom," considers two areas in which the fiscal plight of schools impact school libraries and ultimately students' First Amendment right to receive information in a school library. When schools face financial difficulties, the school library is frequently one of the programs under scrutiny for cutting costs. As a result, school library professional positions are often pink-slipped, with adult library assistants and volunteers taking their place. As the number of school librarians shrinks every year, those remaining are burdened with serving multiple schools; in this model, elementary schools receive the least professional staffing.

As some districts face continued budget shortfalls, spending on school library resources is also declining. Based on the November 2011 *School Library Journal* spending survey, school library budgets dropped on average 4.8 percent for elementary and middle school libraries and 3.4 percent for high school libraries. Public school libraries reported a 6.1 percent budget decline while private school library budgets fell 2.9 percent (Farmer 2012). In the December 2010 survey, responding school librarians calculated that between 11 percent and 30 percent of their collections are outdated. The 2010 *SLJ* survey also reported a trend of school librarians seeking outside funding sources, including book fairs, local businesses, parent groups and grants (Farmer 2011). The result of fewer school librarians and the reduction or stagnation of library budgets is spelled out in the fourth reading.

BYOD and Equitable Access

"Bring Your Own Device (BYOD) and Equitable Access to Technology" is the final reprinted column in Chapter 2. It highlights the need to ensure equity of access to technology for curricular purposes for all students. Many districts have already implemented a BYOD policy, allowing students to bring their personal technologies (such as smartphones, iPads, and wireless-enabled laptops) to school for use in classrooms. Unfortunately, the issue of equity for economically disadvantaged students who cannot afford such devices appears to have a lower priority among decision-makers. The column details possible strategies that school librarians, as defenders of equitable access for all students to technology, can present to administrators.

Other Considerations

As this chapter's readings show, the principles of intellectual freedom are black and white in the profession's policy statements, but they become less distinct shades of gray when applied to situations involving actual students in the school library. Although intellectual freedom and privacy are core values of the profession, how those concepts are applied in real life depends on the response of school library professionals when confronted with the many legal and ethical factors explored in these readings. Students' First Amendment and privacy rights can be supported or denied, but the *Code of Ethics of the American Library Association*, reprinted in Appendix A, is quite clear on the choice that school librarians should make.

REFERENCES

American Association of School Librarians. 2012. "Position Statement on the Confidentiality of Library Records." http://www.ala.org/aasl/aaslissues/positionstatements/conflibrecds (accessed January 18, 2013).

American Library Association. 2008. "Code of Ethics of the American Library Association." Article III. http://www.ifmanual.org/codeethics/ (accessed January 18, 2013).

Farmer, Lesley. 2011. "SLJ's Spending Survey: As the economy limps along and federal dollars dwindle, school librarians are turning into resourceful survivors." *School Library Journal.* http://www.schoollibraryjournal.com/slj/home/889109-312/sljs_spending_survey_as_the.html.csp (accessed January 18, 2013).

Farmer, Lesley. 2012. "Brace Yourself: SLJ's school library spending survey shows the hard times aren't over and better advocacy is needed." *School Library Journal.* http://www.schoollibrary journal.com/slj/articles/surveys/893538-351/brace_yourself_sljs_school_library.html.csp (accessed January 12, 2013).

IF Matters: Intellectual Freedom @ your library®

The "Overdue" Blues: A Dilemma for School Librarians

By Helen R. Adams

Originally published in the IF Matters: Intellectual Freedom @ your library® column, *School Library Monthly*, XXVI (9) (May 2010): 48–49.

Overdue and lost library materials are no joke. Every spring, school library e-lists have questions about handling missing library resources. *School Library Journal* reported the return of two books to a high school library after 51 years. With the book, the anonymous borrower included a $1,000 money order and a note stating, "At 0.02 cents per day it works out at $745.00 for 51 years. I've sent along a few

> **Overdue Humor**
>
> Have you heard this joke?
>
> Q: Why was the T-Rex afraid to go to the library?
>
> A: Because her books were 60 million years overdue. (Multnomah County Library 2009)

more dollars in case the rates changed" (Staino 2009). Although the news report is amusing, the problem of overdue materials is serious for school library professionals.

The "Overdue" Scenarios

Here's the usual situation. A student checks out a book from the school library and fails to return it on time. The school librarian notifies the student, but the item is not brought back. The item may become weeks or even months overdue. In another scenario, the overdue item is returned, but the fines are not paid. In yet another variation, the student gives back a library resource in a damaged condition (or loses the item) and does not reimburse the school. In these circumstances, what are the consequences to students with overdue materials and unpaid library fines or replacement fees? Should students with fiscal obligations be allowed to check out more library materials?

School library professionals have a fiduciary responsibility to ensure that the users of the collection return or pay for the replacement of library resources damaged or lost. Before cutting off borrowing privileges, however, school librarians should consider these points. Students have a First Amendment right to receive information in school libraries. School librarians are ethically and legally responsible to provide access to library resources to all students. "Economic Barriers to Information: An Interpretation of the Library Bill of Rights" cautions school librarians, "All library policies and procedures, particularly those involving fines, fees, or access, should be scrutinized for potential barriers to access" (ALA 1993). Marcia, a school librarian in the Midwest sums up her perspective: "I consider WHY kids have overdue books. I am particularly sensitive to those kids who may have two or three 'homes' such as those who live in split households or those who are homeless and 'stay' with other family members" (WEMTA IFSIG list 2009).

Check the Library's Policy

Most library policies are clear. Overdue books? Borrowing privileges for students are limited or cancelled until the materials are returned. Lost or damaged materials? A replacement fee is charged with options such as payment of a uniform amount based on format (paperback or hardcover book, DVD) or restitution of the partial or full replacement cost. Some policies allow students to bring a suitable substitute for the lost or damaged item. Many libraries charge fines, although others do not because of potential economic inequities. To induce students to take care of library responsibilities, schools may deny attendance at special school events like dances or withhold report cards. In some districts, failure to clear a library record before the end of school or before transferring means the next school is notified of the student's outstanding library obligation. Of all the policy implications, the most damaging is barring students from checking out library resources. This is especially true for economically disadvantaged students who are unable to reimburse the district, may have little or no access to a public library, and may also lack suitable reading materials at home. For these students, stringent policies can mean years of not being able to borrow library resources.

Strategies for Clearing Library Obligations

Students should be held accountable in some way for lost, damaged, or overdue books, but there are many ways to teach the lesson of responsibility. Library policies should be sufficiently flexible to take into account individual students' personal and economic circumstances and to ensure that students have *full access* to library resources. As a first step, discuss with the student the concept of responsibility and the desire to keep the door open to borrowing the library's resources. Marcia uses this approach. "For chronic book losers, we have them check out books but keep them in school. If there is financial hardship and the books are truly gone for good, I'll have students 'work' for me in the library. They actually enjoy it, and it gives me one-on-one time with a student who might really need it" (WEMTA IFSIG list).

Here are other ideas to consider:

- **Generate incentive to return library materials** by giving every student who "clears his/her record" a gum ball. A school with 700 students spent less than $30 on gumballs. Consider a "jelly bean amnesty." Students and teachers earn a jelly bean for every overdue book returned (Unshelved Answers).

- **Set up an "installment plan"** for students to pay for a lost or damaged item.

- **Create an "honor collection"** where students with suspended borrowing privileges may take a book and return it with no official circulation record. Obtain the extra books through book fairs, or buy gently used books at rummage sales.

- **Help families of English Language Learners understand library use**. "Prepare a short translated note explaining when library books must be returned. Include a bar code, a spine sticker, and library stamp on the letter to help parents identify library materials, which must be returned in a timely manner, as opposed to . . . [classroom] materials. If [library] books are overdue, send home a print-out from your catalogue that contains the book cover . . . Visuals can get better results than a translated note simply listing the name of the overdue book" (Jules 2009).

As school librarians struggle to retrieve missing library resources, they should consider the human side of the situation. Not every child or young adult has a stable home life or a good example of adult responsibility in his or her personal life. Students may be homeless, forced to move due to home foreclosures, or evicted because the family is behind on rent payments. Other families have seasonal employment and move several times in a single school year. Students are minors, not adults; and although there are, unfortunately, students who are irresponsible or are trying to "work the system," school librarians should not lose sight of the students who are struggling. Librarians can be proactive and look for creative alternatives to ensure access to library materials for *all* students.

REFERENCES

American Library Association. 1993. "Economic Barriers to Information Access: An Interpretation of the Library Bill of Rights." http://www.ala.org/advocacy/intfreedom/librarybill/interpretations/economicbarriers (accessed January 18, 2013).

Jules, Jacqueline. 2009. "10 Ways to Support ELLs in the School Library." http://www.colorincolorado.org/article/33008 (accessed January 18, 2013).

Multnohmah County Library. "Kids/Fun and Games/Jokes." http://www.multcolib.org/kids (accessed December 30, 2009) [no longer accessible].

Staino, Rocco. 2009. "High school library books returned 51 years late with $1,000 check." *School Library Journal* (November 16, 2009). http://www.schoollibraryjournal.com/article/CA6707200.html (accessed January 18, 2013).

"Unshelved Answers: Getting Books Back at a School Library. [LibraryKerri and MzG]" http://answers.unshelved.com/questions/356/getting-books-back-at-a-school-library (accessed December 30, 2009) [no longer available].

WEMTA IFSIG list. Marcia, November 17, 2009 8:57 AM, Subject: circulation, overdue policies and intellectual freedom.

Privacy Matters

Principals and Confidentiality of Library Records

By Helen R. Adams

Originally published in the Privacy Matters column, *School Library Media Activities Monthly*, XXIV (2) (October 2007): 32.

What can a library media specialist do if the principal asks for a list of all books a student has checked out since enrolling in the school? This happened to a middle school library media specialist in a Midwestern school district. Given her knowledge of what the student had been reading—books related to drugs, weapons, and war—she surmised that the list might be given to law enforcement officers.

First Steps: Check State and Federal Laws

> **Extending Parents' Rights**
>
> In 2008, the Vermont state legislature enacted a library records law that granted custodial parents and/or guardians of youth under age 16 the right to view their children's library records (American Library Association. "State Privacy Laws Regarding Library Records." http://www.ala.org/advocacy/privacyconfidentiality/privacy/stateprivacy [accessed January 18, 2013]).

Before responding to the principal, the library media specialist checked two laws. First, she read her state's library record law to confirm that school library records are protected. State library record laws protect the confidentiality of school library records *except* in Florida, Maine, Connecticut, and Massachusetts (ALA). Next, she reviewed the legal requirements under which library records in her state were accessible. The law allowed the disclosure of records in the following instances: 1) to library staff as part of their duties; 2) with a valid, signed court order; and 3) to parents/guardians of youth to the age of 16 (ALA). In fourteen states including Alaska, Alabama, Colorado, Florida, Georgia, Louisiana, Ohio, New Mexico, South Dakota, Utah, Virginia, West Virginia, Wisconsin, and Wyoming, parents or guardians have access to library records of their minor children or wards (ALA). Neither the principal, nor any other school staff, were listed as persons to whom library records could be disclosed.

> **Update on FERPA and School Library Records**
>
> The Family Policy Compliance Office (FPCO), which offers guidance to schools about the FERPA, now advises those who inquire that library circulation records maintained in a school library are considered *education records*

The library media specialist also examined the provisions of the Family Educational Rights and Privacy Act (FERPA), a federal law protecting the confidentiality of student education records. FERPA has a broad definition of "education records" describing them as "those records, files, documents, and other materials which— (i) contain information directly related to a student; and (ii) are maintained by an educational agency or institution or by a person acting for such agency or institution" (Cornell Law School 2011). FERPA does not specifically list library records, so it is unclear whether library circulation records are considered "education records" under FERPA. As a result, the American Library Association counsels school librarians to inquire how their districts view minors' library records under FERPA (ALA Office for Intellectual Freedom 2006, 328).

FERPA allows the disclosure of the student education records without written consent from the parent, guardian, or student over 18 years of age, under very specific circumstances, i.e., "to comply with a judicial order or lawfully issued subpoena; [to] appropriate officials in cases of health and safety emergencies; and [to] state and local authorities, within a juvenile justice system, pursuant to specific State law" (U.S. Department of Education 1974). Upon reading this point, the school librarian was unclear about how student library records are treated under FERPA in her district and whether the principal's request fit one of FERPA's specific circumstances for release of student records.

under the Act (Scales, Pat. R. 2009. *Protecting Intellectual Freedom in Your School Library: Scenarios from the Front Lines.* Chicago: American Library Association: 75). Under FERPA provisions [34 CFR § 99.31 (a) (1) School Officials], information from students' education records can be released to school officials with a "legitimate educational interest" (VLex. "Under what conditions is prior consent not required to disclose information? http://cfr.vlex.com/vid/prior-consent -not-required-disclose-19755387 [accessed January 18, 2013]). See Chapter 6 "Privacy and Confidentiality in the School Library" for more information.

Guidance from the *Code of Ethics*

The school librarian then pondered the ethics of disclosing the student's reading history. The ALA *Code of Ethics* states, in Article III, that it is the responsibility of library staff to protect the privacy of library users and to hold confidential all records about their use of library materials (ALA Office for Intellectual Freedom 2006, 245). Students check out books with the expectation of confidentiality. How can releasing a list of the student's reading choices be ethical?

From the Principal's Perspective

Having considered the request for a student's circulation history from the library media specialist's point of view, review it from the principal's perspective. He knew the background for the request but shared none of the circumstances or any prior actions taken with the school librarian. The principal is the school's leader and is responsible for the safety of all students and staff. Given the increasing violence in schools, no administrator wants another Columbine or Virginia Tech tragedy.

The Resolution

How did the incident end? The library media specialist met with the principal and explained the provisions of the state's library records law, described the uncertainty with library records under FERPA, and revealed her unease about the ethics of disclosing the student's library reading record. Although the principal listened, he gave no indication of having a court order or of having sought advice from the district's legal counsel. Instead, he simply repeated the request for the

Policy Tip

A school library privacy policy approved by the board of education is critical to protecting the confidentiality of students' library records and to avoiding the situation this school librarian faced.

The policy should detail how students' library records are protected, the conditions under which minors' library records may be released, and who may lawfully receive the records. Once approved by the school board, the policy should be distributed to faculty, support staff, and parents. Proactive school librarians should encourage open dialogue regarding the policy among the faculty, staff, and parents, either in structured forums or individual discussions.

list of books. Faced with this direct order, the librarian prepared to print the list. While still in the library, the principal received a telephone call and told the librarian, "I don't need the list. We have enough evidence."

Given the circumstances, the school librarian followed professional principles by informing the principal of the laws and ethical issues related to the confidentiality of student library records. There was, however, one more action she could have taken before complying with the principal's order. She could have asked the administrator if they could seek legal guidance. After the episode ended, many details surrounding the request remained unknown; however, this case clearly illustrates why school librarians must *proactively* educate principals about the confidentiality of student library records *prior* to a crisis.

REFERENCES

American Library Association. "State Privacy Laws Regarding Library Records." February 2003. http://www.ala.org/advocacy/privacyconfidentiality/privacy/stateprivacy (accessed January 18, 2013).

American Library Association. Office for Intellectual Freedom. 2006. *Intellectual Freedom Manual*, 7th ed. Chicago: American Library Association: 328, 245.

Cornell Law School. *U.S. Code Collection, Family Educational Rights and Privacy Act, Title 20, Chapter 31, Subchapter III, Part 4, X 1232g.* "Family Educational and Privacy Rights." http://www.law.cornell.edu/uscode/html/uscode20/usc_sec_20_00001232—g000-.html (accessed January 18, 2013).

U.S. Department of Education. 1974. "General, Family Educational Rights and Privacy Act (FERPA)." http://www.ed.gov/policy/gen/guid/fpco/ferpa/index.html (accessed January 18, 2013).

IF Matters @ your library

Computerized Reading Programs and Intellectual Freedom

By Helen R. Adams

Originally published in the IF Matters @ your library column, *School Library Monthly*, XXVIII (2) (November 2011): 27–28.

Some school librarians are concerned about the possible consequences that computerized reading programs, such as Accelerated Reader (AR), may have on students' selection of reading materials and their privacy. Although the program can be implemented in various ways, here's a disquieting story from an elementary librarian:

> As the fifth graders enter the library, the teacher announces, "Find an AR book that is on your reading level." While the class browses, one student whispers to me, "Can you help me find a book?" Jim is required to read AR books near his AR-tested third grade reading level. Because the spines of the books are labeled with reading levels, Jim is embarrassed and avoids browsing with his peers, most of whom are reading titles many grade levels above his. Jim comes to me each week, and I know what he might want—a short chapter book that would be of interest to a middle grade boy reading "below" his AR tested reading level, one that doesn't scream "picture book." I discreetly lead him to a book suitable for his reading assignment. (Margaret)

Choice versus Reading Levels and Points

Even though there are thousands of books in the school library's collection, Jim's choice is limited. For his class assignment he may select only a title within his reading level range and for which an AR test is available. After Jim completes the book, he will take a test to earn "points" that then translate into classroom rewards such as a pizza party and also affect individual student grades. Jim doesn't want to be excluded from a class treat, nor does he want a poor grade.

The restriction of choosing a book within his reading level, combined with the lure of earning "points," changes Jim's search from finding an appealing read to hunting for a book with the greatest number of points—even if the book does not engage his interest. Although the library's collection supports classroom instruction, teachers should ensure that reading program assignment guidelines allow students to seek books that pique their intellectual curiosity and correlate with their social and emotional levels. From Margaret's perspective, "AR advocates say that labels on library books will offer students reading success. But I see some kids feeling singled out and cautious about browsing with much of the fun gone" (Margaret).

How Labeling Affects Student Privacy

Traditionally library books are labeled on the spine for subject organization and easier location. Adding the reading level of the book on a book's spine allows others to view the numbers and, thus, threatens student privacy. Only the student, the child's parents, the teacher, and the librarian should know the student's reading capabilities. Jim's reluctance to have his peers know his reading level is understandable: classmates may tease or ridicule a child who reads less skillfully. School librarians, therefore, have ethical and legal responsibilities to protect a student's privacy related to selecting library materials.

Unintended Consequences

In addition to restricting choice and privacy issues, some librarians are being urged to arrange library collections according to reading levels. This non-standard shelving practice makes it difficult for library staff and students to find individual titles. Students using a public library may be confused about how to find a book because those collections are not "leveled." Maintaining the confidentiality of a child's reading level is even more difficult in a leveled collection.

Additional Resources

- American Association of School Librarians. 2011. "AASL Position Statement on Labeling Books by Reading Levels." http://www.ala.org/aasl/aaslissues/positionstatements/labeling/ (accessed January 18, 2013).

- American Library Association. 2009. "Restricted Access to Library Materials: An Interpretation of the Library Bill of Rights." http://www.ifmanual.org/restrictedaccess (accessed January 18, 2013).

- American Library Association. 2010. "Questions and Answers on Labeling and Ratings Systems." http://www.ifmanual.org/labelingratingqa (accessed January 18, 2013).

More information about these resources can be found at the end of the chapter under "Resource Roundup: Intellectual Freedom in Action."

Seeking a Solution

Is there an answer for school librarians? They can consider these steps:

- Resist placing reading level labels on book spines and "leveling" the library collection,
- Advocate for district policies that take into account privacy concerns, and
- Educate the principal and teachers about students' First Amendment right to freely choose library materials.

Whatever the individual school librarian's stand may be on this issue, there should still be reflection on how implementation of a reading management program impacts students' intellectual freedom.

REFERENCE

Margaret (elementary librarian), email message to author, June 9, 2011.

IF Matters: Intellectual Freedom @ your library®

How School Budgets Affect Students' Intellectual Freedom

By Helen R. Adams

Originally published in the IF Matters: Intellectual Freedom @ your library® column, *School Library Media Activities Monthly*, XXIV (3) (November 2007): 30.

The Endangered School Library Professional

It is no secret that as school district financial resources shrink, administrators begin to look for additional cuts in the school budget. Under the No Child Left Behind Act (NCLB), a "highly qualified" teacher must be in every classroom; however, school library media specialists are not included in that classroom designation. School library media positions are, consequently, frequently reduced or eliminated. According to the American Association of School Librarians (AASL), based on statistics from the National Center for Education Statistics (NCES) School and Staffing Survey for the 2007–2008 school year, approximately 63 percent of traditional public schools have a full-time, state certified school librarian providing services to students (AASL).

Elimination of school library professionals in most instances starts with elementary schools. Cuts in elementary library staffing may include situations where all building positions are eliminated, and a single library professional becomes responsible for the library program in *all* the district's elementary schools. If the cost-cutting continues, professional library staff in middle and high school library media centers may be affected. Credentialed library media specialists in many school districts are being replaced with paraprofessional staff or parent volunteers.

> ### School Librarians: Are They Disappearing?
>
> Despite the time lapse since this article's original publication, the NCES survey numbers for 2007–2008 are still the most current national statistics on the number of school librarians. Although anecdotal evidence (including an AASL informal survey of its state affiliate organizations in Spring 2010: http://www.ala.org/aasl/aaslissues/advocacy/advocacy) points to a decline in school librarians in some parts of the country (while other areas hold steady), there is not reliable compiled evidence from an authoritative source. NCES has completed data collection for its 2011–2012 survey and will release the results in 2013.

Access, Instruction, Program, and Resource Cuts

Eliminating the positions of credentialed library media specialists can endanger students' access to information, disrupt information literacy instruction, and hamper their intellectual freedom. According to the ALA's "Access to Resources and Services in the School

> ### Support for Appropriate Staffing in School Libraries
>
> In 2010, AASL adopted a new position statement—"Position Statement on Appropriate Staffing for School Libraries"—to provide support to school librarians

and guidance to school districts considering changing library staffing. The AASL statement recommends at least one full-time school librarian and one library clerk and/or technical assistant in each school in order to provide the level of service described in *Empowering Learners: Guidelines for School Library Programs* (American Association of School Librarians. 2010. "Position Statement on Appropriate Staffing for School Libraries." http://www.ala.org/aasl/aaslissues/positionstatements/appropriatestaffing [accessed January 18, 2013]).

Access to School Libraries

AASL's "School Libraries Count!" survey for 2010 found that school libraries were open fewer hours (thereby reducing student access to library resources and services) than reported in 2009 (American Association of School Librarians. 2010. "School Libraries Count!" 2010: 6. http://www.ala.org/aasl/sites/ala.org.aasl/files/content/researchandstatistics/slcsurvey/2010/slc2010.pdf [accessed January 18, 2013]). The 2011 survey, however, reported libraries being open the same number of hours as 2010 with a decrease in hours only in schools with fewer than 300 students (American Association of School Librarians. 2011. "School Libraries Count!" 2011: 6. http://www.ala.org/aasl/sites/ala.org.aasl/files/content/researchandstatistics/slcsurvey/2011/AASL-SLC-2011-FINALweb.pdf [accessed January 18, 2013]). There were no surprises in the 2012 "School Libraries Count!" data. Library hours remained the same as in 2011 with a small decline for libraries serving over 2,000 students. American Association of School Librarians. 2012. "School Libraries Count!" 2012: 6. http://www.ala.org/aasl/sites/ala.org.aasl/files/content/researchandstatistics/slcsurvey/2012/AASL-SLC-2012-WEB.pdf [accessed January 18, 2013]).

Library Expenditures

AASL's "School Libraries Count!" survey for 2011 found that school library expenditures remained steady for the 4,887 survey respondents with the exception of statistically significant decreases reported in middle and combined school levels. Conversely, there were statistically significant increases in schools with a student enrollment of over 2,000 and schools in the southern area of the U.S.

Library Media Program: An Interpretation of the Library Bill of Rights," "School library media specialists assume a leadership role in promoting the principles of intellectual freedom within the school by providing resources and services that create and sustain an atmosphere of free inquiry" (ALA 2008). (For further information on how school library professionals promote and maintain a climate of intellectual freedom, refer to the "What is Intellectual Freedom?" reading in Chapter 1).

Another consequence of no longer having a school library professional to advocate for the program is that hours of access to the facility are frequently shortened. The library media center may be open only one day per week or only a few hours when a library staff member is onsite. In some schools, the facilities are locked except when a teacher accompanies students to select books. This decreased access to school libraries and their resources is especially disheartening when this may be the *only* library to which a child or young adult has regular access. Loss of the school library program can have a detrimental effect on all students, but especially those who do not have the socioeconomic resources to purchase books, obtain Internet access at home, or regularly use a public library.

In other situations, there may be a library media specialist and a fully functioning school library, but the budget is low or non-existent. Poor financial support results in an inability to purchase new books, update older inaccurate resources, and provide electronic reference materials to students. A school library, in order to have a viable collection, must purchase one book per student per year to maintain its collection and two books per student to grow (IRA 1999). The impact of low budgets, consequently, is seen in the size and age of collections in school libraries. It is estimated nationally that there are 18 books per student in school libraries, but schools in economically depressed areas may have less than one book per child (Holcomb 2007).

The age of collections is also of concern. A study of public school libraries in middle Tennessee revealed that while the average school library had nineteen books per student, the average age of the books was sixteen years old (Robinson 2006).

Insufficient budgets also impede the First Amendment right of minors to receive information in libraries. Harold Howe, former U.S. Commissioner of Education, is often quoted as saying, "What a school thinks about its library is a measure of what it thinks about education"

(American Association of School Librarians. 2011. "School Libraries Count!" 2011:16. http://www.ala.org/aasl/sites/ala.org.aasl/files/content/researchandstatistics/slcsurvey/2011/AASL-SLC-2011-FINALweb.pdf [accessed January 18, 2013]). The AASL 2012 survey revealed that library expenditures for total information resources were slightly less in 2012: $11,827 for 2012 compared to $12,937 in 2011 (American Association of School Librarians. 2012. "School Libraries Count!" 2012:12. http://www.ala.org/aasl/sites/ala.org.aasl/files/content/researchandstatistics/slcsurvey/2012/AASL-SLC-2012-WEB.pdf [accessed January 18, 2013]).

(Logan). This quote should perhaps be rephrased to state that "what the community thinks about school libraries is a measure of what it thinks about education." When there is no access to a credentialed school library media specialist, a current collection, and an adequate school library facility, *students' desire for lifelong learning and their intellectual freedom is affected.*

Strategies to Retain Staff and Resources

Here are three strategies for maintaining qualified staff and building sufficient resources in YOUR library:

1. Utilize AASL's online advocacy tools to develop an Advocacy Plan for the school library program.

   Resource: AASL School Library Program Health and Wellness Toolkit: http://www.ala.org/aasl/aaslissues/toolkits/slmhealthandwellness

2. Provide the learning community and parents with information on the research that links a quality library program with appropriate staffing to student achievement.

   Resource: Keith Curry Lance School Library Impact Studies: http://www.lrs.org/impact.php

3. Increase visibility as a library professional through such activities as providing staff development, serving on curriculum committees, and meeting with the principal frequently.

   Resource: Wisconsin Department of Public Instruction library media program brochures for school library media specialists, principals, and parents: http://www.dpi.wi.gov/imt/lmsstudy.html [no longer available online].

REFERENCES

American Association of School Librarians. "Public and Bureau of Indian Education Elementary and Secondary School Library Media Centers, Results from the 2007–2008 Schools and Staffing Survey." http://www.ala.org/aasl/sites/ala.org.aasl/files/content/researchand statistics/surveydata.pdf (accessed January 18, 2013).

American Library Association. 2008. "Access to Resources and Services in the School Library Media Program: An Interpretation of the Library Bill of Rights." http://www.ifmanual.org/accesslmp (accessed January 18, 2013).

Holcomb, Sabrina. 2007. "Room for Readers." *NEAToday* 25, no. 6: 37. http://www.nea.org/
    home/11466.htm (accessed January 18, 2013).

International Reading Association (IRA). 1999. "Providing Books and Other Print Materials
    for Classroom and School Libraries: A Position Statement of the International Reading
    Association." http://www.reading.org/General/AboutIRA/PositionStatements/Libraries
    Position.aspx (accessed January 18, 2013).

Logan, Deborah. "Quotations about Libraries, Books, and Reading." http://www.deblogan
    .com/quo2/ (accessed January 18, 2013).

Robinson, Dorren. 2006. "Libraries." http://web.archive.org/web/20070919075516/ http://
    research.givingmatters.com/papers/2006/9/6/libraries (accessed January 18, 2013).

IF Matters @ your library

Bring Your Own Device (BYOD) and Equitable Access to Technology

By Helen R. Adams

Originally published in the IF Matters @ your library column, *School Library Monthly*, XXVIII (8) (May/June 2012): 25–26.

Countless recent online communications are devoted to managing use of personal technology devices in schools, and questions abound. Can faculty bring their own mobile technology to work? Are students allowed to connect personal devices to the school's network? Who assumes liability for damage or loss of a student-owned device? Less frequently asked is how will students from impoverished families have equitable access to technology under a "bring your own device" (BYOD) policy?

Equity: An Ethical Dilemma

In public schools, instructional resources and technology should be available equitably to every student regardless of socioeconomic status. Under BYOD, schools face an ethical dilemma when families are financially unable to provide personal technology for their children. The problem is real, and the 2010 statistics for poor and homeless Americans are astonishing:

- 16.4 million or 22 percent of all children lived in poverty, with children of color experiencing higher rates than do white children (UW-Madison).
- More than 18 percent of U.S. children had at least one unemployed or underemployed parent, compared with 9.1 percent in 2007 (Mishel 2011).
- One in 45 or 1.6 million children were homeless, a 38 percent increase since 2007 (National Center on Family Homelessness 2010).

Some educators question whether all students should be restricted from using their personal technology in school because their economically disadvantaged peers do not have similar tools, and the disparity in the "real world" is often cited as justification allowing those with devices to use them.

> **Economic Barriers**
>
> According to "Economic Barriers to Information Access: An Interpretation of the Library Bill of Rights," librarians and their institutional governing bodies such as school boards should be wary of charging fees and fines that result in fiscal barriers to using a library for students living in poverty (American Library Association. 1993. "Economic Barriers to Information Access: An Interpretation of the Library Bill of Rights." http://www.ala.org/advocacy/intfreedom/librarybill [accessed January 18, 2013]). Similar caution should be exercised in districts establishing BYOD policies that do not provide equity in the use of technology for students whose families are unable to afford personal mobile technology.

Parents and BYOD

Parents are partners with schools; to gauge community support for BYOD, Jan, a technology director in the Midwest, disseminated a survey to parents. Amid positive responses, parents had concerns about students' sense of responsibility; the potential for loss, theft, and damage; inappropriate use while in class; the need for upgrades as technology changes; the risk for bullying; and the inequity to families who cannot afford personal technology for school use. A few expressed apprehension about the emotional distress of students without personal devices, with one parent asking, *"what if you are the one kid in a class without a laptop?"* (Jan 2012). Although educators may propose sharing of students' personal devices in a classroom, some parents did not want their child to let others use their expensive technology. Still other parents preferred the district buy the necessary hardware.

Providing Equity in a BYOD World

One District's Solution to Achieve Equity

Annette Smith, technology director for a high school in Wisconsin, led an effort, with the school's technology team, to create a leasing plan for student mobile devices. Students can lease the device for a specified amount, which includes insurance.

Central to the school's BYOD plan is equity. Students who receive *free* lunches receive a netbook at no cost, although the school asks families to contribute to the insurance if they are able. Students who receive *reduced* lunches will pay a percentage of the technology's cost. If a student chooses not to purchase/lease a device, the district has a set of netbooks that are available for daily checkout.

According to Annette, "The devices do not include internet connectivity, but we do keep our library open before and after school. Any student can access the wireless network anywhere in the building as well as on the athletic fields. If the student goes to the public library or any other spot that offers wireless access, they will be able to use the device to connect" (Smith, Annette. Email message to author, April 3, 2012).

As advocates for equitable access, school librarians must exercise leadership and urge study of strategies that will provide technology resources for *all students*. Before a BYOD plan is implemented, consider these ideas:

- **Share:** Honestly assess whether *every* student needs the individual hardware, or whether groups can share a school- or student-owned device. According to Scott Floyd, an instructional technologist in Texas, "Our students do a lot of collaborative work. It's the only way to prepare them for the work world they will enter. Many of our teachers in elementary levels will not allow a [personal] device to be used unless the student is willing to at least share their screen. Sometimes, students with devices will let others take over the driving of it with monitoring by the student who owns it" (Floyd 2012).
- **Purchase/checkout:** In addition to allowing student-owned technology in classrooms, purchase hardware that can be borrowed from the library by a teacher for classroom use by students without personal devices.
- **Seek funding:** Approach community groups, ask foundations, or seek grant opportunities to secure funding of mobile equipment for circulation to disadvantaged students in school.
- **Community purchasing program:** Set mobile device specifications and work with district hardware vendors to offer discounts on new technology for families (Roscorla 2010).

Incorporating strategies for equity into BYOD programs creates a win-win situation for *all* students.

REFERENCES

Floyd, Scott. Email message to author, January 8, 2012.

Jan, "BYOD Parent Survey" and email message to author, January 3, 2012.

Mishel, Lawrence. 2011. "Share of children with at least one unemployed or underemployed parent." September 8, 2011. Economy Policy Institute. http://www.epi.org/publication/share-children-unemployed-underemployed/ (accessed January 18, 2013).

National Center on Family Homelessness. 2010. "America's Youngest Outcasts 2010: State Report Card on Child Homelessness. Executive Summary." http://www.homelesschildren america.org/media/Ex_Summary_for%20map%20page.pdf (accessed January 18, 2013).

Roscorla, Tanya. 2010. "Student Devices Save Districts Money." November 15, 2010. Converge. http://www.convergemag.com/infrastructure/Student-Devices-Save-Districts-Money.html (accessed January 18, 2013).

University of Wisconsin-Madison. Institute for Research on Poverty. "National Poverty Rate for Children. How Many Children Are Poor?" http://www.irp.wisc.edu/faqs.htm (accessed January 18, 2013).

Key Ideas Summary

Readings in this chapter reflect the principles of intellectual freedom in common situations found in school libraries. Major ideas include:

- Economic barriers such as book fines, damaged or lost book charges, or other library fees, threaten access to library materials, especially for students from economically disadvantaged families.

- School librarians can use a variety of creative strategies to teach students responsibility for their lost, damaged, or overdue materials.

- Labeling books with "book levels" and restricting students' reading selections to their tested reading level is an obstacle to students' free choice in a school library.

- Labeling book spines with "book levels" threatens students' privacy; only a teacher, the student, parents/guardian, and the librarian should be aware of a student's reading capabilities.

- In 2011, AASL approved the "Position Statement on Labeling Books by Reading Levels" to support school librarians resisting the labeling of library book spines with "book levels" used by reading management programs and arranging library books by book level, a non-standard shelving practice.

- Every school library should have a board-approved privacy policy that delineates how students' library records are protected legally, who may request records, and under what circumstances records may be divulged.

- The *Code of Ethics of the American Library Association* and AASL's "Position Statement on the Confidentiality of Library Records" provide the ethical framework for protecting student library records.

- Declining school finances can have a direct, negative impact on school libraries.

- Limiting or eliminating students' access to the services of a credentialed school librarian and current library resources greatly diminishes their First Amendment right to read and receive information in a school library and their intellectual freedom.

- In all schools, instructional resources and technology should be available equitably to every student, regardless of socioeconomic status.

- Before "bring your own device" programs are initiated in schools, strategies for equitable access to technology should be in place for economically disadvantaged students.

Resource Roundup:
Intellectual Freedom in Action

- **American Association of School Librarians. 2011. "AASL Position Statement on Labeling Books by Reading Levels." July 18, 2011. http://www.ala.org/aasl/aaslissues/positionstatements/labeling**

  In July 2011, the AASL Board of Directors approved a position statement to support school librarians who are under pressure to label and arrange books in their collections according to reading management program book levels. Student privacy issues related to labeling are also addressed.

- **American Library Association. 2010. "Questions and Answers on Labeling and Ratings Systems." Updated January 16, 2010. http://www.ifmanual.org/labelingratingqa**

  Using this Q & A, school librarians will find answers to their questions on labeling books with reading levels, especially as it relates to reading management programs such as Accelerated Reader and genres in school libraries. There is also an explanation on how ratings systems and labels can inadvertently discourage or restrict use by patrons, or can be used to obtain an endorsement or approval of certain resources.

- **American Library Association. 2012. Intellectual Freedom Committee. "Questions and Answers on Privacy and Confidentiality." Updated January 23, 2012. http://www.ifmanual.org/privacyqa/**

  Originally written to correspond with "Privacy: An Interpretation of the Library Bill of Rights," the Q & A was revised in 2012. Of particular interest to school librarians, the final section on "Minors' Privacy Rights" explains the privacy rights of students in school libraries and stresses the need for an official privacy policy.

- **American Library Association. 2009. "Restricted Access to Library Materials: An Interpretation of the Library Bill of Rights." http://www.ifmanual.org/restrictedaccess**

  This interpretation addresses ways in which resources are restricted in a school library: by book level corresponding to reading management programs, by grade level, by age, and/or by physical barriers such as restricted shelves.

- **Association of Library Services to Children. Intellectual Freedom Committee, 2005–2007. 2007. "Kids, Know Your Rights! A Young Person's Guide to Intellectual Freedom." http://www.ala.org/alsc/sites/ala.org.alsc/files/content/issuesadv/intellectualfreedom/kidsknowyourrights.pdf**

  This attractive four-page document is aimed at children, using age-appropriate language to explain their First Amendment and privacy rights when using a library. The document also defines intellectual freedom and discusses censorship.

- **Cooperative Children's Book Center, School of Education, University of Wisconsin-Madison. "What IF? Questions and Answers on Intellectual Freedom." http://www.education.wisc.edu/ccbc/freedom/whatif/default.asp**

"What IF?" is a Q & A service maintained by a librarian at the CCBC. It provides all types of librarians with the opportunity to ask questions and receive well thought-out answers about intellectual freedom in practice in their libraries. Because school librarians are often the only library professional in the building, "What IF?" serves as a support when intellectual freedom dilemmas occur. Those who submit a confidential question will receive a personal response; some of the questions are also added to the online Q & A database.

Discussion Questions

- Name two main intellectual freedom issues facing school librarians today, and provide rationale for your answer.

- School librarians face a dilemma when students fail to return books and pay for lost or damaged materials. When confronted with this issue, will you cut off borrowing privileges, or follow another course? Describe your plan for maintaining fiduciary responsibility to preserve the collection, teaching students responsibility for materials borrowed, and providing access to library resources.

- Taking into account your state's library records law, the Family Educational Rights and Privacy Act (FERPA), and the ALA *Code of Ethics*, what course of action would you take if confronted with a request from the principal for a student's library circulation history?

- Many school librarians face pressure to label library materials with book levels identified in reading management programs and arrange labeled books by book levels on library shelves. Would you resist this pressure? Describe the rationale you would give a principal for not taking these actions.

- Elementary students like to share the titles and stories of books they are reading with their friends. From your perspective, does having reading levels placed on the spines of library books (to identify them as titles that are part of reading management programs) threaten a student's privacy? Provide the reasoning for your answer.

- Fiscal constraints affect many educational programs including the school library. Discuss three substantive ways in which students' intellectual freedom is impacted by the loss of or restricted access to a credentialed school library professional.

- School librarians support the principles of intellectual freedom and equity of access in *Library Bill of Rights* interpretations, including "Access to Digital Information, Services and Networks: An Interpretation of the Library Bill of Rights" and "Economic Barriers to Information Access: An Interpretation of the Library Bill of Rights." Is it logical to restrict use of students' personal technology in school because their economically disadvantaged peers do not have similar tools? How would you propose to ameliorate inequity and create a positive educational climate for all students?

Chapter 3

Challenges to School Library Resources

Including the Columns

"The Freedom to Question: Challenges in School Libraries"

"Can You Challenge-Proof Your School Library?"

"A Tale of Two Challenges"

"What Happens When You Call the ALA Office
for Intellectual Freedom for Help?"

"The Materials Selection Policy: Defense Against Censorship"

Challenges to School Library Resources

INTRODUCTION

When a challenge—a formal written complaint about a library resource—occurs, the faces of most school librarians become grave, and their apprehension is apparent. Deep inside, each librarian knows that s/he must be prepared for a challenge because it is only a matter of time before a parent or administrator voices a concern about a book or other material. Unless an expression of concern can be resolved directly with the complainant on an individual basis, it can easily become a formal challenge. The columns in this chapter focus on managing challenges to library materials, including where to find support when a challenge occurs and how a school's materials selection policy provides guidance during selection of materials and defense during the reconsideration process.

The Challenge of Challenges

The first three readings—"The Freedom to Question," "Can You Challenge-Proof Your School Library?" and "A Tale of Two Challenges"—were originally published as a series. The words "challenge" and "censorship" are often used interchangeably, although in reality they are very different. The first column explains American Library Association (ALA) terminology to define a wide range of situations from "expression of concern" about a resource to outright "censorship." It also explains the right of complainants to express their misgivings about a library resource. The second column considers whether a school library can be "challenge-proofed." It provides a useful checklist for library professionals to determine if they have taken proactive steps to educate the school community about the selection policy, create an inclusive process for library resource selection, and build positive relationships with the principal, school staff, students, parents, and community members. In the third column, two library professionals tell their stories of challenges and the valuable lessons they learned.

The fourth column, "Making the Call: What Happens When You Call the ALA Office for Intellectual Freedom for Help?" offers guidance on where to find assistance when a formal challenge—or the potential for a challenge—occurs. For many school librarians, the ALA seems distant and intimidating; and as a result, they do not contact the Office for Intellectual Freedom (OIF) for support. In addition to their fear of someone learning about the request for help, there is also a misconception that one must be an ALA or AASL member to ask for help. Untrue: *anyone* may call and receive support. If you were to visit ALA headquarters in Chicago, the OIF is a series of small, crowded offices with files, desks, and chairs overflowing with books and papers. It is amazing that so few staff members working in crowded conditions are responsible for helping librarians, teachers, and others successfully fight censorship in all types of libraries.

The final column in Chapter 3, "The Materials Selection Policy: Defense Against Censorship," reminds school library professionals of the important role the policy plays both during selection and when a concern is raised. The policy used to select library resources is the same document that can be used to defend against challenges during the reconsideration process.

Information about Challenges

Since 1990, the OIF has maintained a *confidential* database of challenges that have been reported by individuals to OIF or gleaned from newspaper or other media sources. Those who are interested can gauge the pattern of challenges to materials in all types of libraries nationwide from four sources:

1. **IFAction**, a no discussion news-only e-list that provides articles about challenges and other intellectual freedom issues;

2. **"Newsletter on Intellectual Freedom,"** the bimonthly subscription-based digital publication from OIF that lists censorship attempts in its "Censorship Dateline" section;

3. *Banned Books Week Resource Guide*, published by ALA Editions every three years; and

4. **"Top Ten Most Frequently Challenged Books,"** an annual list compiled by the OIF staff from individual reporting and media accounts in a single year (ALA).

Are all challenges reported to the OIF? Unfortunately, not even close. It has long been suspected that only a fraction of challenges are reported to ALA, and a small survey conducted in 2011 by a library science student confirmed this presumption. It found that, of the 73 respondents from public, school, and academic libraries, only 20.6 percent of their 160 total challenges were reported to OIF (Houghton 2011).

The OIF provides assistance upon request from *any library professional*, but it also needs help from the library community. To encourage more librarians to report challenges, the OIF began a "Defend the Freedom to Read; It's Everybody's Job" campaign in 2011. The awareness project was the idea of Andy Woodworth, a public librarian in New Jersey, because of his concern over the low rate of reporting these attempts to remove resources from libraries. According to Woodworth, reporting challenges is important because with more accurate knowledge, OIF can better analyze censorship attempts for trends or patterns (Woodworth 2011).

The "Defend the Freedom to Read" promotion urges those who have experienced formal challenges or have knowledge of the attempts of censorship to use ALA's "Online Challenge Reporting Form" (http://www.ala.org/advocacy/banned/challengeslibrarymaterials/challenge reporting/onlinechallengeform) to share their knowledge. There is also a printable form that can be completed and faxed to OIF. All information received from individuals is kept *confidential.*

The OIF is not alone in collecting information on book challenges in school libraries. Annually the American Civil Liberties Union of Texas contacts every public school district and charter school in Texas seeking information about books that have been challenged by a parent, teacher, administrator, or student in schools in the last year. Using that information, the "Free People Read Freely" Banned Books Project creates a report that lists the title, author, reason for challenge, result and current status of a formally challenged item, and whether the book was in a library collection or on a curricular reading list. The report is issued annually in September during Banned Books Week (ACLU of Texas).

Reflections on Challenges

Facing a challenge is a main concern of school librarians. Unlike teachers, most librarians are "singletons" (meaning the only librarian in a school). As a result, when a concern about a library resource is raised, if policy is followed, the school librarian is usually substantially involved in the resolution. Even when the review process is followed, however, a school librarian can experience emotional distress. At times challenges become public debates on what is "appropriate" for a school library collection, and criticism of school employees—including the school librarian—can be vitriolic. Resources listed at the end of this chapter will help school librarians prepare for a challenge and defend against censorship.

How a challenge is resolved depends on the attitudes and actions of administrators, and whether they follow policy meticulously or try to appease the complainant. Although a school librarian cannot "challenge-proof" a library, s/he can prepare for a challenge by laying the groundwork to help the school and community understand how materials are selected and appreciate the place and purpose of each in the collection.

REFERENCES

American Civil Liberties Union of Texas. "We Believe in an Educated Citizenry." http://www.bannedbookstx.org (accessed January 18, 2013).

American Library Association. "Reporting a Challenge." http://www.ala.org/advocacy/banned/challengeslibrarymaterials/challengereporting (accessed January 18, 2013).

Houghton, Sarah. 2011. "Book Challenges and Removals Survey Results." March 8, 2011. Librarian in Black Blog. http://librarianinblack.net/librarianinblack/2011/03/book challenges.html (accessed January 18, 2013).

Woodworth, Andy. 2011. "Defend the Freedom to Read: It's Everybody's Job." October 6, 2011. Agnostic Maybe Blog. http://agnosticmaybe.wordpress.com/2011/10/06/defend-the-right-to-read-its-everybodys-job (accessed January 18, 2013).

IF Matters: Intellectual Freedom @ your library®

The Freedom to Question: Challenges in School Libraries

By Helen R. Adams

Originally published in the IF Matters: Intellectual Freedom @ your library® column, *School Library Monthly*, XXVI (3) (November 2009): 48–49.

Many school librarians fear a challenge to the resources in their libraries. This column begins a three part series on challenges to resources in school libraries. This column will focus on the definition of a challenge, why challenges occur, and what happens during a challenge. The second column will explore the concept of whether a school librarian can "challenge-proof" the collection and will include a checklist for preparing for a challenge. The series will conclude with a column discussing what happens after a district completes its reconsideration process.

What is a Challenge?

Some persons incorrectly call every incident in which an individual or group expresses disapproval or concern about a library resource a *challenge* or *censorship*. The American Library Association's (ALA) Office for Intellectual Freedom (OIF) has more precise terms and definitions for the range of actions that may occur including the following:

- **Expression of concern:** An inquiry that has judgmental overtones.
- **Oral complaint:** An oral challenge to the presence and/or appropriateness of the material in question.
- **Written complaint:** A formal, written complaint filed with the institution (library, school, etc.), challenging the presence and/or appropriateness of specific material. (Note: Within the context of this book, a written complaint is also known as a *challenge*.)
- **Censorship:** A change in the access status of material based on the content of the work and made by a governing authority or its representatives. Such changes include exclusion, restriction, removal, or age/grade level changes (http://www.ala.org/ala/issuesadvocacy/banned/challengeslibrarymaterials/index.cfm).

Challenging Statistics

The number of incidents in which individuals or groups attempt to remove a resource from libraries or classrooms varies.

- Between 2001 and 2008, there were 3,736 challenges reported to the ALA Office for Intellectual Freedom.
- ALA estimates that this is only 20–25 percent of actual challenges since many are unreported.

- More than half of the reported challenges occurred in schools with 37 percent in school library collections and 31 percent in classrooms.
- Parents accounted for 51 percent and administrators 6 percent of challenges reported to the ALA (ALA 2009).

According to Angela Maycock, Assistant Director of ALA's Office for Intellectual Freedom, of the 3,745 challenges to materials reported to ALA:

- 58 percent had unknown outcomes,
- 27 percent resulted in the materials being retained,
- 14 percent ended in materials being removed, and
- 1 percent resulted in materials being stolen or defaced (Maycock 2009).

What is Challenged and Why?

Each year the ALA publishes the "Top Ten List of Most Frequently Challenged Books" to highlight the titles and topics that draw the most censure. In 2008 for the third successive year, *And Tango Makes Three* was the most challenged book reported to the OIF (ALA 2009). Other titles that have been challenged often are also listed on ALA's site (http://www.ala.org/ala/issuesadvocacy/banned/frequentlychallenged/21stcenturychallenged/2008/index.cfm). The reasons why library and classroom resources have been challenged include:

- Offensive language
- Positive portrayal of homosexuality
- Sexual explicitness
- Violence
- Representing religious or political points of view
- Anti-family perspective
- Unsuited to the age of potential readers (ALA http://www.ala.org/ala/issuesadvocacy/banned/frequentlychallenged/21stcenturychallenged/index.cfm)

The Right to Question Library and Classroom Resources

U.S. Constitution, First Amendment

"Congress shall make no law respecting an establishment of religion, or

Most materials selection policies include a "reconsideration process" by which an individual may request that a library or classroom resource be reviewed for possible removal. The basis for the right to question library or classroom resources is the First Amendment, which guarantees that citizens have the right to "petition the

Government for a redress of grievances" (U.S. Constitution). In K–12 education, the "government" is represented by public schools, and the "grievance" is a concern about resources in the school library collection or a classroom (Adams 2008, 121). Although school librarians and other educators may not agree with a request to remove or restrict a resource, the opinions of those expressing concern deserve respect and should be received courteously.

prohibiting the free exercise thereof; or abridging the freedom of speech, or of the press; or the right of the people peaceably to assemble, and to petition the Government for a redress of grievances" (http://www.usconstitution.net/const.html#AmI).

What Happens During a Challenge?

The concept of challenges in schools is simple. An individual or group expresses concern to a principal, teacher, or school librarian that a library resource or classroom novel, film, or other media is not appropriate for a child, preteen, or young adult. Most often the rationale for a challenge is to protect—and prohibit—not just the complainant's child but *all students* from accessing that resource. If personal fears or objections are not allayed through that initial contact, the school employee will explain the formal process through which the resource can be reviewed by a committee that will recommend whether the resource will be retained, moved to another level, restricted in some manner, or removed from the library collection or curriculum. The complainant will be apprised of the fact that, until a formal written complaint is made, no action is taken.

Using his/her First Amendment right to "petition the government," the complainant may submit the official reconsideration form, and that action sets the district's reconsideration process in motion. Following district policy, the principal appoints a reconsideration committee or alerts the standing committee; its members read, view, or listen to the challenged resource. The school librarian provides reviews, analysis of how the resource meets district selection criteria, and a list of awards, if any. Some districts supply a list of questions to guide the committee's discussion. The committee will deliberate, write a recommendation for the disposition of the challenged resource, and forward the report to the school official(s) as noted in the policy (i.e., superintendent or school board). If the complainant does not accept the committee's recommendation, s/he may request that the school official(s) named in the policy review the matter and make a final decision. Whatever the outcome, the complainant(s) have the right to make their opinions known. Judging from the number of challenges reported to the ALA Office for Intellectual Freedom, many citizens are exercising their First Amendment right.

REFERENCES

Adams, Helen R. 2008. *Ensuring Intellectual Freedom and Access to Information in the School Library Media Program.* Westport, Connecticut: Libraries Unlimited.

American Library Association. 2009. "Attempts to Remove Children's Book on Male Penguin Couple Parenting Chick Continue; 'And Tango Makes Three' tops ALA's 2008 Top Ten List of Most Frequently Challenged Books." April 16, 2009. http://www.ala.org/ala/news presscenter/news/pressreleases2009/april2009/nlw08bbtopten.cfm (accessed January 18, 2013).

American Library Association. "Challenges to Library Materials, Definitions to Clarify Terminology Associated with Challenges." http://www.ala.org/ala/issuesadvocacy/banned/challengeslibrarymaterials/index.cfm (accessed January 18, 2013).

American Library Association. "Most Frequently Challenged Books of the 21st Century." http://
       www.ala.org/advocacy/banned/frequentlychallenged/21stcenturychallenged/ (accessed
       January 18, 2013).

Maycock, Angela. Email to author, June 29, 2009.

United States Constitution. First Amendment. 1791. http://www.usconstitution.net/const
       .html#Am1 (accessed January 18, 2013).

IF Matters: Intellectual Freedom @ your library®

Can You Challenge-Proof Your School Library?

By Helen R. Adams

Originally published in the IF Matters: Intellectual Freedom @ your library® column, *School Library Monthly*, XXVI (4) (December 2009): 48–49.

There is a significant fear among many school librarians: facing a challenge to a resource in their libraries. Some try to avoid a challenge by not selecting books that may be considered controversial. Library supervisors or principals who are also concerned about challenges may peruse the titles in a book order and cross out those that seem provocative or controversial.

Although there are books that have been challenged repeatedly in school libraries, *no individual can know for certain what books or other resources will trigger a challenge.* This fact is evident when checking the books listed by the American Library Association (ALA) as the "Frequently Challenged Books of the 21st Century." Titles range from *The Kite Runner* by Khaled Hosseini to the *Captain Underpants* series by Dav Pilkey to *Go Ask Alice* by Anonymous to *Bridge to Terebithia* by Katherine Paterson. A diverse variety of books including *Adventures of Huckleberry Finn* by Mark Twain, *In the Night Kitchen* by Maurice Sendak, and *Arming America: The Origins of a National Gun Culture* by Michael A. Bellesiles have also been targets of censors (ALA http://www.ala.org/advocacy/banned/frequentlychallenged/21stcentury challenged). The practice of self-censorship, not choosing a book because of the fear of potential challenges, is not a practical or an ethical solution. Furthermore, Article VII of the ALA *Code of Ethics* advises librarians that private opinions and biases should not interfere with conducting their professional duties—in this case, selection of library materials (ALA 2008).

> **Lester Asheim: Selection or Censorship?**
>
> Published in the *Wilson Library Bulletin* in 1953, librarian Lester Asheim's article "Not Censorship, But Selection" describes the ways in which librarians may act as censors. Self-censorship practiced during the selection process can be done out of fear of challenges, because of personal bias, or to "protect children" from ideas the librarian finds disturbing. Asheim's memorable essay is available online on the ALA Office for Intellectual Freedom website: http://www.ala.org/offices/oif/basics/notcensorship/.

Is Challenge-Proofing a Collection Possible?

Is there any way other than self-censorship that a school librarian can *guarantee* no resource will ever be challenged? The answer to that question is "no." In reality, *any* book or other library resource may be offensive to and questioned by a parent, principal, teacher, community member, or student. As discussed in "The Freedom to Question: Challenges in School Libraries," the first reading in this chapter, challenges are most frequently initiated by parents and principals. Because no one can predict which books or other resources will be challenged or who will express a concern, a more effective approach is to take proactive steps toward creating a climate where the principles of intellectual freedom are understood and the legal right of minors to receive information in the school library is acknowledged.

The checklist in this column is an attempt to help school librarians develop a school culture where a challenge to a library resource can be managed successfully through school policy. Have school librarians become advocates for intellectual freedom and the First Amendment rights of minors in school libraries? Have they undertaken actions to prepare for a challenge before it occurs? School librarians can determine the vulnerability of their libraries to challenges by completing the "Challenge-Proofing Your School Library Checklist."

Challenge-Proofing Your School Library Checklist

I have . . .	Met	Not Yet or District Level Action	Next Steps
Personal Knowledge			
✓ Educated myself about the First Amendment and court decisions affecting minors' right to receive information in schools and libraries.			
✓ Reviewed ALA policy statements related to intellectual freedom and resisting censorship including, the *Library Bill of Rights* and its interpretations and the *Code of Ethics for the American Library Association.*			
✓ Become a member of a state school library organization and participated in state conferences, workshops, and other professional development opportunities.			
The Materials Selection Policy			
✓ Created a materials selection policy that includes a process for reconsideration of school library resources and requested that it be officially approved by the institution's governing body.			
✓ Posted the materials selection policy on the school's and the library's web pages to inform educators, patrons, and the community how school library resources are chosen.			
✓ Reviewed the reconsideration process and am familiar with the steps and persons involved.			
✓ Worked with principal and other administrators to clarify any steps or responsibilities in the reconsideration process that are not clear.			
✓ Arranged with administrators for opportunities to educate teachers, students, and parents/the community about the selection and reconsideration of school library resources.			
✓ Considered how to proceed if the principal directs me as the school librarian to remove a library resource without following the reconsideration process.			
Educating the Principal and Teachers			
✓ Proactively instructed administrators and teachers about materials selection, reconsideration of library materials, and how to respond to a complaint by a parent or other individual about a library resource.			
✓ Explained to new staff the school's library policies related to materials selection, reconsideration of a resource, circulation of resources, privacy of library records, interlibrary loan, Internet use, and others.			
✓ Reviewed with the principal *annually* the materials selection policy, how materials are selected, and district reconsideration procedures.			

(*continued*)

Challenge-Proofing Your School Library Checklist (*continued*)

I have . . .	Met	Not Yet or District Level Action	Next Steps
✓ Shared with the principal and staff articles, websites, and other resources related to intellectual freedom in the school library and classrooms.			
✓ Selected professional materials related to censorship and made them available to staff.			
✓ Planned collaboratively with teachers and students to create learning experiences incorporating minors' First Amendment speech rights.			
Selection of Materials			
✓ Modeled best practices in selection of library resources by resisting outside pressures (or personal fear) to avoid selecting materials considered by some to be controversial.			
✓ Not permitted personal beliefs or values to interfere with selection of library resources.			
Teaching Students about Intellectual Freedom			
✓ Incorporated into formal and informal student instruction Responsibilities 3.3.7: "Respect the principles of intellectual freedom" from Standard 3 of AASL's *Standards for the 21st-Century Learner* (AASL 2007 http://www.ala.org/ala/mgrps/divs/aasl/guidelinesandstandards/learning standards/standards.cfm).			
✓ Taught students about their First Amendment right to receive information in the school library.			
Educating Parents and the Community			
✓ Described to parents and community members the process used to select library materials.			
✓ Explained the reconsideration process for review of library resources about which a concern has been expressed.			
✓ Practiced positive communication strategies with persons who express concern about a school library resource.			
General Advocacy for the Library Program			
✓ Built positive relationships with the principal, school staff, students, parents, and community members.			
✓ Become knowledgeable about local media and provide positive information and photos about the school library program.			
✓ Contacted legislators regarding the impact of proposed legislation on school libraries and patrons. (Adams 2008, Chapters 2, 3, 6, 9)			

Checklist developed by Helen R. Adams, 2009.

What's Your Score?

If more of your answers fall in the "not yet" column, begin a plan of how to accomplish each task. Achieving every item on the checklist will take time, but the result will be the evolution of a group of knowledgeable allies who will support more readily the retention of a questioned title when a challenge occurs. It will also result in your being a school librarian who is confident, not fearful, when facing a challenge.

REFERENCES

Adams, Helen R. 2008. *Ensuring Intellectual Freedom and Access to Information in the School Library Media Program.* Westport, Connecticut: Libraries Unlimited.

American Association of School Librarians. 2007. *Standards for the 21st-Century Learner.* http://www.ala.org/ala/mgrps/divs/aasl/guidelinesandstandards/learningstandards/standards.cfm (accessed January 18, 2013).

American Library Association. 2008. *Code of Ethics of the American Library Association.* http://www.ala.org/advocacy/proethics/codeofethics/codeethics/ (accessed January 18, 2013).

American Library Association. "Most Frequently Challenged Books of the 21st Century." http://www.ala.org/advocacy/banned/frequentlychallenged/21stcenturychallenged/ (accessed January 18, 2013).

IF Matters: Intellectual Freedom @ your library®

A Tale of Two Challenges

By Helen R. Adams

Originally published in the IF Matters: Intellectual Freedom @ your library® column, *School Library Monthly*, XXVI (5) (January 2010): 48–49.

The final column in the "Challenges" series focuses on two actual challenges: their similarities, their differences, and what the school library professionals learned from their experiences.

Joel's Story

Joel is the Director of Technology and Media Services in a mid-size district, and he describes the following formal challenge that a complainant in his district made against the young adult novel, *TTYL* (Harry N. Abrams, Inc., 2004):

> A complaint was filed against *TTYL* by Lauren Myracle in one of our middle school libraries. Our district has a policy and procedure for handling complaints, and it was followed by the administration and school librarian. A team met with the parent, reviewed the selection process, and discussed concerns. The parent was offered the option of disallowing her child the ability to check out this particular book but was concerned [based on sexual content] also about the availability of the book to others. Following district procedure, a formal committee was assigned the task of reviewing and preparing reports for the school board.
>
> The [reconsideration] process is harder than some believe. People feel quite strongly about the appropriateness of some books and are often on opposite sides ranging from protecting intellectual freedom to protecting children from what each sees as harmful. It is unlikely that people with strong beliefs on either pole will move significantly. Everyone wanted the same thing—what is best for kids—but disagreed on how to achieve it. My goal was to make sure that enough information and conversation flowed to place the issue in a larger context.
>
> The committee created majority and minority opinions, and these documents, along with some context, were provided at a board meeting. The board voted 2-7 to retain the book. (Joel 2009)

What Joel Learned

Joel discovered valuable insights for those experiencing a challenge, including:

- Set up a standing reconsideration committee that meets several times per year rather than one formed when a challenge occurs. We have a fairly straightforward policy/procedure, but looks on paper can be deceiving. Too much happened in a very short timeframe, and I felt unprepared.

- Frame the challenge objectively focusing on the bigger picture. It is easy to think the issue is this book or the passage on page 20. In reality, it is more about the philosophy of the library and approach to selection.

- Support the school librarian going through the challenge. We structured time into department meetings as well as frequent check-ins (Joel 2009).

Jim's Story

The final decision in Joel's district was positive and resulted in, as Joel states, "a very intellectual discussion around how we think about books, the education of our children, social issues in their lives, and conflict" (Joel 2009). Some situations, on the other hand, are more difficult and personal. Jim, a middle school librarian, relates his experience in the following narrative:

In 1996 before widespread use of the World Wide Web and Google, our library media center had limited dial-up access to the Internet, and I selected *The Internet Yellow Pages* for our collection. The parent of a middle school student found this book at home and discovered that, in addition to addresses for useful information, the book provided URLs to such resources as The Anarchist's Handbook and other "questionable" sites. The parent informed my principal that she felt this sort of directory should not be available for students.

The principal felt that this material was so *dangerous,* his exact word, that contrary to the Board-approved policy for reconsideration of materials, he removed the book from the collection immediately. At that point, I felt I had no recourse but to initiate the reconsideration procedure rather than allow him to pull the book. Professional ethics left me no reasonable alternative—none that would allow me to respect myself had I not stood up to his censorship.

The policy called for the local building principal to act as chair for the reconsideration committee, but since *he* was involved in the challenge, a principal from another building stepped in. I contacted ALA's Office of Intellectual Freedom where the late Judith Krug and others helped me with this case. My principal made an attempt to "stack" the committee with parents sympathetic to his view, but in the end, the committee voted 5 to 1 to retain the book. My relationship with this principal was poor to begin with, and I felt this challenge could have cost me my job had the committee not ruled in my favor.

Although I prevailed, my "victory" (and yes, it was personal) cost me dearly with other administrators in the district. There was the perception that I placed principle over common sense, although I didn't see it that way. They also probably perceived me as "difficult" and not a "team player." (Jim 2009)

What Jim Learned

Like Joel, Jim learned some lessons and advises the following:

- Be ready for a challenge. It's not *if* a challenge will happen in your career but rather *when.*

- Have a board approved selection policy with a reconsideration process and know it inside and out.

- Work to build the best possible relationship with your administrator, and let him/her know how important intellectual freedom is to you.

- Build a positive reputation in your community (Jim 2009).

> **The Merritt Fund:
> One Recipient's Story**
>
> The Leroy C. Merritt Humanitarian Fund was established by Judith Krug in 1970 as a safety net to assist librarians whose employment and financial security is in jeopardy based on their active protection of intellectual freedom. Although information about Merritt Fund recipients is kept confidential, occasionally those who have benefitted from Merritt Fund support choose to speak publicly. Former ALA president Carol Brey-Casiano described in a brief video (http://americanlibrariesmagazine.org/al_focus/merritt-humanitarian-fund-40th-anniversary) a situation she encountered in 2011 as a public library director and how the Fund assisted her financially to pay legal fees (American Library Association. 2010. "Merritt Humanitarian Fund 40th Anniversary." AL focus. http://americanlibrariesmagazine.org/al_focus/merritt-humanitarian-fund-40th-anniversary [accessed January 18, 2013]).

The Leroy C. Merritt Humanitarian Fund

Jim felt threatened during the challenge in his district, and there are no statistics for the number of school librarians who feel forced to leave their positions following challenges. Fortunately, there is limited financial assistance available to them. The Leroy C. Merritt Humanitarian Fund provides direct financial support to librarians working in any type of library who either lose their position or are threatened with job loss because they uphold and defend intellectual freedom principles. According to Merritt Fund Trustee Emeritus Martin Garnar, a financial grant from the Fund can be used without restrictions for living expenses, legal fees, or whatever the recipient needs most (ALA 2008). School librarians who need assistance will find a copy of the request form and instructions at the Leroy C. Merritt Humanitarian Fund website (http://www.ala.org/ala/mgrps/affiliates/relatedgroups/merrittfund/assistance/assistance).

Final Thoughts

When challenges occur, Joel, Jim, and other librarians stand firm, sometimes risking their employment and careers in the process. They rely on the advocates they have educated and nurtured in preparation for a challenge, use ALA documents such as the *Code of Ethics* and the *Library Bill of Rights* interpretations for guidance, and ask for assistance from the local library community and the ALA Office for Intellectual Freedom. Those who protect students' First Amendment right to read all types of books in libraries are silent, often unappreciated, heroes.

REFERENCES

American Library Association. "Leroy C. Merritt Humanitarian Fund." http://www.ala.org/ala/mgrps/affiliates/relatedgroups/merrittfund/assistance/assistance.cfm (accessed January 18, 2013).

American Library Association. 2008. "Leroy C. Merritt Humanitarian Fund Transcript." *AL Focus.* Video. http://www.youtube.com/watch?v=8SKD1esyhyY/ (accessed January 18, 2013).

Jim, email to author, August 22, 2009.

Joel, email to author, August 24, 2009.

IF Matters: Intellectual Freedom @ your library®

What Happens When You Call the ALA Office for Intellectual Freedom for Help?

By Helen R. Adams

Originally published in the IF Matters: Intellectual Freedom @ your library® column, *School Library Monthly*, XXVI (7) (March 2010): 47–48.

Challenges to school library resources occur across the United States, and no school library professional is immune. This fact is well documented. According to the American Library Association's (ALA) Office for Intellectual Freedom (OIF) there were 3,736 challenges reported to the ALA Office for Intellectual Freedom between the years 2001 and 2008, with 37 percent occurring in school libraries (ALA 2009). A more graphic representation can be found on the Banned Books Week website. It features a map (http://www.bannedbooksweek.org/mapping-censorship) showing the locations of over 120 challenges selected from the hundreds of challenges reported since 2007 to the OIF, the National Coalition Against Censorship, and the Kids' Right to Read Project (OIF 2009).

Q & A with the Office for Intellectual Freedom

Where do you find help when your principal directs you to remove a book from library shelves on the basis of its content and its potential for a challenge, or when a parent complains about a book? If a concern is raised about a library resource, you have an ally waiting to provide assistance: the ALA Office for Intellectual Freedom. OIF provides confidential assistance to school librarians with actual and possible challenges to books, magazines, and other library resources.

> **Where to Find Help During a Challenge**
>
> 1-800-545-2433, Ext. 4221 (Angela Maycock) or Ext. 4220 (OIF office)
>
> Hours: 8:30–4:30 pm CST, Monday–Friday
>
> Email: oif@ala.org OR amaycock@ala.org
>
> *ALA/AASL membership not required.*

Angela Maycock, Assistant Director for the ALA's Office for Intellectual Freedom, answered my questions about ALA's challenge support services. Angela is the person with whom many librarians and teachers speak or correspond when they contact OIF about a challenge. Questions and answers from the interview with Angela follow.

May any school librarian contact the Office for Intellectual Freedom for assistance, or must the caller be a member of the American Library Association?

Anyone can call the ALA Office for Intellectual Freedom for support. We do not require anyone who contacts us to be an ALA member, and we don't ask for the caller's credentials or affiliation. We provide help to anyone who needs it.

How can a school librarian contact the Office for Intellectual Freedom?

We're available by phone or email. You can call us toll free at—800-545-2433—that's the general number for ALA. Ask for extension 4221, my [Angela Maycock's] direct number, or the Office for Intellectual Freedom, extension 4220. We're also very responsive to emails if a phone is not available to a school librarian during the day. The general office email address is oif@ala.org, and my personal email is amaycock@ala.org.

When a school librarian calls the Office for Intellectual Freedom to whom will s/he speak?

If not calling my direct extension, the phone is answered by our administrative assistant or the office manager. Both are well-trained in handling calls for assistance with challenges because we receive them literally every day. OIF staff will direct the call to me or to the Director of OIF. If neither is available, staff will gather whatever information the caller feels comfortable giving, and we'll call them back.

Our office hours are 8:30 am to 4:30 pm CST. For calls after hours, there is always voice mail or send an email, and we'll respond.

What specific support will the Office for Intellectual Freedom offer school librarians?

Every challenge situation is unique, but when someone calls, the first thing s/he will get is an "open ear." We're available to listen—to find out exactly what is going on and to help strategize about the situation that is unfolding. In addition to listening, I can provide book reviews and supporting information about the challenged resource. I can offer a letter of support directed to the principal, superintendent, or school board; and we compose the letter in collaboration with the librarian. We tailor what we provide to meet the needs of the librarian and the local situation.

Is information that the school librarian gives to you kept confidential?

All information on challenges reported to the Office for Intellectual Freedom by individuals is kept confidential. We take our promise of confidentiality very seriously and will not disclose any information to outside groups. We do compile statistics about the challenges reported to us, but there is never any identifiable information linking a particular materials challenge to an individual, an institution, or a town.

Is legal advice provided?

Our office does not specifically provide legal advice. I'm a librarian, not an attorney. What we can do is give general advice about situations and direct librarians to legal counsel if it is needed. We have a network of attorneys with whom we've worked in the past whom we know will do "pro bono" work [provide free legal counsel].

Are follow-up calls ever made to a school librarian who has sought assistance?

We always do our best to follow-up on challenge situations—whether by a phone call or an email—to ask: did you receive the information, was it helpful, is additional action needed, or how was the situation resolved? We do not always receive a response back from the person. We feel that is OK. We're happy to simply have been able to provide some assistance.

Where can school librarians go on the ALA website to learn more about preparing for and working through a challenge?

The ALA Office for Intellectual Freedom website is huge and is located at http:/www .ala.org/oif/. There is a link on that main page titled "Challenges to Library Materials," and it includes information on essential preparation before a challenge, strategies for responding to a challenge, and getting support from OIF staff.

May school librarians also call about filtering and privacy issues?

Yes, these are clearly intellectual freedom issues, and we deal with them every day. We encourage librarians to call us because privacy and filtering issues are complex in ways that print and/or other physical items are not. Deborah Caldwell-Stone, Deputy Director of the Office for Intellectual Freedom, is an attorney and has particular expertise in the area of privacy. She is also very knowledgeable about filtering laws as they apply to minors.

Do you have any final advice to give school librarians who are seeking assistance from the ALA Office for Intellectual Freedom?

We welcome all contact from librarians needing assistance with an intellectual freedom issue. We are happy to talk through the situation and provide guidance on how to proceed.

> **Other Pro–First Amendment Organizations**
>
> Appendix B contains an annotated list of other pro–First Amendment and privacy advocacy organizations that may also provide support to school librarians.

REFERENCES

American Library Association. "Most Frequently Challenged Books of the 21st Century." http://www.ala.org/advocacy/banned/frequentlychallenged/21stcenturychallenged/ (accessed January 18, 2013).

American Library Association. Office for Intellectual Freedom. 2009. OIF Blog, August 20, 2009. "New Book Censorship Map Reveals National Problem." http://www.bannedbooksweek.org/mappingcensorship (accessed January 18, 2013).

Maycock, Angela. Interview by Helen Adams. Appleton, Wisconsin, October 22, 2009.

IF Matters: Intellectual Freedom @ your library®

The Materials Selection Policy: Defense Against Censorship

By Helen R. Adams

Originally published in the IF Matters: Intellectual Freedom @ your library® column, *School Library Media Activities Monthly*, XXIV (7) (March 2008): 28.

     Picture this scenario. Your principal leaves a note in your mailbox directing you to take a library resource off the shelf because a parent has complained about it. You suffer heart-in-the-throat panic and then stop to think. Remembering the *Code of Ethics*, you realize removing the resource immediately is not the right thing to do. Isn't there a policy to follow in case of a complaint? After a frantic search, you find it in your library policy manual and, thankfully, read through the passages describing the process for reconsidering materials. Initially, the procedures call for trying to resolve the parent's concern informally. No further action should occur unless a formal, written request for reconsideration of the resource is submitted by the complaining party. Other words in the policy stand out: "The challenged material will not be removed from circulation during the reconsideration process." You determine that speaking to the principal as quickly as possible is your next step.

Questions to Ask about Your Policy

Using this scenario as a starting point, ask yourself the following questions:

- Does your school have an officially approved materials selection policy that includes reconsideration procedures?
- Can you locate a copy easily?
- Are you well informed about the various parts of the policy?
- Is the policy current or more than five years old?
- Are the reconsideration procedures detailed enough to offer guidance to you, the principal, and the reconsideration committee during a challenge?
- Is your principal knowledgeable about the policy and what to do when a complaint is voiced?

These are always relevant questions because a materials selection policy is a *working document*, and a challenge could occur in your library media center at any time.

The Value of a Selection Policy

     A formally approved materials selection policy with review procedures is the *legal basis* for selection *and reconsideration* of all instructional materials used within a school including school library resources. Some states, including Wisconsin and Arkansas, require public schools to have materials selection policies and procedures for reconsideration approved by their governing boards. In addition to providing guidance to the school library media specialist, the selection policy gives an explanation to the broader school community as to why certain materials are chosen and others are not.

A materials selection policy contains criteria for selection of *all types* of materials for the collection from books to DVDs to audio book CDs to computer software to electronic databases. The policy provides guidance on the selection of potentially controversial resources. It communicates the school's support for intellectual freedom by endorsing professional association documents such as the American Library Association's (ALA) *Library Bill of Rights* and the *Freedom to Read*, a joint statement of the ALA and the Association of American Publishers. The policy opposes censorship in any form, referring to students' rights to receive information under the First Amendment. Significantly, the policy also includes the process through which materials will be reviewed by a reconsideration committee if a formal written complaint is received.

The selection policy contains the seeds for defense in case of a challenge. When selection criteria are consciously considered while identifying resources to be purchased, those same criteria can be used to justify the acquisition if a formal challenge is filed. The ability to demonstrate how the challenged resource meets approved selection criteria is a powerful argument for retention of the resource. Additionally, drawing on the policy's statements of support for intellectual freedom (i.e., the *Library Bill of Rights*), the reconsideration committee must consider how the withdrawal of the challenged title would affect the First Amendment rights of students to access information or read freely.

If Policy Is Not Followed

A policy is only as effective as the people in charge. If school personnel follow policy, a book or other library resource will not be removed from the collection without due process. If, however, the principal is afraid of challenges and gives in to the pressure to remove an item from the collection without following the reconsideration process, the policy is useless. School administrators or board of education members who do not follow written policy may leave the district open to legal action.

Creating and Revising a Selection Policy

If your school does not have an approved selection policy, take immediate action by discussing this situation with the principal. A school without a selection policy is vulnerable to complaints about library resources with no guidance on how to proceed and little legal basis for protecting students' First Amendment rights.

Because policies do not have an infinite shelf-life, every school or district should develop a schedule for the systematic review of *all* school library media program policies to keep them current. A three-year policy review cycle would be a useful time span. In three years, resources in new formats may be available requiring some modification in selection criteria, selection tools may change, or acquisitions procedures may be altered.

Additional References

Adams, Helen R. "Selection of School Library Media Program Resources." Chapter 3 in *Ensuring Intellectual Freedom and Access to Information in the School Library Media Program*. Westport, Connecticut: Libraries Unlimited, 2008: 37–57.

Chapter 3 details the creation of a school library materials selection policy, which includes a reconsideration process and addresses the selection of materials that some may consider controversial. The practice of self-censorship by school library professionals as a means of avoiding challenges is also discussed.

American Library Association. Office for Intellectual Freedom. "Developing a Materials Selection Policy." *Intellectual Freedom Manual*. 8th ed. Chicago: American Library Association, 2010: 376–380.

Although the manual was written for all types of libraries, this section includes a discussion of the components of a selection policy and procedures for handling informal and formal complaints about library resources.

Intellectual Freedom Committee. New York Library Association. "Self-censorship Checklist." http://www.nyla.org/images/nyla/files/Self-Censorship.pdf.

The eighteen question checklist will assist school librarians who are unsure whether their selection of library resources is veering toward self-censorship. Questions also involve restricting access to materials and violating patron privacy.

Resources to Assist You

There are several resources that may be useful in developing or revising a materials selection policy including the following:

- American Library Association. "Workbook for Selection Policy Writing." http://www.ala.org/Template.cfm?Section=dealing&Template=/ContentManagement/ContentDisplay.cfm&ContentID=57020
- Bishop, Kay. *The Collection Program in Schools: Concepts, Practices, and Information Sources*. 4th ed. Connecticut: Libraries Unlimited, 2007. (Author's note: The 5th edition of this book was published in 2012.)
- Reichman, Henry. *Censorship and Selection: Issues and Answers for Schools*. 3rd ed. Chicago, Illinois: American Library Association, 2001. (Author's note: This book is being revised.)

Key Ideas Summary

Readings in this chapter focus on challenges to school library resources and the role of the school librarian in battling censorship. Major ideas include:

- A formally approved selection policy with a review process is the *legal basis* for selection *and reconsideration* of all print, audiovisual, and digital resources added to the school library collection.

- The selection criteria used to evaluate and select resources for the collection are also used to defend the resource if a concern arises.

- A selection policy should include a means of reconsideration by which materials under scrutiny for appropriateness can be reexamined by a formal committee representing the school community. The reconsideration process ensures that no library resource selected using the district's selection criteria will be removed without due process.

- The First Amendment guarantees citizens the right to "petition the Government for a redress of grievances," which in effect allows those who have a concern about a library resource to request a review or reconsideration of the material.

- Parents and guardians have the right to guide the reading choices of their children or wards, but they may not infringe on the rights of other families to do the same.

- Fearing a challenge, some school library professionals practice self-censorship by not selecting books that could be considered controversial; however, no person can determine for certain which library resources may be challenged.

- Although librarians cannot insulate their collections from the potential for challenges to library resources, they can undertake actions to create a climate in the school and the community that supports the principles of intellectual freedom and minors' First Amendment legal right to receive information in the school library.

- From the first day on the job, the school library professional should prepare for a challenge. In school libraries, the question is more often *when* rather than *if* a concern will be raised about library material; and if not resolved informally, a written challenge may occur.

- The Leroy C. Merritt Humanitarian Fund provides financial assistance to librarians who have lost employment as a result of their stand on intellectual freedom.

- The ALA Office for Intellectual Freedom provides support to any school librarian who asks for help with a library material challenge; one need not be a member of ALA or AASL.

- All contacts made with the OIF are kept confidential, and information received related to challenges is used only for statistical purposes.

Resource Roundup:
Combating Censorship

- **Adams, Helen R. "Challenges to School Library Media Program Resources." Chapter 6 in *Ensuring Intellectual Freedom and Access to Information in the School Library Media Program*. Westport, Connecticut: Libraries Unlimited, 2008: 107–139.**

  Within this comprehensive reference on intellectual freedom in school libraries, chapter 6 topics include understanding the rationale for challenges, handling an oral or written complaint, managing the reconsideration process, acknowledging that some challenges do succeed, and examining whether there is the potential for school librarians to lose their jobs over challenges. The stories of school librarians who faced challenges in public and private schools are woven throughout the text.

- **American Library Association, Office for Intellectual Freedom website. http://www.ala.org/oif**

  This online home of intellectual freedom resources for all types of librarians contains extensive advice on essential preparations before a challenge, working through challenges, effective communication strategies when meeting the complainant, dealing with the media, and information on the most-challenged books by decade beginning with 1990.

- **Cooperative Children's Book Center, School of Education, University of Wisconsin-Madison. "What IF? Questions and Answers on Intellectual Freedom." http://www.education.wisc.edu/ccbc/freedom/whatif/default.asp**

  "What IF?," the Q & A service maintained by a librarian at the CCBC, was introduced as a valuable resource on intellectual freedom issues in Chapter 2. Its searchable database includes questions related to challenges such as "Could I someday lose my job as a school librarian because someone challenges a book in the library?" and "How can I help a colleague who is facing a challenge?"

- **Doyle, Robert P. *The Banned Books Resource Guide*. Chicago: American Library Association Office for Intellectual Freedom.**

  Published every three years, this standard reference includes an annotated "List of Books Some People Consider Dangerous" that reports worldwide censorship attempts going back hundreds of years. Arranged alphabetically by author, the list concentrates on publicly reported recent challenges in the United States and provides such details as the author, title, publisher, date, reason for the complaint, result, and source of the information. A supplement with information on the latest banned and challenged titles is published by the ALA annually and is available from the ALA Bookstore (http://www.alastore.ala.org).

- **National Library of Norway.** *The Beacon for Freedom of Expression.* **http://www.beaconforfreedom.org/index.html**

  Censorship is global. The Beacon for Freedom of Expression, an online searchable international bibliographic database hosted by the National Library of Norway, lists more than 50,000 titles of books, newspapers, radio and television broadcasts, and websites that have been censored by a "state, governing authority or state-related body" for "moral, religious, or political" reasons (Beacon of Free Expression. "What is registered in the database?" http://www.beaconforfreedom.org/liste.html?tid=411&art_id=531 [accessed January 18, 2013]). The site also has cataloged more than 5,000 works about censorship and freedom of expression. Initially documenting censorship in thirty countries including the United States, Japan, Poland, Norway, Russia, Canada, and South Africa, the database also includes the *Index Librorum Prohibitorum,* the list of books banned by the Catholic Church over a four hundred year period (Beacon of Free Expression. "Which countries are featured in the database?" http://www.beaconforfreedom.org/liste .html?tid=411&art_id=548 [accessed January 18, 2013]).

- **Nye, Valerie and Kathy Barco, editors.** *True Stories of Censorship Battles in America's Libraries.* **Chicago: ALA Editions, 2012.**

  With a wide range of the ideas conveyed, the text compiles short vignettes on censorship attempts in all types of libraries. Those who were involved reflect on what they learned, report strategies that were successful, and caution against tactics that failed. In addition to the usual incidents of book challenges, the volume touches on self-censorship, age-appropriateness, cultural expressions, and controversy over book displays.

Discussion Questions

- You are having dinner with a group of local area school librarians. The conversation turns to selecting fiction books with a bit of "edginess" such as *The Hunger Games, And Tango Makes Three, The Absolutely True Diary of a Part-Time Indian,* and *What My Mother Doesn't Know.* One person of the group says, "I don't buy those kinds of books because I know that there are people in the community who would challenge them." How would you respond?

- Expressions of concern and formal challenges are a fact of life for school library professionals. Discuss three ways in which you will prepare for a challenge.

- Although districts' reconsideration processes differ, describe your general role as school librarian during a formal challenge.

- Many school library professionals hesitate to contact the ALA Office for Intellectual Freedom (OIF) for assistance with an actual or potential challenge. Discuss the factors which cause librarians not to request assistance, and articulate the factors that would persuade you to call OIF staff for help.

- ALA acknowledges that only a small percentage of challenges or book removals are reported to the OIF. Since confidentiality is guaranteed, debate whether it is the ethical responsibility of librarians to report censorship attempts to OIF.

- Having a materials selection policy with a reconsideration process is key, both for guidance in selecting materials and for providing direction during an informal oral complaint or a formal written challenge. If a district does not have a selection policy, describe the steps that a school librarian can take to begin a conversation about creating one.

- Real-life school staff Joel and Jim had very different experiences with challenges in their districts. Jim's principal took the unusual step of personally removing from the collection the book he saw as "dangerous" rather than initiating the reconsideration process. Although eventually the reconsideration committee recommended retaining the book, Jim felt that his job could have been in jeopardy if a reverse decision had been made. Debate how far a school librarian should go to uphold professional ethics such as resisting censorship. What factors might cause a school librarian to make the difficult personal decision not to take a greater stand to uphold intellectual freedom principles?

Chapter 4

Intellectual Freedom Online

Including the Columns

"Filters and Access to Information, Part I"

"Filters and Access to Information, Part II"

"Filters and Access to Information, Part III"

"Overcoming Filtering Frustration"

"Dusting Off the Acceptable Use Policy (AUP)"

"Social Networking and Privacy: A Law Enforcement Perspective"

Chapter 4

Intellectual Freedom Online

INTRODUCTION

When the topic of censorship arises, it is usually in relation to books; however, censorship can also occur online, caused by overly aggressive filtering practices in schools that block sites far beyond the requirements of the Children's Internet Protection Act (CIPA) of 2000. The intent of CIPA is to filter *visual depictions* of child pornography, obscenity, and those harmful to minors as defined by federal law. Instead, however, the filtering mandated by CIPA and state filtering laws has created much frustration and debate over how to protect children and young adults from educationally unsuitable content online while at the same time protecting students' First Amendment right to receive constitutionally protected information. Concurrently, modes of social networking, involving popular sites such as Facebook and Twitter, and the exponential use of personal mobile devices for communication have caused a host of new challenges for educators.

Filters and Access to Information

The first three reprinted columns in Chapter 4 were published as a series. "Filters and Access to Information, Part I" provides an overview of CIPA and the Neighborhood Children's Internet Protection Act (NCIPA). It also supplies specific examples of how restrictive filtering impedes instruction for an eighth grade science teacher. Part II in the series explains how excessive filtering can have a detrimental effect on teaching young citizens to seek and evaluate information for themselves, may cause students not to meet the AASL's *Standards for the 21st-Century Learner* (specifically requirements in Standards 1, 2, and 3), and infringes on students' First Amendment right to receive information in a school library. Part III in the series urges school librarians to realize that filtering laws are unlikely to be repealed and to advocate to the school community for less restrictive filtering. Although the basic information in the columns is unchanged, statistics on minors' use of social media, the advent of texting and tweeting, and the use of personal mobile devices has transformed the use of technology; and many school districts are scrambling to keep up.

"Overcoming Filtering Frustration," the fourth column introduces the American Association of School Librarians' Banned Websites Awareness Day, established in 2011 and held annually during Banned Books Week. The fifth reading, "Dusting Off the Acceptable Use Policy (AUP)," provides recommendations from a state school board association policy consultant on updating AUPs to include discussions on Web 2.0 collaborative tools and cyberbullying. The final column, "Social Networking and Privacy: A Law Enforcement Perspective," is based on a 2007 interview with a young law enforcement officer in a small Midwest town who shared his perspective on the dangers of teenagers posting private information on adult social networking sites. Although law enforcement personnel are still very aware of the dangers of online predators, the extreme media hype has dissipated. Cyberbullying and its consequences have replaced cyber predators as an area of major concern in schools.

Clarification on Filtering Requirements

Interpretations of CIPA requirements vary a great deal among schools, with some districts closely following only the three CIPA constraints against obscenity, child pornography, and material harmful to minors and others opting for very strict filtering that amounts to a virtual "lockdown" of the Internet. In August 2011, Karen Cator, the Director of Education Technology at the U.S. Department of Education, spoke candidly in an interview about what CIPA requires and made clarifying comments. Many schools block YouTube, but Cator explained that the site has much content that can be useful in instruction, such as videos of experts explaining complex ideas. As a result, the site *need not be blocked* for teachers using it for instruction. Cator also dispelled the misconception that schools can lose E-rate funding by *unblocking* legitimate, appropriate websites that have been blocked by the school's filtering product. She further counseled that teachers should be trusted in their evaluation of the appropriateness of a blocked website and stated there should be a process for teachers to request the unblocking of a site by an authorized staff member. The Department of Education's "National Education Technology Plan" of 2010 states that students' online safety at school is a primary objective, but filters sometimes also block access to collaborative, creative tools such as blogs, wikis, and social networks that hold the promise of sparking student learning. In this case, Cator stated that more targeted, "nuanced" filters are needed. Finally, Cator re-enforced that schools need to teach students about Internet safety, as required by the Protecting Children in the 21st Century Act approved by Congress in 2008 and described throughout this chapter (Barseghian 2011).

Additional clarification on CIPA and NCIPA requirements was provided in August 2011 when the Federal Communications Commission (FCC) issued its rulemaking for implementation of the 2008 Protecting Children in the 21st Century Act. Although the implementation rule primarily assists districts with adding references into their Internet Safety Policies, to comply with the law's requirement of educating students about Internet safety when using social networking sites and chat rooms and informing them about cyberbullying, the rule also offers clarification on blocking of social networking websites. Section B, number 17 of the rule states:

> Although it is possible that certain individual Facebook or MySpace pages could potentially contain material harmful to minors, we [FCC] do not find that these websites are *per se* "harmful to minors" or fall into one of the categories that schools and libraries must block . . . The U.S. Department of Education recently found that social networking websites have the potential to support student learning, stating that students can "participate in online social networks where people from all over the world share ideas, collaborate, and learn new things." Declaring such sites categorically harmful to

minors would be inconsistent with the Protecting Children in the 21st Century Act's focus on "educating minors about appropriate online behavior . . .". (FCC 2011, 8)

It is now clear that schools are not *required* to block social networking sites, but they must still determine to what extent and under what circumstances social technologies add to student learning and incorporate that information into their own district's AUP.

The ACLU's Legal Challenges to Discriminatory Filtering

In 2009, the American Civil Liberties Union (ACLU) filed the first of two lawsuits over discriminatory filtering of lesbian, gay, bisexual, and transgender (LGBT) websites in schools. The earliest, *Franks v. Metropolitan Board of Public Education* (2009), occurred in Tennessee, and the plaintiffs were several high school students and a high school librarian, Karyn Storts-Brinks. The ACLU-TN was able to make a case that the school district blocked pro-LGBT online content such as the Gay, Lesbian & Straight Education Network (GLSEN) while not blocking anti-LGBT sites. The lawsuit was settled out of court after the ACLU received assurance that the two districts named in the legal action would not, in the future, block student or faculty access to LGBT websites in a discriminatory manner (Storts-Brinks 2010 24, 26–27).

As a result of the lawsuit and the feeling that the Tennessee filtering situation had not been unique, the ACLU launched a national "Don't Filter Me" campaign in February 2011. It encouraged students at public schools to check their school web filtering software and report if it was blocking access to LGBT-positive information while allowing access to negatively portrayed LGBT information. Within only six months, the campaign was very successful. The ACLU "Interim Don't Filter Me Report," filed in August 2011 highlighted the following achievements:

- Confirmed 84 reports of pro-LGBT viewpoint-discriminatory filtering in public schools in 24 states.
- Stopped blocking pro-LGBT websites in 96 schools across the United States, affecting access to information for 144,670 students.
- Worked with five top filtering companies to reform their filtering software (Hampton 2011, 3).

Although many school districts agreed to change filtering practices when contacted by the ACLU, one district chose not to do so. In August 2011, the ACLU filed a lawsuit against the Camdenton R-III School District (Missouri) over its filtering practices that block positive LGBT content while anti-LGBT websites are accessible (Ito). In February 2012, a federal district court issued a preliminary injunction in *PFLAG, Inc. v. Camdenton R-III School District* that the Missouri school district must stop viewpoint-discriminatory censoring of pro-LGBT content (ACLU). The case was settled on March 28, 2012, with the district agreeing to stop filtering non-sexual LGBT websites, pay legal fees and court costs, and have its filtering practices monitored for eighteen months (eSchoolNews 2012).

The "Don't Filter Me" campaign and the legal battles are very important. According to a 2009 GLSEN survey, within the past year 90 percent of LGBT students had been harassed in school and two-thirds felt unsafe in the school environment based on their sexual orientation (Ito 2011). Allowing pro-LGBT information to be accessible on public school computers is critical because this may be the only source of supportive, accurate information for students questioning their sexual orientation or gender identity.

ALA and AASL Responses to Filtering in Schools

As Web 2.0 tools and social networking sites proliferated, many schools blocked access to the emerging interactive sites. With the increasing use of Web 2.0 tools by young people, members of the American Library Association (ALA) Intellectual Freedom Committee wanted a statement to support the right of youth to use Web 2.0 tools, both academically in schools and personally outside of schools. The result is "Minors and Internet Interactivity: An Interpretation of the Library Bill of Rights." Approved by the ALA Council in 2009, the interpretation emphasizes the right of minors to create, share, and interact with others online for academic and personal purposes as an extension of their First Amendment right of expression. The interpretation discourages filtering as a solution to inappropriate use, instead supporting that minors be educated to be safe and ethical digital citizens (ALA 2009). The concept of teaching students to use social media responsibly fits well with the mandate in the Protecting Students in the 21st Century Act to teach students Internet safety, including how to interact appropriately on social networking websites. Refer to the Resource Roundup section at the end of the chapter for an article that provides more information on how the interpretation applies in elementary and high schools.

> **Minors and Internet Interactivity**
>
> ALA's "Minors and Internet Interactivity: An Interpretation of the Library Bill of Rights" interpretation can be found online on the *Intellectual Freedom Manual* companion website at http://www.ifmanual.org/part2section2.

In 2011, the American Association of School Librarians (AASL) Board of Directors voted to spotlight the restrictive filtering practices found in many school districts nationwide by designating one day during the annual Banned Books Week as *Banned Websites Awareness Day* (BWAD). AASL argued that helping students develop online searching and evaluation skills is more productive for digital citizenship than sole reliance on filters. A majority of students use online social media sites to communicate, and incorporating their use into instruction will make learning experiences more authentic and engaging (AASL). The first annual BWAD in September 2011 was a modest success, and other organizations (including the National Association of Secondary School Principals) supported the effort. More information about the BWAD website and resources is available in the fourth reading and the Resources Roundup section at the end of this chapter.

The Best Filter

The filtering debate—some feel the term "battle" is more appropriate—will most certainly continue at the local level. Despite this state of affairs, the Protecting Students in the 21st Century Act requires districts to certify in their E-rate program applications that students are being educated about Internet safety; this is a big win for the proponents of education over solely blocking websites. Michael Gras, chief of technology for the White Oaks Independent School District (Texas) stated it well: "No usable filter is perfect, and *the best filter is achieved through training the child to behave responsibly*" (Adams 2010, 32).

The fact remains that students' education is stunted when filters are too strict. Teachers' ability to use all the legitimate educational sources available to them online for instruction is also hampered unnecessarily through overly aggressive filtering. The long-term result is that students' First Amendment rights to receive information and their freedom of expression online are not fully realized in many schools.

REFERENCES

Adams, Helen R. 2010. "Filtering Texas-Style: An Interview with Michael Gras and Scott Floyd." *Knowledge Quest* 39 no. 1, 30–37.

American Association of School Librarians. "Banned Websites Awareness Day." http://www.ala .org/aasl/bwad (accessed January 18, 2013).

American Civil Liberties Union. 2012. "Court Orders Missouri School District to Stop Censoring LGBT Websites." February 15, 2012. http://www.aclu.org/free-speech-lgbt-rights/court -orders-missouri-school-district-stop-censoring-lgbt-websites (accessed January 18, 2013).

American Library Association. 2009. "Minors and Internet Interactivity: An Interpretation of the Library Bill of Rights." http://www.ala.org/advocacy/intfreedom/librarybill/interpreta tions/minorsinternetinteractivity (accessed January 18, 2013).

Barseghian, Tina. 2011. "Straight from the DOE: Dispelling Myths About Blocked Sites." April 26, 2011. Mind/Shift. http://mindshift.kqed.org/2011/04/straight-from-the-doe-facts-about-blocking-sites-in-schools (accessed January 18, 2013).

eSchoolNews. 2012. "School District, ACLU Reach Settlement in Filtering Lawsuit." March 29, 2012. http://www.eschoolnews.com/2012/03/29/school-district-aclu-reach-settlement-in-filtering-lawsuit/2 (accessed January 18, 2013).

Federal Communications Commission. 2011. "In the Matter of Schools and Libraries Universal Service Support Mechanism," CC Docket No. 02.6 and A National Broadband Plan for Our Future, GN Docket No. 09-5, page 8. August 10, 2011. http://transition.fcc.gov/Daily_ Releases/Daily_Business/2011/db0819/FCC-11-125A1.pdf (accessed February 22, 2012 [no longer accessible]).

Hampton, Chris. 2011. "Don't Filter Me Interim Report." September 28, 2011. American Civil Liberties Union. http://www.aclu.org/lgbt-rights/dont-filter-me-interim-report (accessed January 18, 2013).

Ito, Suzanne. 2011. "ACLU Sues Missouri School District for Illegally Censoring LGBT Websites." August 15, 2011. Blog of Rights. http://www.aclu.org/blog/free-speech-lgbt-rights/aclu -sues-missouri-school-district-illegally-censoring-lgbt-websites (accessed January 18, 2013).

Storts-Brinks, Karyn. 2010. "Censorship Online: One School Librarian's Journey to Provide Access to LGBT Resources." *Knowledge Quest* 39 no. 1: 22–29.

IF Matters: Intellectual Freedom @ your library®

Filters and Access to Information, Part I

By Helen R. Adams

Originally published in the IF Matters: Intellectual Freedom @ your library® column, *School Library Media Activities Monthly*, XXV (1) (September 2008): 55.

Why Are These Sites Blocked?

Students, teachers, and library media specialists in many schools are frustrated daily when they find legitimate educational websites blocked by their schools' filters. An 8th grade science teacher in the Midwest gave these examples of recent searches where access was denied:

- "Sites that I use for animal research papers are sometimes blocked, depending on how you try to access them. These include such scandalous sources as the San Diego Zoo and the University of Michigan Zoological Museum."

- "I was helping an 8th grader with a social studies assignment and tried to call up a map of Canada. Blocked."

- "Nearly all Google searches are blocked" (Anonymous 2008).

Mary, a Wisconsin library media specialist said, "Recently students were doing an assignment for music class that involved Internet research on their favorite guitar player. Quite a few of the students had everything about their favorite musician blocked. . . . Our district uses the most restrictive filtering possible, which results in many educationally necessary sites being blocked" (Mary 2008).

School Libraries Count! Filtering and Online Access

The American Association of School Librarians (AASL) has been engaged in "School Libraries Count!," a national longitudinal study of school library programs at the elementary and secondary levels since 2007. In addition to standardized tracking questions, AASL asks school librarians several topical questions. In 2012, the additional questions focused on filtering and online access in schools (AASL. "School Libraries Count!" http://www.ala.org/aasl/researchandstatistics/slcsurvey/slcsurvey [accessed January 18, 2013]).

AASL's most recent data from the 2012 survey provided a "snapshot" of Internet filtering in schools. From the 4,299 respondents, AASL learned that 98% of schools filter Internet content using multiple approaches including: installing filtering software (94%), having an acceptable use policy (87%), and supervising of students while online (73%). Survey respondents reported that four types of content are heavily blocked: social networking sites (88%), IM/online chat (74%), online games (69%), and video services such as YouTube (66%). Data suggest that many schools are filtering beyond the requirements of CIPA. Although the majority of school librarians (92%) can ask to have wrongly blocked sites unblocked, the response rates vary greatly: unblocked within a few hours (27%), one to two days (35%), two days but less than five (17%), or wait times of one week or longer (20%). According to survey respondents, filters impact student learning by inhibiting student research (52%), ignoring the social process involved in learning (42%), and discouraging collaboration (25%) (American Association of School Librarians. 2012 "Filtering in Schools: AASL Executive Summary." http://www.ala.org/aasl/researchandstatistics/slcsurvey/filtering-schools [accessed January 18, 2013]). The 2012 complete survey report is available with other School Libraries Count! results dating back to 2007 (http://www.ala.org/aasl/researchandstatistics/slcsurvey/slcsurvey).

The Challenge for Administrators

While there are incredible resources on the Internet for K–12 students and teachers, there is also plenty of cyber-garbage. Administrators and technology staff struggle to keep students safe while online at school *and, at the same time,* retain their districts' eligibility for federal and state funding. According to the National Association of Secondary School Principals, "School leaders face the triple challenge of protecting their students against online predators while safeguarding students' First Amendment rights and encouraging use of the Internet as a legitimate pedagogical tool" (National Association of Secondary School Principals 2007).

CIPA and NCIPA Requirements

There are filtering requirements for any public or private school that accepts specific types of federal funding. In December 2000, Congress passed the Consolidated Appropriations Act (PL 106-554), which included the Children's Internet Protection Act (CIPA) and the Neighborhood Children's Internet Protection Act (NCIPA). CIPA requires that elementary and secondary schools that accept discounted services under the federal Schools and Libraries Program of the Universal Service Fund (the E-rate Program) or direct federal funding through the Elementary and Secondary Education Act (ESEA), as amended in 2001, certify that they have installed "technology protection measures" or filters on *all computers used to access the Internet* by minors and adults to protect against *visual depictions* that are obscene, contain child pornography, or material "harmful to minors" as defined under federal law. CIPA does not require that districts filter text or audio. CIPA does require schools to certify the existence and implementation of an Internet safety policy and that this policy must include monitoring the online activities of minors. Under CIPA and NCIPA, minors are considered to be those less than 17 years of age (Bocher 2004, 2, 3, 4, 6, 11).

NCIPA applies only to schools and libraries receiving E-rate discounted services and specifies that schools must create and implement an Internet safety policy that addresses the following:

(i) access by minors to *inappropriate matter* on the Internet and World Wide Web;

(ii) the safety and security of minors when using electronic mail, chat rooms, and other forms of direct electronic communications;

(iii) unauthorized access, including so-called 'hacking,' and other unlawful activities by minors online;

(iv) unauthorized disclosure, use, and dissemination of personal information regarding minors; and

(v) measures designed to restrict minors' access to materials harmful to minors . . . (Public Law 106-554, Section 1732 (1) (1) (A) (i)–(v) 2000).

While CIPA provides a definition for the term "harmful to minors," NCIPA does not provide a definition for "*matter inappropriate for minors.*" Instead, it allows the local school board or governing body to determine what is and is not inappropriate for minors to access under its Internet safety policy, often referred to as an acceptable use policy or AUP (Public Law 106-554, Section 1732 B (2) 2000).

State Filtering Laws

In addition to CIPA and NCIPA, many states have filtering laws that apply to schools. Most call for school boards to adopt Internet use policies to prevent minors from accessing sexually explicit, obscene, or harmful materials. Some also require the installation of filtering software on school computers and may tie eligibility for specified types of state funding to compliance. According to the National Conference of State Legislatures, other states such as Virginia, require instruction in Internet safety (http://www.ncsl.org/programs/lis/cip/filterlaws.htm). The statutes vary widely, so it is important for library media specialists to know their individual state's filtering laws. One source for this information is the National Conference of State Legislatures website (http://www.ncsl.org/programs/lis/cip/filterlaws.htm).

REFERENCES

Anonymous, mail message to author, May 7, 2008.

Bocher, Bob. 2004. "FAQ on E-Rate Compliance with the Children's Internet Protection Act and the Neighborhood Children's Internet Protection Act." February 19, 2004. http://pld.dpi .wi.gov/files/pld/pdf/cipafaq.pdf (accessed January 18, 2013).

Mary, email message to author, May 7, 2008.

National Association of Secondary School Principals. Nov. 2, 2007. "NASSP Board Position Statement on Internet Safety" (Note: revised Nov. 4, 2010 as "Internet and Wireless Safety"). http://www.nassp.org/Content.aspx?topic=55883 (accessed January 18, 2013).

National Conference of State Legislatures. "Children and the Internet: Laws Relating to Filtering, Blocking and Usage Policies in Schools and Libraries." http://www.ncsl.org/ programs/lis/cip/filterlaws.htm (accessed January 18, 2013).

Public Law 106-554. 2000. Subsection C. Neighborhood Children's Internet Protection Act. http://ifea.net/cipa.html (accessed January 18, 2013).

IF Matters: Intellectual Freedom @ your library®

Filters and Access to Information, Part II

By Helen R. Adams

Originally published in the IF Matters: Intellectual Freedom @ your library® column, *School Library Media Activities Monthly*, XXV (2) (October 2008): 54.

Years after the passage of the Children's Internet Protection Act (CIPA) and the Neighborhood Children's Internet Protection Act (NCIPA) in 2000, the battles about accessibility to educational websites for instruction and student research continue. Last month's column provided insights into the daily frustrations of teachers and library media specialists who find needed sites blocked. When filters are set at a stringent level, much legitimate and legal information protected under the First Amendment is inaccessible.

Filters' Effect on "Citizens in Training"

Federal and state legislators have passed and continue to sponsor filtering legislation in an effort to keep minors safe while using the Internet; however, except in rare instances such as in Virginia, they have overlooked the power of education versus use of filters. Thomas Jefferson wrote, "A democratic society depends upon an informed and educated citizenry" (Doyle 2007, 200). Minors are educated to make them knowledgeable, productive citizens capable of making critical decisions in a representative democracy. In effect, schools "grow" citizens who must develop skills to evaluate information from all types of sources in multiple formats, *including the Internet*. When filters are restrictive, students are unable to view diverse viewpoints on a topic, and they gain little experience in sorting authoritative sources from those that are dubious. In addition, filters protect minors only when they are using the Internet *in schools and libraries*, not during their Internet use outside those locations.

Americans do not automatically acquire the knowledge and skills necessary for citizenship when they reach the age of 18; therefore, it is essential that library media specialists and other educators teach students the information literacy skills needed to be effective citizens, including those related to Internet use. In 2007, the American Association of School Librarians (AASL) introduced its four *Standards for the 21st-Century Learner*. The following three Standards state, "Learners use skills, resources, and tools to:

> **NASSP Supports Less Restrictive Filtering**
>
> "Using Mobile and Social Technologies in Schools" is a position statement approved by the National Association of Secondary School Principals (NASSP) Board of Directors in May 2011. It recommends decreasing Internet filtering "to maximize student access to online learning tools and to provide opportunities to exercise judgment in the selection of those [educational social] tools" (National Association of Secondary School Principals. 2011. "Using Mobile and Social Technologies in Schools." http://www.nassp.org/Content.aspx?topic=Using_Mobile_and_Social_Technologies_in_Schools/ [accessed January 18, 2013]).

- Inquire, think critically, and gain knowledge.
- Draw conclusions, make informed decisions, apply knowledge to new situations, and create new knowledge.
- Share knowledge and *participate ethically and productively as members of our democratic society* [emphasis added] (AASL 2007, 3). [Excerpted from *Standards for the 21st-Century Learner* by the American Association of School Librarians, a division of the American Library Association, copyright © 2007 American Library Association. Available for download at www.ala.org/aasl/standards. Used with permission].

These Standards may not be met if school filters continue to block Internet resources far beyond what is required by CIPA.

Filters have a detrimental effect on youthful citizens' access to information on the Internet and on their intellectual freedom. For example, high school students in the Midwest complained to their library media specialist that the results of most Google searches are blocked; they are unable to download a shop manual for 4-wheelers and cannot access any blogs or wikis (Anonymous). In another district, Sandra, a school library professional, reported the following sites as causing the biggest battles in her high school: "NY Times editorials, our county library's blog, biography.com, the American Memory Project at the Library of Congress, and a Teenreads.com article about Harper Lee to name a few" (Sandra 2008).

These experiences are not unique. The authors of *Internet Filters: A Public Policy Report*, published by the Brennan Center for Justice in 2006, concluded that filters over-block huge amounts of information often in illogical, and sometimes biased, ways (Heins, Cho, and Feldmans 2006, ii). Filters make arbitrary decisions for minors on what they may access and do not allow them to make their own choices or mistakes. The American Library Association's "Free Access to Libraries by Minors: An Interpretation of the Library Bill of Rights" states, "Children and young adults unquestionably possess First Amendment rights, including the right to receive information through the library in print, nonprint, or digital format. Constitutionally protected speech cannot be suppressed solely to protect children or young adults from ideas or images a legislative body believes to be unsuitable for them" (ALA 2008).

Snapshot of Filtering Effects from a Student Perspective

Since 2003, Project Tomorrow's annual Speak Up National Research Project has been gathering data to provide a national picture of technology use in classrooms. The Speak Up 2011 survey gathered information from more than 416,000 K–12 students, teachers, and parents, and the contrast between the most recent answers and those from an earlier year continues to show the influence of filtering on students' access to the Internet. In 2005, the major complaint of sixth graders was that the Internet was too slow in their schools. In 2010 their major complaint was that filters block websites needed to complete assignments with 62 percent of middle school students and 71 percent of high school students agreeing that better Internet access to content blocked by Internet filters and firewalls would make their use of technology easier (Project Tomorrow. 2011. "The New 3 E's of Education: Enabled, Engaged, and Empowered: How Today's Students Are Leveraging Emerging Technologies for Learning." Speak Up 2010 National Findings. K–12 Students and Parents. April 1, 2011. http://www.tomorrow.org/speakup/pdfs/SU10_3EofEducation_Students.pdf [accessed January 18, 2013]).

In the 2011 survey, filtering is still considered a limiting educational factor with nearly 50 percent of middle school students and almost 60 percent of high school students reporting that valuable websites are blocked. Slightly more than 50 percent of high school students also report that Facebook and other social media are inaccessible on school computers. (Project Tomorrow. 2012. "Personalized Learning in 2012—The Students & Parent Point of View." Speak Up 2011 National Findings. K–12 Students and Parents. April 24, 2012. http://www.tomorrow.org/SPEAKUP/pdfs/Infographic_PersonalizedLearning2012.pdf [accessed January 18, 2013]).

The Experience in Scandinavian Countries

Recently a delegation sponsored by the Consortium of School Networking (COSN) traveled to the Scandinavian countries and learned that most schools there use filtering only for protection from viruses or spam (Stansbury 2008). According to Julie Walker, AASL's executive director, "Over there, thanks to solid teaching, the filters are in the students' heads. Students come into school with a sense of responsibility for their learning and a sense of why they're there. Ultimately, that's where we need to be too" (Villano 2008). Unfortunately, U.S. legislators have forced schools receiving selected types of federal funding to choose a different path, one that focuses on filters rather than a combination of educational strategies for America's citizens-in-training.

REFERENCES

American Association of School Librarians. 2007. *Standards for the 21st-Century Learner*. American Library Association.

American Library Association. 2008. "Free Access to Libraries by Minors: An Interpretation of the Library Bill of Rights." http://www.ala.org/advocacy/intfreedom/librarybill/interpre tations/freeaccesslibraries (accessed January 18, 2013).

Anonymous, email message to author, May 7, 2008.

Doyle, Robert D. 2007. *Banned Books: 2007 Resource Book*. Chicago: American Library Association.

Heins, Marjorie, Christina Cho, and Ariel Feldman. 2006. *Internet Filters: A Public Policy Report*. 2nd ed. Brennan Center for Justice at NYU School of Law. http://www.fepproject.org/policyreports/filters2.pdf (accessed January 18, 2013).

Sandra, email message to author, May 14, 2008.

Stansbury, Meris. 2008. "U.S. Educators Seek Lessons from Scandinavia." March 3, 2008. *eSchool News*. http://www.eschoolnews.com/2008/03/03/u-s-educators-seek-lessons-from -scandinavia (accessed January 18, 2013).

Villano, Matt. 2008. "What Are We Protecting Them From?" May 2008. *The Journal.* http://the journal.com/articles/2008/05/01/what-are-we-protecting-them-from.aspx (accessed January 18, 2013).

IF Matters: Intellectual Freedom @ your library®

Filters and Access to Information, Part III

By Helen R. Adams

Originally published in the IF Matters: Intellectual Freedom @ your library® column, *School Library Media Activities Monthly*, XXV (3) (November 2008): 55.

Since it is unlikely that the Children's Internet Protection Act (CIPA) and the Neighborhood Children's Internet Protection Act (NCIPA) will be repealed or changed substantially in the near future, living with a filtering system is a fact of life in K–12 schools. This does not mean, however, that school library media specialists should accept that students and faculty are automatically blocked from accessing worthwhile online educational resources. Instead, they must develop strategies to advocate for use of the Internet in an educationally sound manner to ensure students and staff access to constitutionally protected information.

Strategies to "Live" with Filters

In practical terms, what is the first step? Library media specialists can start by reviewing the district's current board-adopted acceptable use policy (AUP) for inclusion of issues like responsible use by students and staff, access to legal information based on student First Amendment rights, student instruction on safe and effective Internet use, protection of personal privacy, and recognition of the educational uses of Web 2.0 social technologies. They can also champion revising the AUP to make it comprehensive and proactive.

Over-blocking too many Internet websites can be the impetus for collaboration with teachers to incorporate *all* types of library media center resources including those found on the Internet. Library media specialists can assist teachers in developing pathfinders or Webquests with clickable links to carefully selected online information for curricular units. They can also develop a library media program website with links to educational materials as well as to the school's subscription-based online databases. Through ongoing instruction to classes and one-on-one "just in time" coaching, the use of fee-based online resources can be promoted as a high quality alternative to the open Internet. In addition, library media specialists can promote purchasing a search tool such as netTrekker [www.nettrekker.com] or Web Feet [www.galeschools.com] (discontinued Gale product) as a means of guiding teachers and students to pre-selected Internet sites.

Internet resources are valueless if they are inaccessible to teachers when they need them for instruction. It is important to encourage administrators and technology staff to set filters at the least restrictive position as well as to create a workable decision-making process for teachers to request that erroneously blocked websites be unblocked *on a timely basis* for use in classroom and library research. Criteria should be developed for valid staff requests to override the filter.

Educating Students about Internet Use

The importance of student instruction over reliance on filters cannot be over emphasized. As part of a school's K–12 information and technology literacy curriculum, the focus should be on implementing a school-wide program centered on safe and ethical use of Internet resources. For example, i-SAFE is a non-profit foundation whose goal is "to educate students on how to avoid dangerous, inappropriate, or unlawful online behavior" (www.isafe.org/). The i-SAFE curriculum provides age-appropriate lesson plans and activities for K–12 students on a wide range of topics from email and text-messaging to cyberbullying to the ethical use of intellectual property. Kathy, a middle school library media specialist in Wisconsin, states, "I used the personal safety section of the i-SAFE curriculum with 6th, 7th, and 8th grade students this year. . . . The program teaches students about choosing good screen names and strong passwords. It points out how predators lurk in chat rooms and may learn enough to find you just from simple conversation that gives away information like school name, mascot, athletic scores, your jersey number, or the city and state you live in. It is very positive about using the Internet, but strongly urges using it with caution. . . ." (Kathy 2008).

> ### Protecting Children in the 21st Century Act
>
> Since CIPA was signed into law in 2000, opponents of restrictive filtering have been promoting Internet safety instruction as a more long-lasting and effective alternative. The Protecting Children in the 21st Century Act, approved by Congress in 2008, now requires school districts receiving E-rate discounts to certify that their Internet safety policies include teaching students about Internet safety (Broadband Data Improvement Act. 2008. Title II. Protecting Children in the 21st Century Act. October 10, 2008. http://frwebgate.access.gpo.gov/cgi-bin/getdoc.cgi?dbname=110_cong_public_laws&docid=f:publ385.110.pdf [accessed January 18, 2013]).

Advocating for Reduced Filtering

Library media specialists should talk with their principals and give specific examples of blocked Web resources experienced by both teachers and students. According to CIPA, 47 USC § 254 (H), recipients of E-rate program funding may disable filters only for adults for purposes of bona fide research. However, if a district over-blocks beyond the requirements of CIPA, district staff can be allowed to unblock websites *for minor students* engaged in legitimate research if the sites do not include visual depictions of child pornography, obscenity, or material legally defined as "harmful to minors" (Adams 2008, 145). This proactive stance allows students to access legal information for assignments in a timely manner. According to Liz, a high school library media specialist in the Midwest, "I am constantly selecting materials that my patrons will find useful to complete assignments. Who better to decide if a website is a good match than a library media specialist?" (Liz 2008). For specific legal questions about local filtering situations, library media specialists and their administrators should seek advice from the district's legal counsel.

> ### When Filters Overblock
>
> According to Theresa Chmara, legal counsel for the Freedom to Read Foundation, "Given that minors have explicit First Amendment rights, it would be prudent for schools—particularly school libraries—to have a system in place to unblock sites that do not constitute obscenity, child pornography, or material harmful to minors" (Chmara, Theresa. 2010. "Minors' First Amendment Rights: CIPA & School Libraries." *Knowledge Quest* 39 no. 1: 21).

Library media specialists can reach out to parents by providing varied educational opportunities and resources, including informative classes, newsletter articles, safety brochures, and books in the library media center about safe and beneficial Internet use by children and young adults. This approach provides parents with information about safe Internet use and helps protect students outside school.

Although federal and some state laws require filtering as a condition of receiving specific types of funding, it is still critical to ensure student access to legal information on the Internet. When the school community works cooperatively, the negative effects of filtering may be lessened, and students will learn Internet skills that are useful throughout their lives.

REFERENCES

Adams, Helen R. 2008. *Ensuring Intellectual Freedom and Access to Information in the School Library Media Program*. Westport, Connecticut: Libraries Unlimited.

Children's Internet Protection Act. Public Law 106-554. 2000. 47 USC § 254(H) (D) (A) (i). http://codes.lp.findlaw.com/uscode/47/5/II/II/254 (accessed January 18, 2013).

I-SAFE. http://www.isafe.org/ (accessed February 15, 2013).

Kathy, email message to author, July 7, 2008.

Liz, email message to author, May 12, 2008.

IF Matters @ your library®

Overcoming Filtering Frustration

By Helen R. Adams

Originally published in the IF Matters @ your library® column, *School Library Monthly*, XXIX (1) (September/October 2012): 29–30.

It has been four years since this column focused on filtering of Internet websites and the restrictions and frustrations heavy-handed filtering causes for teachers, students, and librarians. Filters are not always accurate; they both over-block (restricting access to legitimate educational websites) and under-block (allowing access to sites that may contain material that is obscene, child pornography, and harmful to minors). Here's the dilemma: filters are required under the Children's Internet Protection Act (CIPA), but they frequently block access to constitutionally protected information students have a right to receive under the First Amendment. A balance must be found, and in many schools, evenhandedness is lacking.

AASL Takes Positive Action

After CIPA was enacted, the American Association of School Librarians (AASL) became aware of the problem of over-zealous filtering based on schools' desire to protect children, fear of parental complaints, and misinterpretation of the law's requirements. According to AASL past president Carl Harvey, "In the summer of 2011, a proposal was brought to the Board asking AASL to consider designating a day during Banned Books Week to highlight the educational websites and online tools unavailable to students because of blocking software. The Board agreed and voted to establish the first Banned Websites Awareness Day (BWAD) in September 2011" (Harvey).

Carl feels strongly that BWAD is an important event for AASL to sponsor because, "Relying solely on filters does not teach young citizens how to be savvy searchers or how to evaluate the accuracy of information. As school librarians taking the lead in providing this instruction for our students, we know how often the tools and websites they need for projects are blocked and inaccessible. It makes filtering a relevant issue for AASL and BWAD an event to generate awareness. The day allows school librarians to lead activities in their schools to help raise the awareness of what blocking access to useful educational websites does for student learning" (Harvey).

AASL BWAD Activities for 2012

The first AASL BWAD was celebrated on September 28, 2011 with an AASL website, multiple blog posts, a "Don't Filter Me" activity, and links to articles about the negative effects of filtering. Informally, the National Association of Secondary School Principals supported BWAD. In early adopter schools, 2011 BWAD activities ranged from a "graffiti debate" about online censorship to sending email messages to administrators about the blocking of social media sites (Hu 2011).

The AASL 2012 Banned Websites Awareness Day event on October 3, 2012 keeps the focus on reducing restrictive filtering that hampers teaching and learning, but the event's components have expanded to include:

- an official AASL "Unlock the Internet" logo designed by a Connecticut high school student,
- a complimentary AASL webinar, "How to be a Ninja Warrior Filter Fighter!" presented by middle school teacher librarian and "Daring Librarian" blogger Gwyneth Jones on October 3, 2012 at 7 pm EST. Check the BWAD website for details.
- the BWAD hashtag #bwad12 to be used across social media,
- AASL "Promotional Partnerships" with organizations including the American Civil Liberties Union and AASL's state affiliate organizations, and
- daily AASL blogs on filtering and related topics written by leaders in the school library and technology world and posted throughout Banned Books Week (September 30–October 6, 2012).

What Actions Can YOU Take?

Here are a few ideas to recognize BWAD in your school:

- Present your principal with real-life examples of ways in which your school's current filtering practices impede teachers' and students' access to useful sites for instruction and completing assignments.
- Begin a "dial back the filter" dialog with stakeholders (including students), and advocate for filters to be set at less restrictive levels.
- Plan with administrators and teachers to ensure that digital citizenship instruction is carried out annually.
- Collaborate with teachers to develop WebQuests and pathfinders incorporating carefully selected online resources for instructional units.
- Make presentations to parents about Internet use in schools and how Web 2.0 tools can be used to spark students' creativity and collaborative learning.

Take a step toward lowering the level of too strict filtering in your school by supporting Banned Websites Awareness Day on October 3. Your teachers and students are counting on you to help "unlock the Internet."

> **Banned Websites Awareness Day Resources**
>
> **AASL 2012 BWAD:** www.ala.org/aasl/bwad
>
> **AASL BWAD Essential Links:** aasl.ala.org/essentiallinks/index.php?title=Banned_Websites_Awareness_Day
>
> **AASL Blog:** http://www.aasl.ala.org/aaslblog
>
> **AASL 2011 BWAD Vintage Blog:** "Seven Myths about Internet Filters" by Doug Johnson http://www.aasl.ala.org/aaslblog/?s=Seven+Myths+about+Internet+Filters&searchbutton=go%21

REFERENCES

Harvey, Carl, email message to author, June 2, 2012.

Hu, Winnie. 2011. "A Call for Opening Up Web Access at Schools." September 28, 2011. *New York Times.* http://www.nytimes.com/2011/09/29/education/29banned.html?_r=1&scp=3&sq=new%20canaan&st=cse (accessed January 18, 2013).

IF Matters: Intellectual Freedom @ your library®

Dusting Off the Acceptable Use Policy (AUP)

By Helen R. Adams

Originally published in the IF Matters: Intellectual Freedom @ your library® column, *School Library Media Activities Monthly*, XXV (4) (December 2008): 56.

The Children's Internet Protection Act (CIPA) requires those schools that accept discounted services under the E-rate Program or direct federal funding through the Elementary and Secondary Education Act (ESEA) to certify the existence and implementation of an Internet safety policy. The Neighborhood Children's Internet Protection Act (NCIPA) also specifies that schools must create and implement an Internet safety policy that addresses minors' access to "inappropriate matter" on the Internet, safety and security of minors while online, unlawful online activities, and protection of minors' personal information (CIPA and NCIPA 2000). In most districts, the Internet safety policy is known as an *acceptable use policy* or AUP and specifies the rights and responsibilities of Internet users in a school, describes ethical use of technology resources, defines unacceptable uses, and states the consequences of violating the policy.

Children and Young Adults Online

In 2007, the National School Board Association published a study that revealed 9–17 year olds spend an average of 9 hours a week on social networking including updating personal websites or profiles, posting messages and photos, blogging, and related activities (NSBA

> **New Federal Requirements for the AUP**
>
> In 2008, President Bush signed into law the Broadband Data Improvement Act, which incorporates the "Protecting Children in the 21st Century Act" in Title II. It requires schools that receive E-rate discounts to include in their Internet safety policies (also known as AUPs) references to educating its students about Internet safety, including interacting on social networking websites and in chat rooms, as well as teaching about cyberbullying. Under the Federal Communications Commission (FCC) rule announced in August 2011, school districts were required to have their revised policy and procedures in place by July 1, 2012 (Broadband Data Improvement Act. 2008. Title II. Protecting Children in the 21st Century Act. October 10, 2008. http://frwebgate.access.gpo.gov/cgi-bin/getdoc.cgi?dbname=110_cong_public _laws&docid=f:publ385.110.pdf and Federal Communications Commission. 2008. "In the Matter of Schools and Libraries Universal Service Support Mechanism. CC docket No. 02.6 [accessed January 18, 2013] and A National Broadband Plan for Our Future, GN Docket No. 09-5. October 10, 2008: 3–4. http://transition.fcc.gov/Daily_Releases/Daily_Business/2011/db0819/FCC-11-125A1 .pdf [accessed February 19, 2012. No longer available]).

> **Social Networking at a Young Age**
>
> According to the Project Tomorrow results from its Speak Up 2010 survey, more than 50 percent of sixth grade girls and more than 30 percent of boys of the same age regularly update their social networking information; this constitutes an over 125 percent increase since 2005. The irony is that these students are under the age thirteen threshold required by Facebook and other social

networking sites (Project Tomorrow. 2011. "The New 3 E's of Education: Enabled, Engaged, and Empowered: How Today's Students Are Leveraging Emerging Technologies for Learning." April 1, 2011. Speak Up 2010 National Findings. K–12 Students and Parents. http://www.tomorrow .org/speakup/pdfs/SU10_3EofEducation_Students.pdf [accessed January 18, 2013]).

2007). Therefore, it may be time for districts to update AUPs to address use of Web 2.0 collaborative tools that support learning in an *educational* setting while also ensuring safe and responsible use.

Recommendations for Updating an AUP

When updating an AUP, Erin Harvey, policy consultant for the Wisconsin Association of School Boards, recommends the following:

Resource for Updating the AUP

With the many advances in technology, schools are revising their AUPs to include guidelines for the use of students' and teachers' personal mobile devices in school to meet the "bring your own device" (BYOD) trend described in Chapter 2. The Consortium for School Networking (CoSN) helps schools update their policies with their "Acceptable Use Policies in the Web 2.0 and Mobile Era: A Guide for School Districts." Online and in a pdf format, the document offers guidance to districts on safety and access issues related to student use of Web 2.0 tools and Web-enabled mobile devices. The guide includes links to articles on the topic, exemplary policies, and summaries of state laws on filtering and cyberbullying (Consortium for School Networking. 2011. "Acceptable Use Policies in the Web 2.0 and Mobile Era: A Guide for School Districts." Updated September 13, 2011. http://www.cosn.org/ Initiatives/Web2/AUPGuide/tabid/8139/ Default.aspx?utm_source=feb18_ aupguide&utm_medium=eblast&utm_ campaign=aupguide [accessed January 18, 2013]).

- **Social Networking Sites**. Districts should include language about the use of social networking sites and blogs in order to protect themselves against the possible violation of a student's First Amendment rights. For example, if a district states in its AUP that the use of social networking sites is prohibited during school hours, a student who posts something offensive on a social networking site while at school can be punished for violating the AUP, not because of the content of his/her speech. Prohibiting the use of social networking sites at school also helps to keep students safer from online predators. On the other hand, some districts see social networking sites and blogs as potential learning tools for their students. In these cases, the AUP should state that such sites and Web 2.0 tools will only be used at school under the permission of the supervising teacher.

- **Cyberbullying**. With the increasing use of social networking sites and blogs, the amount of cyberbullying has risen, and districts should make sure that students and staff are educated about its negative effects. The AUP should state that cyberbullying will not be tolerated when using the district's network.

- **Compatibility with District Philosophy**. Every school or district is different—both in terms of the technology available and in terms of who has access to the network and Internet resources.

When updating an AUP, make sure that the policy fits the goals and needs of the district and that the district can actually enforce the policy. It is always a good idea to solicit opinions from teachers, parents, and the community about what they would like to see addressed in the AUP.

- **Signature Form**. Many districts require students to read the AUP and turn in a signed form that states that they have read the AUP and are willing to abide by its rules. This is a worthwhile safeguard if a student ever tries to claim that they "didn't know what the rules were" or that they "never got a copy of the AUP" (Harvey 2008).

Harvey also counsels, "Since the Internet is constantly evolving, an AUP cannot anticipate every possible situation. I advise districts to make sure their AUPs can be easily revised as new issues arise and to review them every year" (Harvey 2008).

The Value of an AUP

In addition to providing guidance on the use of technology resources, the AUP is also a means of ensuring students' access to information and their intellectual freedom. During the AUP review process, the library media specialist should urge that the policy protect students' First Amendment right to receive information. The American Library Association's "Access to Digital Information, Services, and Networks: An Interpretation of the Library Bill of Rights" states:

> Information retrieved, utilized, or created digitally is constitutionally protected unless determined otherwise by a court of competent jurisdiction. These rights extend to minors as well as adults. (ALA 2009)

The right of privacy also includes users' intellectual freedom; therefore, it is critical that the AUP acknowledge the limitation of privacy when using district-owned computers, network resources, and the Internet at school. Finally, having a current, proactive AUP that assures students' First Amendment rights is another way to ensure that students acquire the information and technology skills necessary to be effective citizens in a democratic society.

REFERENCES

American Library Association. 2009. "Access to Digital Information, Services, and Networks: An Interpretation of the Library Bill of Rights." http://www.ala.org/advocacy/intfreedom/librarybill/interpretations/accessdigital/ (accessed January 18, 2013).

Harvey, Erin, email message to author, August 5, 2008.

School Discipline and Students' Off-Campus Free Speech Rights

In 2012, the U.S. Supreme Court refused to review three lower court contradictory decisions involving discipline of students who used social media to parody administrators or encourage cyberbullying directed toward a peer. The three cases were *J.S. v. Blue Mountain School District*, *Layshock v. Hermitage School District*, and *Kowalksi v. Berkeley Count School*. Collectively they raised the issue of the ability of schools to impose a penalty on students for off-campus speech that the three educational institutions alleged created substantial disruption within their schools. Unfortunately, the Supreme Court's decision leaves schools with uncertainty about their authority to discipline students related to their off-campus speech (National School Board Association. 2012. Legal Clips: "Supreme Court Declines to Hear Student Internet Speech Cases." January 19, 2012. http://legalclips.nsba.org/?p=11474 [accessed January 18, 2013]).

Although the legal terrain is currently unclear, the public has opinions on this issue. According to the 2012 State of the First Amendment survey published by the First Amendment Center, 57 percent of survey respondents do not believe that administrators should have the right to discipline students for "offensive" free speech when made off school grounds using their own computers. On the other hand, 34 percent feel that school officials should have this authority (First Amendment Center. 2012. "The State of the First Amendment: 2012." http://www.firstamendmentcenter.org/madison/wp-content/uploads/2012/07/SOFA-2012.pdf [accessed January 18, 2013]).

National School Boards Association. 2007. "Creating & Connecting: Research and Guidelines on Online Social and Educational Networking." July 2007. http://socialnetworking.procon .org/sourcefiles/CreateandConnect.pdf/ (accessed January 18, 2013).

Public Law 106-554. 2000. Sections 1701-1731 (4) [CIPA and NCIPA]. http://ifea.net/cipa.html (accessed January 18, 2013).

Privacy Matters

Social Networking and Privacy: A Law Enforcement Perspective

By Helen R. Adams

Originally published in the Privacy Matters column, *School Library Media Activities Monthly*, XXIII (10) (June 2007): 33.

According to the Pew Internet and American Life Project national survey released in January 2007, 55 percent of all American youth aged twelve through seventeen use adult online social networking sites (SNS) such as MySpace and Facebook. The survey further found that girls use the sites to continue existing friendships while boys use the sites to find new friends and flirt (Pew 2007). Some SNS allow users as young as thirteen to create personal profiles and invite "friends" to view their information and photos, comment, and engage in chat and IM (Instant Messaging).

Officer Wilson's Mission

A year ago [2006], Officer Joshua Wilson of the New London [Wisconsin] Police Department began working proactively with middle and high school students on the dangers inherent in posting private information on adult social networking sites and presenting educational programs to parents. According to Wilson, "Privacy is a hard issue for kids using these sites to understand. They don't have credit cards or checkbooks and don't understand the ramifications of identity theft. How do you explain to them don't post profiles so that ten years down the road when you want to buy a house someone will already have your information and possibly have used it in an illegal way?" (Wilson 2007). Equally important is the fact that school administrators, police officers, employers, and college admissions officers are also checking these sites for possible school code of conduct violations, background information, or evidence of crimes. Wilson does not think it is illegal or unethical for a policeman to check SNS because students have posted their information in public Internet space much like a billboard in the offline world.

> ### Social Media Use by Youth
>
> When this column was written, preteens were already registering with adult social networking sites and creating profiles with inaccurate birth dates. According to a 2011 Pew Internet and American Life Project report, 95 percent of teens are online, and 80 percent are engaged in social networking (Lenhart, Amanda, et al. 2011. "Teens, Kindness, and Cruelty on Social Network Sites." November 9, 2011. http://www.pewinternet.org/Reports/2011/Teens-and-social-media/Summary/Findings.aspx# [accessed January 18, 2013]).
>
> Although Facebook accounts remain popular, teens have added "microblogging" to their online communications. A July 2011 Pew Internet and the American Life Project report shows teens use Twitter in part to escape the scrutiny of family members with Facebook accounts and pressure to "friend" unwanted others. They are not using their real names, and the short 140 character posts are similar to texting (Irvine, Martha. 2012. "Teens Migrating to Privacy—Sometimes for Privacy." Updated January 30, 2012. Associated Press. Today Tech. http://today.msnbc.msn.com/id/46182268/ns/today-today_tech/t/teens-migrating-twitter-sometimes-privacy/#.TybBh4I4edA [accessed January 18, 2013]).

An Invitation to Identity Theft

Recently Wilson found that a local boy had posted his learner's permit and his driver's license with his photograph on Xanga.com (social networking and blogging site). Wilson said, "He was so proud he had gotten his driver's license. He thought he was safe blocking out his driver's license number, but his name, address, date of birth, and physical description were there. I showed him how easy it was for me to recreate his driver's license with my photo using his name and address." While the young man has removed this information from the website, Wilson explained, "Once a photo goes on the Internet, it is there forever. There is no magic number to call to say take my picture off the Internet" (Wilson 2007).

The New Meaning of "Friend"

There are other privacy and safety issues with SNS. Commenting on a young teenage girl's profile found on Facebook, Wilson said, "For adult predators, it's like a map to an individual kid. It (the profile) had the student's name, address, phone number, cell phone number, school schedule, so if I wanted to find this girl, I knew exactly where she was. From reading the comments in the profile, I knew exactly what she was interested in, what her friends were talking about." He further notes that the term, "friend," online can have a different connotation from that term in a teen's offline life. As Wilson explained, "On the social networking sites, you have to be invited into each other's profile area—to become a 'friend.' You have to ask for approval. It becomes a popularity contest" (Wilson 2007).

Furthermore, many teens are indiscriminate about adding "friends," frequently approving persons whom they do not personally know for the sake of having a large "friends" list. Youth of this age are trusting and accept information online as being a fair representation of another teenager. They often feel invulnerable and do not suspect a predator may be lurking behind an innocent "friend." There is a false sense of security created since teens feel they are "just hanging out" online with friends.

Profiles: Privacy and Safety Issues

Wilson stated that about 50 percent of youth with whom he has contact have private profiles; the others are open to the world. There has always been a feeling of anonymity on the Internet. Wilson says, "Since the beginning, I can go on the Internet without anyone really knowing who I am. That's why for the criminals, it's such a safe place to go." Wilson added, "Young girls register as 28-year-olds, so everyone can see their profiles. The frustrating thing is how to get the message to kids how dangerous this is" (Wilson 2007). There are no safeguards to keep underage students from posting profiles. One is asked to enter date of birth, but no one verifies truthfulness. Next, there is a box to check that the information is accurate.

Wilson tries to impress privacy and safety issues upon students after viewing their profiles. He said, "They're embarrassed, upset I'm looking at MySpace, think it's an invasion of their privacy. Yet, they posted the embarrassing pictures with drinking, smoking, guns, kids passed out next to a toilet. Underage drinking has been going on for years, but no one had a camera. Now everyone has a [cell phone] camera, and the party's on MySpace the next day. I try to explain the ramifications could be your future employment. It can come back to haunt them, and they don't realize that" (Wilson 2007).

The Education Solution

What does Wilson suggest? He would like to have schools initiate Internet safety instruction, including the use of social networking sites, beginning in 7th grade or at about the age of twelve and continuing through high school. According to Wilson, "I want teachers and administrators to know it's out there, not going away, and will only get bigger. We are missing a bus by not teaching about MySpace and computer safety. The kids are a step ahead of the parents" (Wilson 2007).

REFERENCES

Pew Internet & American Life Project. 2007. "Social Networking Websites and Teens." http://www.pew internet.org/PPF/r/198/report_display.asp (accessed January 18, 2013).

Wilson, Joshua, email interview with author, January 2007.

Officer Wilson's Perspective 5 Years Later

Officer Josh Wilson continued to do presentations to parents and students on personal privacy cautions when posting on social networking sites. In a 2012 follow-up to his 2007 interview, Wilson stated, "Technology has exploded the last couple of years with the development of tablets and smart phones. The privacy portion of my message continues to be the same, and the issue I see after following teens and preteens on their Facebook pages for several years is there appears to be a turning point in their privacy expectations when they turn about 16 years old. The younger kids want to be seen and heard on the Internet and lie about their age to do so" (Wilson 2012).

He went on to provide a chilling reminder for the need to not only teach students appropriate and healthy Internet habits, but to remind them (and their parents) that nothing on the Internet can be guaranteed "private": "The best example I use in my current presentation is from a search online in the *Appleton Post-Crescent* [local newspaper] for youth sports news. I found a young female student from our community and was able to get a Google street image of her house. The final image I show is looking down the driveway of the house where she resides. I learned where she lives even though all her Facebook information was set to private" (Wilson, Joshua, email message to author, March 14, 2012).

Key Ideas Summary

Readings in this chapter focus on intellectual freedom online and more specifically on the requirements of the Children's Internet Protection Act (CIPA) and the Neighborhood Children's Internet Protection Act (NCIPA), how these laws are interpreted by schools, the effects of overly restrictive filtering, updating an AUP, and privacy as an aspect of social networking. Major ideas include:

- CIPA requires that schools and libraries receiving specific types of federal funding certify that they have installed "technology protection measures" or filters on *all computers used to access the Internet* by minors and adults to protect against *visual depictions* that are obscene, contain child pornography, or material "harmful to minors" as defined under federal law. *CIPA does not require that districts filter text or audio.*

- Less well known, the Neighborhood Children's Internet Protection Act (NCIPA), calls for schools accepting E-rate discounted services to create and implement an Internet safety policy with specific provisions. NCIPA does not provide a definition for "*matter inappropriate for minors*" but rather allows the local school board or governing body to determine what is and is not appropriate for minors to access under its Internet safety policy.

- Based on fear, many schools limit students' access to legitimate educational websites far beyond CIPA's requirement. These limitations make it difficult for students to meet AASL's *Standards for the 21st-Century Learner*, especially selected requirements in Standards 1, 2, and 3.

- The purpose of a school is to educate young citizens. Restrictive filtering does not allow K–12 students to access websites necessary to obtain and evaluate information from diverse points of view.

- Filters are not infallible. Under-blocking can expose students to content and visual images that are educationally unsuitable and that may fit federal definitions of obscenity, child pornography or being harmful to minors. On the flip side, over-blocking of legitimate educational websites threatens minors' First Amendment rights to receive information in a school library.

- School librarians can exhibit leadership and build coalitions among teaching colleagues to advocate with administrators for less restrictive filtering.

- In 2011 AASL created Banned Websites Awareness Day (BWAD) to spotlight the over-blocking of legitimate education websites by filtering software in many schools.

- BWAD is observed annually during Banned Books Week.

- The Protecting Children in the 21st Century Act requires districts receiving E-rate discounts on Internet access to include, in their AUP, a provision stating that the district is educating minors about appropriate online behavior, while on social net-working sites and in chat rooms, and cyberbullying.

- Districts must revise their AUPs frequently to include new forms of online interactive tools such as social media sites and microblogging. The AUP should also address cyberbullying and use of personal mobile devices in schools.

- The AUP should acknowledge the limitation of student personal privacy when using district-owned computers, network resources, and the Internet in a school setting.

- The use of social networking sites by youth continues to grow, and students must be educated to use good judgment to protect their confidential personal information and photos when posting online.

Resource Roundup: Intellectual Freedom Online

- **Adams, Helen R. 2010. "Filtering Texas-Style: An Interview with Michael Gras and Scott Floyd."** *Knowledge Quest* **39 no. 1: 30–37.**

  This interview centers, in part, on the educational philosophy of a chief of technology whose district filters to meet the requirements of CIPA but trusts its staff when making requests to unblock websites for instruction and planning purposes. Scott Floyd, the district's technology integrator, describes how he works with teachers at all grade levels to facilitate the use of Web 2.0 tools with students.

- **American Association of School Librarians (AASL). Banned Websites Awareness Day (BWAD) website. http://www.ala.org/aasl/bwad**

  AASL's website includes a history of the event and links to activities and resources to help school librarians draw attention to the censorship overly strict filters cause online. BWAD is observed annually during Banned Books Week.

- **American Library Association. 2012. "Libraries and the Internet Toolkit." http://www .ifmanual.org/litoolkit**

  Updated in 2012, the downloadable Toolkit is available on the *Intellectual Freedom Manual* (8th edition) companion website and includes information on CIPA and its requirements, filtering, legal challenges to filtering, the use of social media in libraries, and developing policies related to Internet use. The Toolkit also provides clickable links to additional resources.

- **Chmara, Theresa. 2010. "Minors' First Amendment Rights: CIPA and School Libraries."** *Knowledge Quest* **39 no. 1: 16–21.**

  This exceptionally well-written article explains the progression of minors' First Amendment rights in schools beginning with the Supreme Court decisions of *Tinker v. Des Moines*

Independent Community School District (1969) to *Board of Education v. Pico* (1982). Chmara extrapolates from the Supreme Court decision in the *United States v. American Library Association* case involving filtering only in public libraries to minors' rights online in a school library.

- **Lamb, Annette. 2010. "Everyone Does It: Teaching Ethical Use of Social Technology."** *Knowledge Quest* **39 no. 1: 62–65.**

Prolific author Annette Lamb addresses the need to teach students about the ethical use of social media and to guide them through a decision-making process leading to their becoming good digital citizens. Referencing AASL's *Standards for the 21st-Century Learner* (2007), her article lists the skills needed by young people and provides strategies and resources for school librarians to help students make good choices online.

- *Pew Internet & American Life Project.* **http://pewinternet.org/**

In 1999 the Pew Charitable Trusts created the Pew Internet & American Life Project to provide reliable data about the social impact of the Internet on Americans. Since that time, the Pew Internet and American Life Project has reported on the digital divide, use of social media and mobile technology by teens and adults, and home use of broadband, among other topics, giving decision-makers a snapshot of online life. School librarians can glean needed information about online trends from these reports and can sign up to be notified by email each time a new report is released.

- **Stripling, Barbara, et al. 2010. "Minors and Internet Interactivity: A New Interpretation of the LBOR."** *Knowledge Quest* **39 no. 1: 38–45.**

This four-author article addresses how the interpretation fits into the progression of minors' legal First Amendment right to freedom of expression, where the new interpretation fits among other ALA intellectual freedom statements, and its application to elementary school, high school, and public library settings.

Discussion Questions

- School districts vary in the strictness of their filtering practices based on local interpretation of the Children's Internet Protection Act (CIPA). What is *your interpretation* of CIPA's filtering requirements for schools that accept E-rate discounts under the Schools and Libraries Program of the Universal Service Fund? Conversely, what does CIPA *not require* schools to filter?

- Enumerate three reasons why districts filter Internet content in schools. Discuss whether the reasons are logical or are based on fear.

- As a teacher or school librarian, what experiences have you had with Internet filtering over-blocking or under-blocking websites? Describe a situation in which filtering has interfered with your instruction or with students' access to information needed for assignments.

- Filtering can be an ethical dilemma for librarians trying to follow the ALA *Code of Ethics* and the *Library Bill of Rights*. The "open" Internet makes available many sites that are inappropriate for children and young adults. On the other hand, filters over-block legitimate websites that can be useful to students for academic purposes and personal information seeking. From another perspective, filters notoriously under-block some Internet content. Discuss the circumstances under which you could support filtering taking into account student age and that filters can be configured for levels of restrictiveness.

- Put forth two arguments you would present to a principal to encourage a move from filtering at a stringent level to a less restrictive level.

- Describe one way your school can participate in Banned Websites Awareness Day.

- Examine your/a district's AUP. From your perspective, describe items related to interactive Web tools and use of technology that should be added, or highlight those that are already included.

- Many minors under the age thirteen threshold required by social networking sites have accounts on adult social networking sites. Discuss the ways in which the social media world has changed since Officer Wilson was interviewed in 2007.

Chapter 5

Serving Students with Special Needs

Including the Columns

"Access for Students with Disabilities"

"Welcoming America's Newest Immigrants: Providing Access to Resources and Services for English Language Learners"

"Serving Homeless Children in Your School Library, Part I"

"Serving Homeless Children in Your School Library, Part II"

Chapter 5

Serving Students
with Special Needs

INTRODUCTION

Who is considered a student with *special needs*? The definition generally refers to individuals with physical, cognitive, and learning disabilities, as well as chronic illnesses and disorders, although those considered disabled under federal education law varies (Adams 2008, 175). In this chapter, the description is broadened to include English language learners (ELL) and homeless children and young adults. In theory, the definition could also comprise incarcerated and detained youth, gifted students, and unwed mothers. There are still other K–12 students who face challenges in schools and libraries due to their unique family relationships. These include minors living in foster care, youth with a parent in the military, children and young adults whose families have been affected by personal disasters (such as home fires) and/or natural disasters (such as hurricanes or tornados) and currently living in temporary housing, children being raised by grandparents, and youth with a parent in prison (Huntington 2005).

Librarians and Students with Special Needs

"Access for Students with Disabilities" is the first reading in Chapter 5. It describes three federal laws that require K–12 schools to meet specific provisions for the education of disabled students. State laws also lay out requirements for schools to meet the needs of disabled students. Beyond the legal requirements, the American Library Association's (ALA) "Services to Persons with Disabilities: An Interpretation of the Library Bill of Rights," is introduced and states, "A person's right to use the library should not be denied or abridged because of disabilities" (ALA 2009). The column provides practical ideas for school librarians to provide access to the school library's facility, resources, and services for students with varying disabilities.

Reading two, "Welcoming America's Newest Immigrants: Providing Access to Resources and Services for English Language Learners (ELL)," highlights tips from eleven school librarians who currently offer resources and services for ELL students. The column reveals how the school library becomes a safe haven for students who are adjusting to a new country, culture, and language; and it also emphasizes the role of the school librarian in ensuring a welcoming atmosphere and solid academic support.

The final two readings in the chapter, "Serving Homeless Children in Your School Library, Parts I and II," introduce the McKinney-Vento Act, a federal law that defines who is considered a "homeless student" and how their needs must be met by public schools. Two school librarians and a school social worker who work with homeless students describe the situations of homeless children and young adults and the impact of insecure housing on their lives. The series provides proven strategies to help support students' academic efforts and also highlights the library as a safe, stress-free location for homeless students in a school.

Incarcerated and Detained Youth

The United States has the largest prison population in the world with approximately 2.4 million inmates of all ages in correctional facilities (Rudolf 2011). In 2010, the total American juvenile population was 308,745,538 (Puzzanchera 2011). Of that number, 70,792 were part of the juvenile justice system and held in public or private residential correctional facilities (U.S. Department of Justice 2010). Although none of the readings in this chapter focus on library services to incarcerated youth, students in juvenile detention centers, jails, and prisons also need library services.

Approved in 2010, the ALA's "Prisoners' Right to Read: An Interpretation of the Library Bill of Rights" speaks to the issue of library services to incarcerated persons stating, "When free people, through judicial procedure, segregate some of their own, they incur the responsibility to provide humane treatment and essential rights. Among these is the right to read" (ALA 2010). The title seems to center the interpretation on "reading"; however, in this case, reading equates with access to print, non-print resources, electronic references, and information found on the Internet. Libraries in correctional institutions need selection policies, but their creation and subsequent selection of materials is complicated by the requirement to meet various state and federal laws, as well as layers of regulations.

Largely unknown to most school librarians, there is a contingent of active, passionate librarians who provide direct or support library services for incarcerated and detained youth. One of their professional associations is the Association of Specialized and Cooperative Library Agencies (ASCLA), a division of ALA. ASCLA has a Library Services for Incarcerated Youth Interest Group that is very active online, and interested persons *need not* be ASCLA members to join. The Library Services for Incarcerated Youth Interest Group currently aspires to revise ASCLA's *Library Standards for Juvenile Correctional Facilities*, which has not been revised since 1999. Another goal is to create tools to advocate for more services and the intellectual freedom of youth in custody (ASCLA 2011a). More information about ASCLA and its website is

Additional Resources for Library Services for Incarcerated and Detained Youth

- Austin, Jeanie. 2012. "Critical Issues in Juvenile Detention Center Libraries." *Journal of Research on Libraries and Young Adults.* July 26, 2012. http://www.yalsa.ala.org/jrlya/2012/07/critical-issues-in-juvenile-detention-center-libraries/.

  Originally presented as a research paper at a Midwinter Meeting 2012 event sponsored by the Young Adult Library Services Association (YALSA), the author provides an overview of the many challenges faced by librarians serving young people in detention centers and a portrait of their youthful patrons.

- Library Services for Youth in Custody. http://www.youthlibraries.org

  Developed by Colorado State Librarian, Camden Tahg, the site includes booklists, collection development policies, opportunities for professional development including webinars, and online discussions for those serving or interested in youth who have been detained or incarcerated. The site is hosted by the Colorado State Library and not officially associated with ASCLA.

- **ASCLA. 1999. *Library Standards for Juvenile Correctional Facilities*. Chicago, Illinois: American Library Association.**

  Although admittedly in need of revision, the Standards include information on the role of the library in a correctional facility, library administration, budget, collection, and services, and reprints copies of ALA intellectual freedom documents such as the *Library Bill of Rights*, "Free Access to Libraries for Minors: An Interpretation of the Library Bill of Rights," and the *Freedom to Read* statement. The Standards are still available from the ALA Store (http://www.alastore.ala.org/).

- **ALA Discussion Groups for Librarians Serving Incarcerated Individuals**

  ◦ **Library Services for Incarcerated Youth Interest Group:** The ASCLA interest group "meets" for discussion purposes in ALA Connect, which is an ALA online collaborative committee work and discussion space for groups with various interests. Participants are not required to be a member of ASCLA or ALA. For information about how to set up a free ALA Connect account to enable participation, go to http://connect.ala.org/about (ASCLA 2011b).

  ◦ **prison-l, the Library Services to Prisoners listserv:** This ASCLA forum is reserved for ALA members. Visit http://lists.ala.org/wws/info/prison-l.

  ◦ **YALSA-Lockdown:** http://lists.ala.org/wws/info/yalsa-lockdown This Young Adult Library Services Association discussion group centers on those who serve incarcerated and detained youth. ALA membership is required.

available in the resources section near the end of this chapter.

A Caring Library

The introduction to Chapter 5 begins with an expanded definition of students with special needs. For most, there are economic and emotional components that add to the strain of their circumstances and make life more difficult for them.

Whoever is being served, school library users need a *caring library* staffed by those who exhibit sensitivity and compassion when working with all students. Lori Franklin, a school librarian at Olathe East High School (Kansas) described her view of the necessary attitude and atmosphere:

> I work in a large, suburban high school with approximately 2,100 students. We strive to make the LMC a warm, welcoming place for our students. We (our library staff) often remind one another that a word of encouragement may be the first nice thing a child has heard directed at them that particular day.

From my perspective, school library staff create a *caring library* by:

- greeting each student and asking how they are doing,
- learning students' names and using them,
- sharing successes (not empty praise),
- going the extra mile to help make sure their assignment needs are met (they don't have money for the copier, they are rushing to electronically turn in an assignment at the last minute, they need glue sticks, they have formatting problems, they need to call a parent, etc.),
- inviting them to eat lunch in the library and occasionally sharing a meal with them (some students need this safe environment as an alternative; others choose to socialize in a setting they already enjoy),

- providing thinking games (Chess, Scrabble, etc.) in various locations around the library,
- feeding them sometimes; whether we make nachos for a surprise, or provide peanut butter, jelly and bread for students who might not otherwise eat a meal that day,
- seeking their opinions regarding book and periodical purchasing,
- listening to their comments/concerns,
- contacting the appropriate parties within the school network for extra help (psychologist, social worker, special education teacher, student advocate, etc.),
- delivering requested books to them in person, and finally,
- acknowledging their presence and sharing a conversation upon seeing them out in public. (Franklin 2011)

I tell others the school library functions as a type of gas station/convenience store. Everyone who crosses our threshold has a different need, and it is our job to help them recognize that need and to help them fulfill it from the varied resources we access. (Franklin 2012)

When school librarians see students as Lori and her colleagues do, the *caring library*, where students are viewed empathetically as individuals, becomes a reality.

REFERENCES

Adams, Helen R. 2008. *Ensuring Intellectual Freedom and Access to Information in the School Library Media Program.* Westport, Connecticut: Libraries Unlimited.

American Library Association. 2010. *Intellectual Freedom Manual.* 8th ed. "Prisoners' Right to Read: An Interpretation of the Library Bill of Rights." http://www.ifmanual.org/prisoners (accessed January 14, 2013).

American Library Association. 2009. "Services to Persons with Disabilities: An Interpretation of the Library Bill of Rights." http://www.ifmanual.org/servicesdisabilities (accessed January 14, 2013).

Association of Specialized and Cooperative Library Agencies. Library Services for Incarcerated Youth Interest Group. 2011a. "ASCLA Library Services for Youth in Custody Interest Group Purpose." December 12, 2011. ALA Connect. http://connect.ala.org/node/162509 (accessed January 14, 2013).

Association of Specialized and Cooperative Library Agencies. 2011b. "Resources for Libraries Serving Incarcerated Youth." December 14, 2011. ALAConnect. http://connect.ala.org/node/162509 (accessed January 14, 2013).

Franklin, Lori. November 2011. AASL Forum "caring library" thread.

Franklin, Lori, email message to author, March 14, 2012.

Huntington, Barbara. 2005. "Chapter 10: Youth in Alternative Family and Home Situations." *A Resource and Planning Guide for Wisconsin Public Libraries.* Wisconsin Department of Public Instruction. http://pld.dpi.wi.gov/files/pld/pdf/ysn-10.pdf (accessed January 14, 2013).

Puzzanchera, C., A. Sladky, and W. Kang. 2011. "Easy Access to Juvenile Populations: 1990-2010." Online. http://www.ojjdp.gov/ojstatbb/ezapop/ (accessed January 14, 2013).

Rudolf, John. 2011. "Drug Sentencing Reforms Halt Decades of Prison Population Growth." December 1, 2011. *Huffington Post.* http://www.huffingtonpost.com/2011/10/29/prison-growth-drug-law-reforms_n_1064250.html (accessed January 14, 2013).

U.S. Department of Justice's Office of Juvenile Justice and Delinquency Prevention. 2010. Easy Access to the Census of Juveniles in Residential Placement: 1997–2010. "Detailed Offense Profile in Public and Private Facilities in United States, 2010." http://www.ojjdp.gov/ojstatbb/ezacjrp/asp/Offense_Facility.asp (accessed January 14, 2013).

IF Matters: Intellectual Freedom @ your library®

Access for Students with Disabilities

By Helen R. Adams

Originally published in the IF Matters: Intellectual Freedom @ your library® column, *School Library Media Activities Monthly*, XXV (10) (June 2009): 54.

In the past, few school librarians served students with disabilities in their libraries. This situation changed, however, when Congress passed the following three major laws that impact how students with disabilities are educated:

- **The Rehabilitation Act of 1973:** This act and its subsequent reauthorizations prohibit discrimination against disabled persons in institutions that receive federal funds (U.S. Department of Justice 2005). As a result, schools must provide students with disabilities with access to the programs, activities, and services offered to their peers, and Section 504 calls for schools to develop specific plans to meet the needs of individual students (Civil Rights Legislation 1992).

- **The Individuals with Disabilities Education Act (IDEA):** IDEA requires "public schools to make available to all eligible children with disabilities a free appropriate public education in the least restrictive environment appropriate for their individual needs" (U.S. Department of Justice 2005). Students with disabilities must be considered for assistive technology use if it is needed to meet the requirement for free and appropriate public education (Assistive Technology Online Training Project 1990).

- **The Americans with Disabilities Act of 1990 (ADA):** Under Title II of the ADA, public schools must supply disabled students with equal opportunities to programs and services. Additionally, for any new construction or renovation projects, schools must follow specific architectural standards. The law does not, however, require public schools to make accommodations that would cause undue "financial and administrative burdens" (Guide to Disability Rights Laws 2005).

Snapshot of School Library Users with Special Needs

As an online instructor, I asked graduate students in the Fall 2011 term to list the types of student disorders for which their library was providing resources and services. The list included:

- Attention Deficit Disorder
- Attention Deficit Hyperactivity Disorder
- Audio Processing Disorder
- Autism/Autism Spectrum Disorder
- Bipolar Disorder
- Low Vision
- Cerebral Palsy
- Cystic Fibrosis
- Hearing Problems
- Down's Syndrome
- Dyslexia
- Fetal Alcohol Syndrome
- Gifted and Talented
- Mentally Retarded
- Multiple Sclerosis
- Neurologically Impaired
- Turret's Syndrome

School librarians must be knowledgeable about the individual needs of their students, and teaming with special education teachers is an excellent strategy.

Because of these laws, students with disabilities are educated with their peers instead of being isolated and can be active users of the school library media center.

State Laws and Requirements for Educating Students with Disabilities

State laws also provide requirements for educating students with disabilities. For example, in 2000, Kentucky passed the Accessible Information Technology Act (AIT). The law requires that public schools provide students with disabilities access to information technology "that is equivalent to the access provided individuals who are not disabled" (Noble 2005). No two state laws are the same; therefore, school library professionals should collaborate with their school's special education staff to ensure that state requirements are implemented in the school library.

Librarians' Ethical Responsibilities

In addition to legislative requirements, school library professionals have ethical responsibilities to ensure access not only to the physical facility but also to its resources and services for students with a range of disabilities. The *Code of Ethics of the American Library Association* states in Article I, "We provide the highest level of service to all library users through appropriate and usefully organized resources; equitable service policies; equitable access; and accurate, unbiased, and courteous responses to all requests" (ALA 2008). *Every student*, regardless of whether he/she has a disability, has a First Amendment right to receive information in the library media center, and it is the responsibility of the school library professional to protect that right. Access to the library media program and its resources and services is an integral part of the intellectual freedom of students with disabilities as reflected in "Services to Persons with Disabilities: An Interpretation of the Library Bill of Rights" (http://www.ifmanual.org/servicesdisabilities).

Strategies for Providing Access to School Libraries

Library media professionals provide access to the library media program for students with disabilities by:

Resources for Working with Students with Disabilities

- **Cummings, Edward O. 2011. "Assistive and Adaptive Technology Resources."** *Knowledge Quest* 39 no. 3: 70–73.

  The theme of the January/February 2011 *Knowledge Quest* issue is "Everyone's Special: Equal Opportunities for All Students to Learn." Selected as one example of the content, this article is comprised of online assistive and adaptive technology resources that school librarians can use when working with students with physical and learning disabilities in the library or that can be recommended to teachers serving this population. Titles, descriptions, and Web addresses are provided for a wide range of organizations, products, and staff development/workshop options, including webinars.

- Meeting the requirements of federal and state laws relating to students with disabilities

- Eliminating physical barriers that prevent student users from entering the library media center and/or obtaining resources and services (i.e., heavy entrance doors, insufficient width between shelving units, shelving that is too high, furniture set too closely together for free movement across the facility)

- Creating a welcoming atmosphere for *all* students

- Being knowledgeable about positive learning strategies and the needs of individual students

- Selecting resources in various formats that fit students' intellectual and physical abilities
- Building a collection that includes resources that reflect accurate information about persons with disabilities
- Ensuring that students with disabilities can locate, retrieve, and use the selected resources successfully (i.e., clear signage, adequate lighting)
- Procuring assistive technologies that allow those with special needs to work as independently as personally possible (i.e., magnification devices, text-to-voice software)
- Providing differentiated instruction in library media and technology skills to ensure students with disabilities are successful lifelong information seekers
- Collaborating with special education staff and
- Advocating for the budget, staff, and services to meet the needs of students with disabilities using the library media center (Adams 2008, 175–192).

REFERENCES

Adams, Helen R. 2008. *Ensuring Intellectual Freedom and Access to Information in the School Library Media Program.* Westport, Connecticut: Libraries Unlimited.

- **Library of Congress. National Library Service for the Blind and Physically Handicapped. http:// www.loc.gov/nls**

  Available for every state, this website explains and promotes a national free library program for persons of all ages who are blind or whose physical handicap results in their inability to read print materials. The program provides recordings of books, magazines, and newspapers, as well as playback equipment, postage-free to eligible individuals including children and young adults.

- **National Dissemination Center for Children with Disabilities. http://nichcy.org**

  Useful to school librarians without experience with all types of disability in youth ages 3–22, this website offers fact sheets on specific disabilities, information on the laws that govern the education of disabled children, and research-based information to improve learning opportunities.

- **University of Washington. Center for Universal Design in Education. http://www.washington .edu/doit/CUDE**

  Although aimed at faculty and staff working at the post-secondary educational institutions, this website shares many ideas that can be adapted for use in a K–12 setting. Two resources will be of particular interest to readers: 1) "Universal Access: Making Library Resources Accessible to People with Disabilities" (http://www.wash ington.edu/doit/UA/PRESENT/libres.html#L3) and 2) "Applications of Universal Design in Elementary and Secondary Education" (http://www.washington.edu/ doit/CUDE/app_sec.html).

American Library Association. 2008. *Code of Ethics of the American Library Association*, Article I. http://www.ala.org/advocacy/proethics/codeofethics/codeethics (accessed January 14, 2013).

American Library Association. 2009. "Services to Persons with Disabilities: An Interpretation of the Library Bill of Rights." http://www.ala.org/advocacy/intfreedom/librarybill/interpre tations/servicespeopledisabilities (accessed January 14, 2013).

Assistive Technology Online Training Project. 1990. "Schools and AT." http://atto.buffalo.edu/ registered/ATBasics/Foundation/Laws/schools.php (accessed January 14, 2013).

Civil Rights Legislation. 1992. "The Rehabilitation Act of 1973, Section 504, (P.L. 93-112)." http://atto.buffalo.edu/registered/ATBasics/Foundation/Laws/civilrights.php#rehab2 (accessed January 14, 2013).

Noble, Steve. 2005. "The Kentucky Accessible Information Technology in Schools Project." August 2005. *Information Technology and Disabilities* XI, no. 1. http://people.rit.edu/easi/itd/itdv11n1/noble.htm (accessed January 14, 2013).

U.S. Department of Justice, Civil Rights Division, Disability Rights Section. 2005. "A Guide to Disability Rights Laws." September 2005. http://www.ada.gov/cguide.htm (accessed January 14, 2013). Note: This resource was updated in 2009, and the 2005 guide is no longer available.

IF Matters: Intellectual Freedom @ your library®

Welcoming America's Newest Immigrants: Providing Access to Resources and Services for English Language Learners

By Helen R. Adams

Originally published in the IF Matters: Intellectual Freedom @ your library® column, *School Library Monthly*, XXVII (1) (September/October 2010): 50–51.

America has always been a nation of immigrants, and many school libraries serve students whose first language is not English. In the American Association of School Librarian's 2009 School Libraries Count! survey, 14 percent of the 5,824 respondents reported a student population with 25 percent or more English language learners (ELL). Yet 91 percent reported that less than 5 percent of their collections are in a language other than English. Unfortunately, 36 percent reported they used no special strategies to serve their ESL student populations (AASL 2009).

The lack of resources and services tailored to English language learners (ELL) impacts the students' First Amendment right to receive information in a school library. "Access to Resources and Services in the School Library Media Program: An Interpretation of the Library Bill of Rights" points out the responsibility of school librarians in this area stating, "Schools serving communities in which other languages are used make efforts to accommodate the needs of students for whom English is a second language" (ALA 2008).

> **The English Language Learner Population**
>
> How many English language learners are there in the United States? According to the National Center for Education Statistics, *The Condition of Education* report, in 2009, 11.2 million students, whose ages ranged from five through seventeen, did not speak English at home and were considered English language learners. In determining English fluency for those students, survey respondents used a sliding scale from using English "very well" to "not at all." Any student assessed as less than "very well" in oral fluency was determined to have "difficulty" speaking English. Of the 11.2 million total ELL students, 2.7 million or 5 percent spoke English with some difficulty (U.S. Department of Education, National Center for Education Statistics. 2011. "Children Who Spoke a Language Other Than English at Home." *The Condition of Education 2011* (NCES 2011-033). http://nces.ed.gov/programs/coe/indicator_lsm.asp [accessed January 14, 2013]).

Supporting Students' Academic Achievement

Debbie, a school librarian in Pennsylvania, describes the unique position of school librarians to assist ELL students, "Librarians can play a vital role in acting as liaisons with other teachers to provide supplemental materials to support the ELL students' academic needs. Working closely with the ESL teacher is a natural alliance. We should be aware of the power we have to enhance a student's life and educational achievement" (Rentschler 2010).

Supporting ELL's academic achievement requires analyzing school library resources and services from the perspective of *the ELL student*. Following are some practical ideas shared by school librarians working with ELL students:

Find Resources: For ELL students homesick for anything familiar, ensure there are current materials on their home countries. Provide copies of translated children's and young adult fiction in a highly visible area. For those building their English language skills, high interest low readability books are especially popular. When possible, offer translated curricular materials in core subjects such as science and social studies. Select subscription databases and online encyclopedias that are available in other languages as well as those with built-in translators. Create an ELL section on the library's website with links to online translators, dictionaries, and foreign newspapers. Create a link to the International Digital Children's Library (http://en.childrenslibrary.org/) where students can read books in more than 50 languages (Summers, Davis, Donahue 2010).

Utilize Audio Technologies: Purchase mp3 players or other audio devices to help students learn English. Obtain a permission slip signed by the parent promising to take responsibility, then download a book the student's class is reading or one of personal choice from http://www.audible.com [subscription-based]. Check out the same book so the student can follow along with the audio version (Heller 2010). Another librarian states, "I buy Playaways for all required texts so that the students can listen while they read since students can understand spoken English before written English" (Teixeira 2010).

Collaborate with ELL Teachers: Librarians often find themselves collaborating with ELL teachers as they seek resources to meet state standards and prepare students for required state tests. Jamie, an elementary librarian explains, "To satisfy Virginia's Literacy Standards of Learning, third graders need to be able to distinguish between historical fiction and fantasy but may not always be able to read and/or understand what their classmates are reading. I collaborate with teachers to find appropriate genres on the reading level needed" (Chapman 2010).

Encourage Students: Lisa, a high school librarian, explains, "Our students arrive without any familiarity about school libraries. I have revamped my orientation for these students, teaching them about what a library offers" (Teixeira 2010). Efforts to support non-native English speakers pay off as Nancy, a senior high school librarian, states, "We have nearly a hundred ELL students, mainly from India, Haiti and Turkey. I have helped them complete homework, get information for their school projects, proofread any writing they were assigned, helped them find books to read independently, and assisted them with their job searches. I was involved with students making Animoto video slide shows of their home countries [http://animoto.com]. These students are among my most loyal patrons. I see very many of them every single day, before school, at lunch, during study halls, and when they come in with their general classes, their reading classes, and with their ESL teachers" (Summers 2010).

Libraries as a Haven

"Librarians can often be the first line of defense in helping ELL students feel secure, welcome, and safe in their new environment," declares a school librarian in Pennsylvania. "My first ELL student was from Turkey, and he was initially bullied by another student. I stepped in and kept a close watch over this unwanted behavior" (Rentschler 2010). School library professionals can create an inviting atmosphere through simple actions such as these:

- Welcome each new ELL student personally, and enlist them to work in the library (Hill 2010).
- Learn to greet students in their first language. Laurie, a school librarian shares, "I have shown an interest in the students, so they have been trying to teach Spanish to me. They laugh right along with me when I can't pronounce the words correctly. They enjoy being the 'teacher' for a change" (Miller 2010).
- Obtain "welcome" and "read" posters from ALA in the native languages of ELL students (Hill 2010).
- Display "materials for holidays and heritage celebrations such as Native American Month in November, Kwanzaa, Hanukkah, Christmas, Divali, or Ramadan so that teachers and students will find them and discuss their significance" (Chapman 2010).
- Provide email access to help students keep in contact with relatives and friends in their home countries (Davis 2010).
- Celebrate events such as National Foreign Language Week by displaying student-created posters depicting the flags of students' home countries with the word "hello" and a pronunciation guide (Tabit 2010).
- Offer space to community groups who provide after school tutoring (Teixeira 2010).
- Invite a public librarian to introduce ELL students to public library services and facilitate their obtaining library cards (Popuri 2010).

As communities and schools become increasingly diverse, school librarians find themselves stretched to meet the needs of English language learners. Article I of the ALA *Code of Ethics* reminds school library professionals, they must provide high quality service and appropriate resources for *all library users* (ALA 2008). Every positive action taken to support ELL students' use of school libraries helps them understand that access to information in libraries is part of America's democratic tradition and their First Amendment right.

REFERENCES

American Association of School Librarians. 2009. "School Libraries Count! Supplementary Report on English Language Learners." http://www.ala.org/ala/mgrps/divs/aasl/researchandstatistics/slcsurvey/2009/ell2009.pdf (accessed January 14, 2013).

American Library Association. 2008. "Access to Resources and Services in the School Library Media Program: An Interpretation of the Library Bill of Rights." http://www.ala.org/advocacy/intfreedom/librarybill/interpretations/accessresources/ (accessed July 13, 2012).

Resources for Working with English Language Learners

- **Colorin Colorado!** http://www.colorincolorado.org/librarians This bilingual (English/Spanish) site provides information to librarians serving Spanish-speaking families. A key article for librarians is "10 Ways to Support ELLs in the School Library" by Jacqueline Jules (2009). Although aimed at a Spanish-speaking population, the ideas will translate well with other language groups. REFORMA, an affiliate of the ALA is noted, with links to this association promoting library services to Latinos and Spanish-speakers.

- **National Association for Bilingual Education** http://www.nabe.org With membership comprised of teachers, researchers, parents, and policy makers, the organization promotes bilingual education that values native languages and incorporates cultural diversity. It publishes NABE News online, and past issues are available to non-members.

- **National Education Association** http://www.nea.org/home/32346.htm One section of the NEA's website is devoted to articles, tools, resources, and news related to teaching students for whom English is a second language.

American Library Association. 2008. *Code of Ethics of the American Library Association*, Article I. http://www.ala.org/advocacy/proethics/codeofethics/codeethics (accessed January 14, 2013).

Email exchanges between school librarians Jamie Chapman, Betsy Davis, Jane Donahue, Susan Heller, Lin Hill, Laurie Miller, Usha Popuri, Debbie Rentschler, Nancy Summers, Linda Tabit, and Lisa Teixeira and the author, May 5–19, 2010.

IF Matters: Intellectual Freedom @ your library®

Serving Homeless Children in Your School Library, Part I

By Helen R. Adams

Originally published in the IF Matters: Intellectual Freedom @ your library® column, *School Library Monthly*, XXVII (3) (December 2010): 52–53.

As we prepare for the upcoming holidays, we should consider that not all children in our schools will be celebrating in comfortable surroundings. According to the Institute for Children & Poverty, it is estimated there are over 1.35 million homeless children in 600,000 families in the United States and another 3.8 million adults and children in "precarious" housing situations (Institute for Children & Poverty). The Department of Education reported that over 956,000 homeless students were enrolled by local public education agencies in 2008–09, a 20 percent increase over the 2007–08 school year (National Center for Homeless Education 2010).

Providing an Education for Homeless Children

In 1987 Congress passed the McKinney-Vento Homeless Education Act which requires schools to provide a free, appropriate education to homeless children. The federal law established the "Education of Homeless Children and Youth" (EHCY) program in all states. State educational agencies apply for funding to ensure that all homeless children receive an education comparable to their housed peers, including preschool education. Because of the downturn in the U.S. economy and recent weather-related disasters such as hurricanes, floods, tornadoes, and fires, many districts have homeless students. School districts can apply for grants (administered through their states) to support student enrollment and placement, referrals for support services, outreach activities, transportation, school supplies, before and after school as well as summer education programs, and coordination among local service agencies (National Coalition for the Homeless 2009).

Children and Poverty: The Numbers and Their Impact

Homelessness is a result of extreme poverty and has been exacerbated by the severe economic downturn from which the United States is still struggling to recover. Analysis of the most recent census data by the Carsey Institute at the University of New Hampshire estimates there were 15.7 million children living in poverty in 2010 compared to 13.1 million children in 2007, representing a 20.6 percent increase in childhood poverty. Even more dramatic is the estimate that one in four children under age six live in poverty (Carsey Institute. University of New Hampshire. 2011. "Press Release: One Million More Children Living in Poverty Since 2009, New Census Data Released Today Shows." September 22, 2011. http://www.eurekalert.org/pub_releases/2011-09/uonh-omm092211.php [accessed January 14, 2013]).

These horrifying statistics have implications for the education of poor children at a time when many public schools are also experiencing decreasing funding. Children living in strained economic circumstances will be less ready to learn and more likely to suffer from poor nutrition and lack of health care. Many will have no early experience with books, a circumstance far different from their more economically privileged peers.

The McKinney-Vento Act defines homeless students as "Children and youth who lack a fixed, regular, and adequate nighttime residence" (McKinney-Vento 2002). The law further describes the situations in which these students find themselves:

- "Sharing the housing of others due to loss of housing, economic hardship, or a similar reason
- Living in motels, hotels, trailer parks, camping grounds due to lack of adequate alternative accommodations
- Living in emergency or transitional shelters
- Abandoned in hospitals
- Awaiting foster care placement
- Living in a public or private place not designed for or ordinarily used as a regular sleeping accommodation for human beings
- Living in cars, parks, abandoned buildings, bus or train stations, or similar settings
- Migratory children . . . living in the above circumstances" (McKinney-Vento 2002).

Under the federal law, school districts are responsible for such actions as appointing a district-level homeless liaison, enrolling students identified as homeless even if medical and academic records are not available, providing transportation to the school if requested by the parents or guardian, and ensuring district policies and procedures have no barriers for homeless students (Wisconsin Department of Public Instruction 2009).

What Does Being Homeless Mean to Children?

Because of their mobility and precarious living conditions, homeless children and young adults face many educational challenges. Moving from school to school or not being enrolled for extended periods disrupts their social network and interrupts their learning. The impact of frequently changing schools or not attending school regularly results in their being "nine times more likely to repeat a grade, four times more likely to drop out of school, and three times more likely to be placed in special education programs than their housed peers" (National Coalition for the Homeless 2009).

According to Mary Maronek, education consultant for the Wisconsin Education for Homeless Youth and Children (EHYC) program, "Children who are homeless face problems daily that housed children don't experience. These issues may include: developmental delays, emotional difficulties, more health problems with lack of access to health services, exposure to violence, less cultural experiences than their housed peers, and concerns about meeting basic needs. . . . Also, many children may be suffering from trauma due to their homelessness" (Maronek 2010).

Patty, an urban elementary school librarian in the Midwest, described the effects of homelessness on her students:

A student who becomes homeless may show signs that students undergoing any type of emotional stress will show. He or she may become listless and not seem to care about school-related or library-related activities, or may become depressed and isolate himself or herself, or may become easily angered and lash out at others verbally or physically . . . again, any of the signs associated with extreme distress. These signs cause me to go to a student's classroom teacher both to let the teacher know about the behavior

I observed and to see if the teacher has any suggestions or insights that will help me understand what the student is experiencing.

Sometimes students will share their [housing] situations with me. It often happens if there are library materials that are overdue, and I am asking the student where the materials are. It is very difficult for a student who comes home from school to find the door to his or her apartment bolted by the landlord and all of the family's belongings locked inside. Sometimes landlords just throw everything away including library books. The student has no control over this . . . so it's difficult to restrict access to library materials for something [unreturned books] the student cannot fix.

Sometimes a student will share if we are privately discussing his or her behavior. I will often ask why the student is acting in a certain way, and the student may explain his or her living situation, usually tearfully.

For me, it is important to remember that homelessness for an elementary student is not his or her fault. School, especially the school library, may be the only location a homeless student can count on as a place that is safe, comfortable, and full of books, magazines, online resources, and more that can bring enjoyment and respite from the daily stresses in his or her life. (Patty 2010)

Responsibilities of Librarians

All homeless children and young adults have the same legal right to an education as their housed classmates. Libraries promote access to resources and services, and the American Library Association's Policy 61. "Library Services to the Poor" states:

The American Library Association promotes equal access to information for all persons, and recognizes the urgent need to respond to the increasing number of poor children, adults, and families in America. (ALA)

It is important to take the time to reflect on the many issues facing homeless students and the ways in which the library can support their learning. The January 2011 "IF Matters@ your library" column (next reading in this chapter) will provide guidance and resources for school librarians working with homeless students.

REFERENCES

American Library Association. "ALA Policy 61. Library Services to the Poor." http://www.ala .org/aboutala/governance/policymanual/updatedpolicymanual/section2/61svctopoor (accessed January 14, 2013).

Institute for Children & Poverty. "Quick Facts: National Data on Family Homelessness." http:// www.icpny.org/index.asp?CID=7 (originally accessed September 13, 2010). [no longer available]

Maronek, Mary, email interview with author, August 10, 2010.

McKinney-Vento Homeless Education Act. 2002. http://center.serve.org/nche/downloads/ mv_full_text.pdf (accessed January 14, 2013).

National Center for Homeless Education. 2010. "Education for Homeless Children and Youth Program: Data Collection Summary." June 2010. http://center.serve.org/nche/ibt/sc_data.php (accessed July 4, 2012) [no longer available at this link].

National Coalition for the Homeless. 2009. "Education of Homeless Children and Youth." September 2009. http://www.nationalhomeless.org/factsheets/education.html (accessed January 14, 2013).

Patty (elementary librarian), email message to author, August 12, 2010.

Wisconsin Department of Public Instruction. 2009. "Requirements of the McKinney-Vento Homeless Assistance Act." October 2009. http://homeless.dpi.wi.gov/files/homeless/pdf/mv_require.pdf (accessed January 14, 2013).

 **IF Matters: Intellectual Freedom @ your library®**

Serving Homeless Children in Your School Library, Part II

By Helen R. Adams

Originally published in the IF Matters: Intellectual Freedom @ your library® column, *School Library Monthly*, XXVII (4) (January 2011): 52–53.

Since the economic downturn began, homelessness is occurring more frequently from metropolitan areas to suburbs from rural localities to small towns and cities across America. In December 2008 a company in Wisconsin closed its plant. Approximately 4,000 General Motors and satellite business employees lost their jobs in Janesville, Wisconsin; and the economic ripple in the community of 60,000 created financial hardship for many families (Greenhouse 2010). As a result, the School District of Janesville is serving an increasing population of students who are homeless, and the eight-minute video "Homeless" tells their story (http://www.janesville.k12 .wi.us/Departments/PublicInformation/VideoGallery/VideoPlayer/TabId/1322/VideoId/8/ Homeless.aspx).

School Policies and Homeless Students

According to Ann Forbeck, a homeless liaison for the School District of Janesville,

Many students in poverty and homeless students especially, live in chaos and focus only on surviving from day to day. In that environment, it is very difficult for families to keep track of important papers, like birth certificates and school records. It is rarely on the radar for these families to take care of getting library books back to school on time, if at all.

I have run into situations where students were denied access to school records or permission to graduate due to an unpaid fee for a missing book [NOT in Janesville]. These are the kind of policies that cause homeless students to give up on their educations. It is also illegal to discriminate against students who are homeless. . . . I have worked with high school students who left school books in unsafe places where they had stayed temporarily, and they have been afraid to go back to those residences to retrieve the books. It is very important that school libraries have policies that allow for students to have access to the materials without penalizing them for situations that are beyond their control. (Forbeck 2010)

"Economic Barriers to Information Access: An Interpretation of the Library Bill of Rights" reminds school library professionals to be aware that the policies for overdue materials and replacement of lost and damaged materials can be an impediment to poor and homeless students' using school libraries (ALA 1993). School librarians must balance their fiduciary responsibility to maintain a collection with open access for all students.

School District Efforts

Janesville school librarians have developed policies that fulfill *Library Bill of Rights* principles and consider homeless students' needs. Kathy Boguszewski, Janesville Library Media and Instructional Technology Coordinator, affirmed:

> We encourage all children to check out books. We want the children to become better readers, and to become better readers, they need to read. The key is getting books in the hands of students. If items do not come back, due to many circumstances, they (librarians) do what they can to encourage the students to return materials. But what does not come back is just the cost of doing business. I know I can speak for all our school librarians. *Literacy is our business.* We do not limit access to materials or checkouts. (Boguszewski 2010a)

To enable some students to complete homework, the [Janesville] school district placed computers and printers in two homeless shelters (Forbeck 2010). Boguszewski agrees this action is helpful but asserts, "I would like to see all of our school libraries open beyond school hours. The homeless shelters are not an ideal learning environment. Our libraries are" (Boguszewski 2010b).

Practical Strategies for School Librarians

School libraries have traditionally been safe havens for at-risk students and can also make a difference in the lives of students who are homeless. According to Mary Maronek, education consultant for the Wisconsin Education for Homeless Children and Youth program, "School librarians or any school staff should not assume (because of age or grade level) the understanding a student may have on any subject. Nor should they assume that a child can take homework home and that s/he has the resources to complete school assignments" (Maronek 2010).

Practical strategies school librarians can use to help homeless students include:

- Welcome new students and provide a library map, brochure describing library usage policies, a brief tour, and orientation to library resources.
- Assign a library buddy for elementary students.
- Stock basic school supplies commonly needed to complete assignments.
- Set clear, consistent rules that provide structure to library use (adapted from "How Teachers Help Homeless Students," Wisconsin, 2009).
- Provide individual support and frequent encouragement to students as they seek resources and work on assignments.
- Provide the one-on-one attention homeless students often desire (Maronek 2010).
- Respect students' privacy in library usage and personal confidences.
- Help students plan where library books can be stored safely, and provide a calendar showing the day library books are due (Forbeck 2010).
- Seek ways to give students books to keep. Janesville elementary school librarian Karen Forst recounts, "I give away books nearly every week. After story time, I choose two students to answer story-related comprehension questions, and they are allowed to choose a book to keep ("forever and ever!" as some little ones say). I also post trivia questions

with books as the prize and ask third to fifth graders Dewey questions with book rewards (Forst 2010).

- Seek alternate ways to replace lost/damaged books such as asking a local service organization to establish a small fund for that purpose or offering students the option to work in the library to pay for a fine or book replacement (Adams 2008, 69).

- Select books on poverty and homelessness to enable homeless students to see themselves in the collection and their housed peers to learn about those conditions.

- Share lesson plans and resources with teachers about students living in poverty and experiencing homelessness.

> **Resources About Homelessness**
>
> - **National Coalition for the Homeless:** Fact Sheets & Lesson Plans
>
>   http://www.nationalhomeless.org/factsheets/index.html
>
> - **Institute for Children, Poverty, and Homelessness:** Reports & Uncensored (free downloadable magazine)
>
>   http://www.icphusa.org/
>
> - **National Center for Homeless Education:** Issues Briefs
>
>   http://center.serve.org/nche/briefs.php
>
> - **National Center for Children in Poverty:** Fact Sheets
>
>   http://www.nccp.org/

Librarianship with Compassion

Providing library resources and service to students who are homeless is a mix of applying professional ethics, recognizing students' First Amendment right to receive information in a school library, and meeting a legal requirement to provide an education equal to that of housed students. Ann Forbeck says it best when she states, "There are no easy answers to helping homeless students succeed in school. However, it is possible to change punitive policies regarding lost and late books with compassion for the very difficult lives of students who are homeless or living in poverty" (Forbeck 2010). To contribute to this effort, school librarians can start by reviewing and fine-tuning library policies. They can then greet homeless students in the school library with a friendly smile, offer a safe space with resources, establish flexible policies, and administer them with empathy.

REFERENCES

Adams, Helen R. 2008. *Ensuring Intellectual Freedom and Access to Information in the School Library Media Program.* Westport, Connecticut: Libraries Unlimited.

American Library Association. 1993. "Economic Barriers to Information Access: An Interpretation of the Library Bill of Rights." http://www.ala.org/advocacy/intfreedom/librarybill/interpretations/economicbarriers (accessed January 14, 2013).

Boguszewski, Kathy. 2010a, email message to author, August 12, 2010.

Boguszewski, Kathy. 2010b, email message to Nancy Anderson, August 9, 2010.

Forbeck, Ann, email message to Kathy Boguszewski, August 16, 2010.

Forst, Karen, email message to Nancy Anderson, August 22, 2010.

Greenhouse, Steven. 2010. "Janesville Wisconsin." January 8, 2010. http://www.granta.com/Online-Only/Janesville-Wisconsin/ (accessed January 14, 2013).

Maronek, Mary, email interview with author, August 9–10, 2010.

Wisconsin Department of Public Instruction. October 2009. "How Teachers Can Help Homeless Students." http://homeless.dpi.wi.gov/files/homeless/pdf/teach_help_hmls_stud.pdf (accessed January 14, 2013). Note: This resource was updated in February 2011.

Key Ideas Summary

Readings in this chapter focus on providing library services to students with special needs including those with disabilities, English language learners, and homeless youth. Major ideas include:

- In the past, few school librarians considered how to accommodate students with disabilities in their school libraries, although the situation changed when Congress and state legislatures passed laws that set forth how students with disabilities must be educated in public schools.

- Today, Article I of the *Code of Ethics of the American Library Association* and "Services to Persons with Disabilities: An Interpretation of the Library Bill of Rights" remind school librarians of their ethical responsibility to provide resources and services *to all library users,* including students with physical, cognitive, emotional, and learning disabilities as well as chronic conditions.

- Many school librarians serve English language learners (ELL) among their library users. Although providing print and digital resources in multiples languages can be a strain on the library budget, "Access to Resources and Services in the School Library Media Program: An Interpretation of the Library Bill of Rights" states that schools, and by inference *school libraries* in communities where multiple languages are spoken, should seek to provide materials in languages used by their ELL populations.

- School libraries often serve as a refuge for ELL students who are adjusting to a new country. The school librarian must establish a welcoming atmosphere and ensure that academic assistance and personal support are available.

- Likewise, school libraries are frequently a sanctuary for homeless and at-risk students, and school librarians can practice *librarianship with compassion* by creating a secure environment with access to resources, technology, and basic school supplies.

- The McKinney-Vento Homeless Education Act of 1987 defines a "homeless student" and lays out the strict requirements for providing homeless students with a free, appropriate education comparable to that of students with stable lodging.

- Homeless children and young adults face overwhelming developmental, emotional, health, and academic issues unknown to their housed peers. Librarians and teachers should acquaint themselves with these hardships to ensure that these subjects are addressed.

- School librarians can establish flexible library policies for overdue, lost, and damaged library materials to ameliorate the economic barriers of homeless children in schools and enable them to continue benefiting from their library experiences.

- Youth held in custody in juvenile detention centers, prisons, jails, or other segregated facilities must be educated in conditions that include access to a library of age appropriate resources and services.

Resource Roundup:
Serving Students with Special Needs

- **American Library Association. Social Responsibilities Round Table's Hunger, Homeless, and Poverty Task Force and the Office for Literacy and Outreach Services. 2012. "Extending Our Reach: Reducing Homelessness Through Library Engagement." http://www.ala.org/offices/olos**

  The combined efforts of two ALA entities created a resource aimed at public librarians who work with homeless patrons; however the toolkit also contains information useful for school librarians serving homeless children and young adults. The toolkit includes definitions of common terms related to homelessness, a discussion of ways in which library policies may deny homeless persons equity of access to resources and services, and recommendations for providing library services to young people. The resource is downloadable as a PDF from the OLOS website (http://www.ala.org/offices/extending-our-reach-reducing-homelessness-through-library-engagement).

- **American Association of School Librarians. 2012. *Knowledge Quest* Themed Issue: "Caring is Essential." XXXX no. 5.**

  The May/June 2012 issue of *Knowledge Quest* is devoted to the topic of caring and empathy for the "school's human resources": its students, teachers, and administrators who face big challenges in school and outside its walls. Articles of particular usefulness are: "The Transformative Power of Care" (with its "How We Demonstrate Care" table written by former Brooklyn [New York], school librarian Olga M. Nesi) and "Quotes on Caring" by school Librarians from Henrico County Public Schools (Virginia).

- **Association of Specialized and Cooperative Library Agencies (ASCLA) website. http://www.ala.org/ascla**

  A division of the American Library Association, ASCLA is an association for librarians working with persons who are physically handicapped, experience behavioral problems, suffer from mental illness, or are incarcerated. Resources on the association's website include an "Understanding the Language" list of terms and definitions of value to those new to working with persons with disabilities (http://www.ala.org/ascla/asclaprotools/thinkaccessible/language), tip sheets on library accessibility issues when serving library patrons with autism and spectrum disorders (http://www.ala.org/ascla/asclaprotools/accessibilitytipsheets), and tools such as the "Internet and Web-based Content Accessibility Checklist" (http://www.ala.org/ascla/asclaprotools/thinkaccessible/internetwebguidelines). Another valuable resource is its "ASCLA Interface," an online communication tool where information is shared with members and other site visitors, and all messages are archived for later retrieval. The association also offers webinars, online courses, and other professional development opportunities.

- **National Coalition for the Homeless. http://www.nationalhomeless.org**

  This informative advocacy site includes resources for school librarians and other educators to help understand the issues related to homelessness including a free five module "Faces of Homelessness" ecourse. There are fact sheets and lesson plans for grades K–2, 3–5, 6–8, and high school to help teach students about homelessness. The site also includes online publications and toolkits for assisting homeless families.

- **National Council of Teachers of English. 2008. "English Language Learners: A Research Policy Brief." http://www.ncte.org/library/NCTEFiles/Resources/ PolicyResearch/ELLResearchBrief.pdf**

  Although aimed at language arts teachers, this eight page PDF will be very useful to school librarians who provide services and resources for students for whom English is a second language. It includes an overview, statistics, and myths about the diverse group of students termed "English language learners" and research-based recommendations on how to teach and support these students.

- **National Council of Teachers of English. "English Language Learners: Supplemental Resources for NCTE's Policy Research Brief." http://www.ncte.org/library/NCTE Files/Resources/PolicyResearch/ELLClips.pdf**

  This brief four-page supplement provides a skeletal outline of concerns about "English language learners," misconceptions about them as students, and strategies for helping them succeed as well as links to resources.

- **Wrightslaw.com. http://www.wrightslaw.com**

  Librarians need to learn about special education law and those relating to homeless students. Pete and Pam Wright, adjunct law professors from William and Mary Law School (Virginia), maintain this site that provides legal information on educating homeless students and a links to understandable explanations of terms and requirements of special education law.

Discussion Questions

- As an educator, school librarian, parent, sibling, or citizen, what experiences have you had with disabled students or adults? Are their needs being recognized and met in our society? Provide an explanation for your answer.

- Visualize your school's library and analyze it through the eyes and experiences of a student with special needs whether they have a physical, emotional, or learning disability; chronic illness; language barrier; or are homeless lacking a safe, quiet environment.

Imagine a student with at least one of these characteristics, and describe how you would change the library to meet the special needs of such a student.

- Persons with disabilities want to be treated like everyone else in society. Discuss best practice communication strategies for working with students in wheelchairs, those who are sight-impaired, and the deaf or hard of hearing.

- In addition to disabled, ELL, and homeless students, what other groups of students could be considered by school librarians as having "special needs" in a school library? Provide a rationale for their inclusion.

- Given that minors have First Amendment rights to receive information in a school library, should schools be required to provide materials in the native language of its ELL students? Provide reasoning for your opinion.

- Review the policy for overdue materials, fines, and damaged or lost items in your school or for a school library with which you are familiar. Does the policy provide flexibility for the economic hardships and other challenges faced by homeless students? If not, how can it be changed?

- Consider this scenario: You are a school librarian with one adult female library assistant. She has difficulty in working well with students who have physical and learning disabilities. She is abrupt and does not represent the welcoming attitude you expect for library program staff. Describe two strategies you can use to improve this situation.

Chapter 6

Privacy and Confidentiality in the School Library

Including the Columns

"Confidentiality"

"The Age of the Patron and Privacy: Elementary Students"

"The Age of the Patron: Privacy for Middle and High School Students"

"The Ebb and Flow of Library Privacy"

"The Troubled Student and Privacy"

"How Circulation Systems May Impact Student Privacy"

"More Privacy Concerns about Technology Use in the Library Media Center"

"Protecting the Privacy of Student Patrons"

"Retaining School Library Records"

"Privacy Checklist: Evaluating Privacy in Your School Library Media Program"

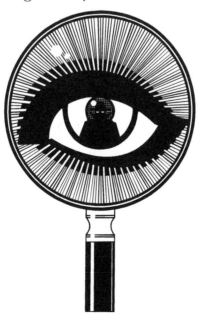

Chapter 6

Privacy and Confidentiality in the School Library

INTRODUCTION

Article III of the *Code of Ethics of the American Library Association* states, "We protect each library user's right to privacy and confidentiality with respect to information sought or received and resources consulted, borrowed, acquired or transmitted" (ALA 2008). Privacy in a school library is a difficult topic for school librarians. One of the primary complications is interpreting how the widely varying state library records laws and the federal Family Educational Rights and Privacy Act apply to minors' public school library records. Add to the mix the myriad of situations in which school librarians find themselves protecting students' privacy or trying to keep students' library use records confidential. Most school libraries have no school board-approved library privacy policy, so school librarians are often without official guidance and are uncertain what to do, for example, when a teacher asks whether a student checked out a particular book. Under what circumstances can a student's circulation record be shared legally?

Although there are references to state and federal laws in this chapter, the information and analysis should not be considered as legal advice. Instead, readers with specific legal questions about local situations should consult their school's legal counsel.

What's in This Chapter?

Chapter 6, the longest in the book, includes ten reprinted columns. The readings combine basic information about privacy and confidentiality in school libraries with guidance for handling situations that a school librarian may face. Sidebars provide updates with new information.

1. The first reading, "Confidentiality," defines the difference between *privacy* and *confidentiality* in a library context. It introduces ALA and AASL policy statements about protecting patrons' privacy and explains the expectations students have for privacy in a school library.

2. "The Age of the Patron and Privacy: Elementary Students" discusses privacy of young students in elementary libraries. It is linked with the third reading, in that they both ask whether *age* makes a difference in extending privacy to school library users.

3. "The Age of the Patron: Privacy for Middle and High School Students" considers the rationale for why older students may need more privacy and rely on school librarians to keep their research on such sensitive topics as sexual orientation confidential.

4. In 2007–2008, four states proposed changes to their library record confidentiality laws. "The Ebb and Flow of Library Privacy" reports on the proposed changes and what they mean for minors.

5. School librarians observe students using the school library and come to know many of them well. "The Troubled Student and Privacy" describes how significant changes in behavior and mood (that may be witnessed by the library staff) can be cause for infringing on a student's privacy and possible courses of action.

6. Automated circulation systems have been a boon to school librarians, helping them computerize clerical tasks associated with managing circulation of materials; however, they have another side. "How Circulation Systems May Impact Student Privacy" discusses the potential for circulation systems to threaten the confidentiality of students' library records.

7. "More Privacy Concerns about Technology Use in the Library Media Center" introduces radio frequency identification (RFID), biometrics, and surveillance cameras and their connections to library privacy.

8. The article "Protecting the Privacy of Student Patrons" describes the single most productive action a school librarian can take to protect the privacy of students using the school library and the confidentiality of their library records—create a school library privacy policy.

9. "Retaining School Library Records" considers another means of protecting the confidentiality of student library records, keeping minimal records and purging unneeded data. The value of a creating a school library records retention policy is also examined.

10. The final reading, "Privacy Checklist: Evaluating Privacy in Your Library Media Program," includes a checklist of twenty-six different aspects of privacy for the school librarian who wants to gauge the privacy of students using his/her library.

State Library Records Laws

Forty-eight states and the District of Columbia have laws that protect the confidentiality of patrons' library use records. Hawaii and Kentucky do not have library records laws, but their attorneys general have issued opinions that library circulation records are to remain confidential. Text of the laws and the legal opinions are accessible on the ALA Office for Intellectual Freedom website (http://www.ala.org/offices/oif/ifgroups/stateifcchairs/stateifcinaction/stateprivacy).

The laws in each state vary a great deal in the types of libraries (public, academic, school) whose records are shielded, the specific records protected, and when the records may be disclosed. For example, Connecticut's library records law covers the library records in public and private libraries but does not protect the records in school and academic libraries. Pennsylvania's law protects the records of public, university, college or other educational institutions, and public school libraries. The Pennsylvania law is very narrowly written to protect only library users' circulation records and to allow release of the records only with a court order related to a criminal proceeding (ALA). In contrast, Arkansas's law protects the records in public, school, academic, and special libraries and library systems that are publicly funded, but the law is far more inclusive than the Pennsylvania statute. The Arkansas library records law shields a laundry list of services and materials beginning with a phrase that indicates the protected items are not limited to protecting only the listed types of materials and services, which include circulation of library materials, use of electronic databases, interlibrary loan requests, reference questions, photocopying, reserves, and use of audiovisual resources. With the words "*including but not limited to*," the Arkansas legislature wisely left the door open for protecting other types of records not yet known. Arkansas library records can be legally disclosed to the patron, to an individual who displays the written consent of the user, and to officials from law enforcement or a civil court who produce a search warrant (ALA).

Because the text and coverage of state library records laws are unique to each state, a school librarian must read carefully to interpret whether the state law protects school library records, what types of records are safeguarded, and when the record may be divulged. It should be noted that not all state library records laws protect the confidentiality of school library records.

The Family Educational Rights and Privacy Act (FERPA)

The Family Educational Rights and Privacy Act (FERPA) is a federal law that guarantees the confidentiality of students' education records. Under the law, *education records* are considered "those records, files, documents, and other materials which—(i) contain information directly related to a student; and (ii) are maintained by an educational agency or institution or by a person acting for such agency or institution" (EPIC. 1974. FERPA, S. 1232g. Family educational and privacy rights. A (4) (A) (i) (ii)).

Students' school library use records are not among the records listed as examples of education records; however, staff in the Family Policy Compliance Office, which oversees the implementation of FERPA, now interpret public school library records to be student *education records* under FERPA (Scales 2009, 75). Because FERPA was not specifically intended to protect library records in the same way that state library records confidentiality laws do, it understandably offers less protection. The education records of K–12 students under the age of eighteen may be released without parental consent to "school officials including teachers" with "legitimate educational interests," with a valid court order or subpoena, in "health or safety" emergencies, and to persons in the "juvenile justice system" in accordance with state laws (EPIC. 1974. FERPA, S. 1232g. Family educational and privacy rights. (b) (1) (A-I)).

Fifteen states permit parents and/or guardians access to their minor children's or wards' library records; however, under FERPA, parents of children under the age of eighteen have the right to review their education records. When the minor reaches eighteen, that right is transferred to the student. Although the records may be examined, FERPA does not demand that schools give parents copies of the records and may require a fee be paid (U.S. Department of Education).

The Need for Privacy-Related Policies

Most state library records laws can be interpreted to shield minors' library records better than FERPA does; however, for school librarians, the difficulty lies in determining how state library records laws and FERPA *together* impact minors' school library records. Trying to sort out which law takes precedence in specific situations can be a conundrum. For example, state library records laws do not permit release of records to educators, but FERPA permits access to school officials (including teachers) who are determined by their schools to have a legitimate educational interest or need. Which law should be followed and in what circumstances?

A majority of school libraries do not have a policy that lays out the rationale for granting privacy to minors or describes how their library resources and services use records will be kept confidential. The lack of a library privacy policy leaves school librarians uncertain about whether to comply with a request to disclose a student's library record. A school library privacy policy should not only protect students' privacy and the confidentiality of their library records but also supply guidance to a school librarian on how the state's library records law and FERPA will be applied. Because there are state and federal laws involved, administrators should seek the advice of the district's legal counsel during the policy development process.

Later in the chapter, "Protecting the Privacy of Student Patrons" and its accompanying sidebars offer direction and resources for creating a privacy policy. The "Retaining School Library Records" column provides advice on creating *a records retention policy*, based on the concept of keeping minimal library use records and expunging records when they are no longer needed.

Final Thoughts on Privacy

The answer to many questions about school library privacy and the confidentiality of students' school library records' situations is "It depends." The quip should not be considered ducking the questions. The answers depend on a state's library records law, how a district is implementing FERPA with regard to library records, the age of the student, the district's legal counsel's interpretation of the state and federal laws, the specific situation, and a school's privacy policy (if one exists). It is not possible to give the clear-cut answers I have always hoped to provide. As a long-time student of school library privacy practices, I am coming to accept that the firm answers or really *interpretations of the laws in specific situations* are best given by district legal counsel. My recommendation is to advocate for a school library privacy policy to begin the conversation about student library privacy and the confidentiality of student library records. Having a board-approved library privacy policy will provide a school librarian with clear direction for protecting students' library privacy.

REFERENCES

American Library Association. 2008. *Code of Ethics of the American Library Association.* http://www .ala.org/advocacy/proethics/codeofethics/codeethics (accessed January 14, 2013).

American Library Association. Office for Intellectual Freedom. "State Privacy Laws Regarding Library Records." http://www.ala.org/offices/oif/ifgroups/stateifcchairs/stateifcinaction/ stateprivacy (accessed January 14, 2013).

Electronic Privacy Information Center. 1974. "Family Educational Rights and Privacy Act (Buckley Amendment). 20 USC S. 1232g. S.1232g Family Educational and privacy rights." http:// epic.org/privacy/education/ferpa.html (accessed January 14, 2013).

Scales, Pat R. 2009. *Protecting Intellectual Freedom in Your School Library: Scenarios from the Front Lines,* Chicago, Illinois: ALA Editions.

U.S. Department of Education. "General: Family Educational Rights and Privacy Act (FERPA)." http://www2.ed.gov/policy/gen/guid/fpco/ferpa/index.html (accessed January 14, 2013).

 **Privacy Matters**

Confidentiality

By Helen R. Adams

Originally published in the Privacy Matters column, *School Library Media Activities Monthly,* XXIII (1) (September 2006): 33.

Defining Privacy and Confidentiality

In a library context, the term, *privacy,* is defined as "the right to engage in open inquiry without having the subject of one's interest examined or scrutinized by others" (ALA 2002). Closely associated with this concept is the term *confidentiality.* Library records hold much personally identifiable information about student patrons, and the library media specialist is often privy through observation and interaction with students to additional knowledge about them. "Confidentiality exists when a library (and its staff) . . . keeps that information private on their (patrons') behalf" (ALA 2002).

Support for Privacy in Libraries

The library community has a strong commitment to providing and protecting the privacy of students using school libraries. This obligation is evident in American Library Association (ALA) and American Association of School Librarians' (AASL) policy statements.

The ALA *Code of Ethics* states:

"We protect each library user's right to privacy and confidentiality with respect to information sought or received and resources consulted, borrowed, acquired or transmitted." (ALA 2008)

The AASL "Position Statement on the Confidentiality of Library Records" further affirms:

"The library community recognizes that children and youth have the same rights to privacy as adults." (AASL)

It should be noted, however, that the right of privacy for minors is not always supported in state or federal laws.

School Library Privacy Expectations for Students

What expectations of privacy and confidentiality may students have in a school library media center? The first expectation is that *all* students will be granted the right to read, borrow, and use electronic resources from the library collection free of scrutiny regardless of age. Like adult library users, students must feel confident that their privacy will be respected in the school library. They need to know that the school library staff will keep the titles of books checked out, interlibrary loan requests made, and reference questions asked confidential.

The second expectation of students using school libraries is the right to seek information and have the topics they are researching remain private. Since school libraries provide both curricular and recreational resources, they are the sole place in a school where a student can freely investigate subjects of personal interest without undue oversight. The Supreme Court has ruled that minors' First Amendment liberties include the right to receive information. The policy statement, "Privacy: An Interpretation of the Library Bill of Rights" from the ALA website reminds us that as library media professionals we are committed "to an ethic of facilitating, not monitoring access to information" (ALA 2002).

Protecting Students' Privacy

Not only should school library media specialists protect student patrons' privacy while using the library, but they should also educate them about how to guard their own privacy in the cyber and physical day-to-day worlds. Development of an effective school library media center privacy policy should tell patrons what data is collected about them, how it is used, and how their privacy will be protected. In addition to these privacy concerns connected with library media center use, library media professionals must also help school administrators and teachers understand student privacy rights under state and federal laws. In summary, *all students* using a school library media center should be extended the maximum privacy possible under state and federal laws, the ALA *Code of Ethics*, and best practice.

REFERENCES

American Association of School Librarians. "Position Statement on the Confidentiality of Library Records." http://www.ala.org/aasl/aaslissues/positionstatements/conflibrecds (accessed January 14, 2013).

American Library Association. 2008. *Code of Ethics of the American Library Association.* Article III. http://www.ala.org/advocacy/proethics/codeofethics/codeethics (accessed January 14, 2013).

American Library Association. 2002. "Privacy: An Interpretation of the Library Bill of Rights." http://www.ala.org/advocacy/intfreedom/librarybill/interpretations/privacy (accessed January 14, 2013).

Privacy Matters

The Age of the Patron and Privacy: Elementary Students

By Helen R. Adams

Originally published in the Privacy Matters column, *School Library Media Activities Monthly*, XXIII (7) (March 2007): 35.

Does the **age of the patron** make a difference in extending privacy rights? The AASL "Position Statement on the Confidentiality of Library Records" affirms "The library community recognizes that children and youth have the same rights to privacy as adults" (AASL). Most ALA policy statements including the Library Bill of Rights interpretations and the ALA *Code of Ethics* do not distinguish between minor and adult patrons. State library records laws and the Family Educational Rights and Privacy Act (FERPA) also do not differentiate between younger and older students unless the students is determined to be an adult (defined in state and federal legislation at varying ages of 16, 17, or 18).

Should Elementary Students Have Privacy Rights?

Should age be considered when granting privacy rights to students in an elementary library? Here are some questions to consider. Do young children know that they have privacy rights in libraries, and are they concerned about their privacy? Does it matter if the library media specialist (LMS) calls out the names of children because they have unreturned library books? Is it a serious breach of privacy for the child if a peer overhears the name of the overdue item? Does it compromise a child's privacy if a teacher assists in locating a student's overdue book? These examples may seem like innocuous situations where a child's right to privacy need not be stringently enforced.

On the other hand, compromising privacy may be a slippery slope. While elementary students may have difficulty remembering to return books or even the titles they checked out, they are worthy of our respect. Where will they learn about their rights to privacy in a library unless we begin teaching them now? It is my belief that one of the expectations of privacy for students in a school library is that *all* will be granted the right to read and borrow free from scrutiny, *regardless of age*.

Parents and Students' Privacy

In a practical sense, how can a LMS maintain privacy for elementary age library patrons while still teaching them about their responsibility to return borrowed materials? When a book is overdue for several weeks, sending a friendly non-threatening note home about overdue items including the title of the book, date due, replacement cost, and LMS contact information is one way to enlist parent assistance in the return of books and still address privacy concerns. Parents of young children will likely be receptive to this type of gentle reminder.

Many children's lives are very complicated. Their overdue materials may be found in many different places. By obtaining the cooperation of parents, the overdue materials will probably be returned quickly. It is a win-win situation with little loss of privacy for the child and includes a lesson in accountability.

Teachers and Students' Library Privacy

Can an elementary teacher become involved in the hunt for a missing book and still preserve the privacy of the child involved? The answer is yes, although it is *very important* that the LMS communicate to teachers the need to protect the child's privacy to the fullest degree possible by not "exposing" the titles and corresponding students' names to the entire class.

Here is a manageable strategy for making teachers partners in the search for missing library books and still maintaining student privacy. A list can be sent by the LMS to a teacher stating that a number of books are missing and including the names of the children who checked them out. The teacher may then speak discreetly to the children with missing books, help them check their desks or backpacks, check to see if the books were lent to friends, thereby, moving the search to other students' desks and backpacks. If not located, a full classroom search may be instituted. If the books are found and returned to the library, there is a win-win situation with little loss of confidentiality for those involved.

> **FERPA and School Officials**
>
> **In answer to the question whether an elementary teacher may be included in a search for an overdue or missing book,** under FERPA provisions (34 CFR § 99.31 (a) (1) School Officials), information from students' education records can be released to school officials with a "legitimate educational interest" (VLex. "Under what conditions is prior consent not required to disclose information? http://cfr.vlex .com/vid/prior-consent-not-required -disclose-19755387 [accessed January 14, 2013]). Each district must determine locally who has an educational interest. In one district in Wisconsin, for example, FERPA is interpreted in such a way that only its school librarians have a "legitimate educational interest" in students' library records.

Teaching Young Students about Privacy

The LMS should take advantage of opportunities to teach elementary students about their rights to privacy and confidentiality in the library. If a student is searching for a particular title and it is not on the shelf, he or she may ask who has checked out the item. The LMS can explain that the name of the person who has borrowed the item is private, but the LMS will put the item on reserve for the student. By taking this action, the LMS is demonstrating that each child has the right to read what he/she chooses and can share that information if they wish. But YOU as the LMS will not divulge who has checked out the title being sought.

Reflecting on Privacy for Young Children

As LMSs, our goal is to make the principles of privacy and confidentiality work in a practical way in an elementary library. The previous examples demonstrate ways to help young children be responsible in the borrowing of materials and, at the same time, learn how library staff can guard the privacy of those who check out materials. In reality, there are few secrets among elementary children about what they are checking out. Yet, it is in these situations that LMSs begin to train young children about their right to privacy in a library.

REFERENCE

American Association of School Librarians. "Position Statement on the Confidentiality of Library Records." http://www.ala.org/aasl/aaslissues/positionstatements/conflibrecds (accessed January 14, 2013).

Privacy Matters

The Age of the Patron: Privacy for Middle and High School Students

By Helen R. Adams

Originally published in the Privacy Matters column, *School Library Media Activities Monthly*, (23) (8) (April 2007): 38.

Library media specialists (LMS) have the responsibility, both legally and ethically, to protect the privacy and confidentiality of their patrons, no matter their ages. Protecting student privacy begins with knowing state library records law and how it relates to school library records. The next step is recognizing the U.S. Supreme Court ruling in the 1982 *Board of Education, Island Trees School District v. Pico* decision that states minors have a First Amendment right to receive information and ideas (Hudson 2002). While intellectual freedom principles protect access to information, there is a corollary concept stating that minors have the right to use resources and library services *free from scrutiny*. When we allow middle and high school students to read, research, and check out materials on a wide range of topics without comment or sharing that information with others, we are honoring the twin principles of privacy and confidentiality in libraries.

Why Privacy Matters

One of the responsibilities of the school librarian is to create a library environment where students will feel free to seek information without concern that someone will question their purpose or right to that knowledge (Adams 2005, 109). There may be topics that teenagers want information about but do not feel comfortable asking their parents. Consequently, the school library may provide the ONLY source for accurate information, and a trusted LMS may be one individual they can turn to when

---

FERPA and School Library Records

When this column was written in 2007, the author assumed that the primary legal protection of K–12 students' school library records was given by state library records laws, and there was uncertainty over whether students' school library records were considered *education records* under the Family Educational Rights and Privacy Act (FERPA). As noted earlier, staff in the Family Policy Compliance Office, whose responsibility it is to oversee the implementation of the FERPA, now state that library records are considered *education records* as defined in the law. Under specific conditions, FERPA allows review of library records where state library records laws would not. Institutions, however, are not *required* under FERPA to create records or disclose them. A strong board-approved school library privacy policy is the best protection of students' library records (American Library Association. 2012. "Questions and Answers on Privacy and Confidentiality." January 23, 2012. http://www.ala.org/advocacy/intfreedom/librarybill/interpretations/qa-privacy [accessed January 14, 2013]).

Creating a "Privacy-Friendly" Environment in a High School Library

Geri, a high school librarian in Connecticut, established an area in the library where students can read about sensitive topics without feeling exposed. She stated, "This might sound simplistic, but one of the things I've done in my library is to move some furniture. I've become more aware of the students who check out books on LGBT, or other 'personal' issues. I wanted to make it easier for these kids to find a spot to sit with a book in relative privacy, so I pulled a couple of our 'comfy' chairs and put each one in a nice area by our glass wall, by a big plant. The spaces make me think of how my cats curl up in a sunny corner. I've also made a point of bringing in more books about these topics that discuss issues at a more personal level, rather than from a political or medical perspective" (Geri, online discussion with author, December 8, 2011).

researching sensitive topics. Any student's reference question brings a weighty responsibility on the part of the LMS to abide by the ALA *Code of Ethics*, Article III, which calls for protecting the privacy of library users as they pursue their research (ALA 2008). It is important to remember that just because a student asks for information on abortion, teen pregnancy, drugs and drug use, or some other social issue does not mean that he/she is pregnant, using drugs, or engaged in other risky behavior. Equally sensitive topics may be sought for a school assignment for personal reasons. As LMSs, we should respect our students' right to privacy and not ask *why* the information is needed.

On the other hand, there may be times when an LMS must apply common sense rather than the ALA policy and ethics statements because of a concern for the student's welfare. Just as educators are required to report cases of child abuse, there are times when concern for a student may move the LMS to seek the advice of another school professional bound by confidentiality such as a guidance counselor. Intervening to potentially save the life of a student transcends student privacy.

Strategies for Maintaining Confidentiality

Because there are so many physical, intellectual, and emotional changes for students during the middle and high school years, a sense of responsibility is not yet well developed. There are ways, however, that the LMS can help students return materials in a timely fashion. Giving quiet oral reminders when students are using the library is a first step. Printed notices, folded and stapled with the student's name at the top, delivered to a homeroom teacher are another. Some schools use a quarterly reward system to encourage adolescents to work toward improving grades and acting responsibly. Returning overdue materials can also become part of the criteria for gaining participation in a special activity. A middle school LMS recently told me that this is a very positive way to encourage responsibility, and few books remain unreturned by the end of the year. In some intractable cases, letters may need to be sent to parents requesting return of books, noting the cost of the item(s), and contact information for the LMS.

While students in middle and high school have developed a desire for privacy, they do not yet comprehend how to protect their personal information. In addition to protecting minors' right to privacy in a library setting and the confidentiality of their records, the LMS should teach students how to guard their own privacy in their physical daily lives as well as online. This instruction may be a part of the information and technology literacy curriculum.

Age does have *some* place in how LMSs extend privacy to student patrons, but student First Amendment rights, the *Library Bill of Rights*, the ALA *Code of Ethics*, and other policy statements tell us that granting privacy to students is the right thing to do. As middle and high school students grow and mature, providing scrutiny free access to information and keeping their interests and intellectual pursuits confidential is a matter of keeping faith with them as well as honoring our professional ethical codes.

REFERENCES

Adams, Helen R., Robert Bocher, Carol Gordon, Elizabeth Barry-Kessler. 2005. *Privacy in the 21st Century: Issues for Public, School, and Academic Libraries.* Westport, Connecticut: Libraries Unlimited.

American Library Association. 2008. *Code of Ethics of the American Library Association.* http://www .ala.org/advocacy/proethics/codeofethics/codeethics (accessed January 14, 2013).

Hudson, David L., Jr. 2002. "Book Censorship." April 1, 2002. *First Amendment Center.* http://www .firstamendmentcenter.org/book-censorship (accessed January 14, 2013).

Privacy Matters

The Ebb and Flow of Library Privacy

By Helen R. Adams

Originally in the Privacy Matters column, *School Library Media Activities Monthly*, XXIV(10) (June 2008): 31.

For the past two years, this column has reported on issues related to privacy of patrons using resources and services in a school library media center. A look at proposed and new state privacy legislation across the United States in 2007–2008 shows both positive and negative changes.

Connecticut: In July 2007, Connecticut's legislature increased confidentiality requirements for library records in public and private libraries of all types *except for records in schools and academic libraries*. Library records for school libraries were not protected under previous law and are not included in this one (Connecticut 2007). While this is a privacy victory for other types of libraries and their patrons, it is unfortunate that confidentiality requirements for school and academic library records were not contained in this strong legislation.

> **Update on Pennsylvania Library Records Law Revision**
>
> In Pennsylvania, the proposed legislation to join fifteen other states in allowing parents and guardians to view their minor child's/wards' library records remained in legislative committee and expired without further action being taken (American Library Association. "State Privacy Laws Regarding Library Records." http://www.ala.org/offices/oif/ifgroups/stateifcchairs/stateifcinaction/stateprivacy [accessed January 14, 2013]).

Pennsylvania: Pennsylvania's library records law shields circulation records stating they may be divulged only by court order in a criminal proceeding (ALA State Privacy Laws). Proposed legislation introduced in October 2007, will grant, if approved, parents and guardians the right to view their minor child's library record. (Pennsylvania 2007). There is no age-limiting language, so presumably the provision would extend until a minor becomes 18. The bill is currently in the House State Government Committee.

Vermont: In December 2007 Senator Claire Ayer introduced Senate Bill 220, "Confidentiality of Library Patron Records," to create a new statute protecting library records of public and academic libraries. The original text *did not include school library records*, but that addition is being requested as an amendment by the Vermont School Library Association (VSLA). The bill includes exemptions under which library records may be released including: by written permission by the patron, to library staff as needed for administrative purposes, by a court order, and to custodial parents or guardians of patrons under the age of thirteen for the purpose of collecting fines or return of overdue materials. VSLA is also seeking an exemption to allow school libraries to release patron records to custodial parents and/or guardians of minors in accordance with provisions of the Family Education Rights and Privacy Act (Vermont 2007).

Trina Magi, library associate professor at the University of Vermont and chairperson of the Vermont Library Association Intellectual Freedom Committee, stated, "The Vermont Library Association was the first state library association to go on record opposing the USA PATRIOT Act. Our concern about that law focused our attention on the issue of confidentiality of library records in general, and we came to realize that our state [library records] law was not as clear and strong as it could be. Various librarians, state officials, and members of law enforcement seemed to interpret the existing law in different ways, creating confusion and leaving the people of Vermont unsure about how their library records would be protected" (Magi 2008).

Wisconsin: Protection of library circulation and other patron use records in public, academic, and school libraries remains in place. However, in November 2007, the Wisconsin legislature enacted a law that allows law enforcement officers to obtain, without a warrant, records that show alleged criminal conduct in the library when recorded by a surveillance device under the control of the library. Wisconsin statute 43.30 (5) states, "Upon the request of a law enforcement officer who is investigating criminal conduct alleged to have occurred at a library supported in whole or in part by public funds, the library shall disclose to the law enforcement officer all records produced by a surveillance device under the control of the library" (Wisconsin 2007). Because public school library media programs are financed by "public funds," this law includes records gathered by surveillance devices in school libraries.

The Results of Legislative Activity

What do these changes in legislation relating to library records mean for school library media specialists and their patrons? An analysis of the actions of the four state legislatures shows the majority

---

Update on the Vermont Library Records Law

The Vermont library records law was strengthened substantially for adult library patrons, and the conditions under which minors' library records may be released are very clear. The law includes the following exemptions for release of confidential library records: 1) with written permission of the library user; 2) to library staff for administrative purposes; 3) with a court order or warrant; 4) to custodial parents/guardians of library users under age 16; and 5) to custodial parents/guardians "in accordance with the federal Family Education [sic] Rights and Privacy Act, by the library at the school the student attends" (Vermont Statutes Online. 2008. Title 22 "Libraries, History, and Information Technology." Chapter 4 "Library Patron Records." 22 V.S.A. § 172. Library record confidentiality exemptions. http://www.leg.state.vt.us/statutes/fullsection.cfm?Title=22&Chapter=004&Section=00172 [accessed January 14, 2013]).

Christine, a school librarian in Vermont, is satisfied with the new library confidentiality law stating:

The Vermont Patron Confidentiality Law has been more helpful than I ever would have realized prior to its passage. As librarians, we are trained to think about safeguarding our patrons' confidentiality and freedoms, and of course, we have our professional *Code of Ethics*. But in a school environment, there are sometimes a number of pressures that can impinge on the principles of confidentiality. Our teaching colleagues, for instance, are used to sharing information with each other about student behavior and learning in the classroom, and they sometimes innocently request information from the school librarian about a student's use of the library. The way schools are structured can also present challenges with something as simple as overdue book notices, so that the notices must go to the teacher instead of directly to students. It's not uncommon that a teacher may read aloud from a list of overdues, trying to encourage responsibility among students but with utter disregard to confidentiality. Time pressures also add to breaches of confidentiality in school settings, where harried teachers with many students may feel that measures of confidentiality are simply an unnecessary hassle.

Having patron confidentiality measures in (state) law means that these issues are not just the preference or fixation of the librarian but have the force and standing of law. As the lone librarian in an organization, it can be hard to uphold philosophical values that others around you don't share and aren't informed of. Codifying patron confidentiality into law moves the issue out of personal or even professional ethics and into a matter of shared community values, and this is of great worth to librarians. Confidentiality (of library records) law gives us a starting point for conversation with our administrators and colleagues that can help us shift our schools toward best practices in privacy and confidentiality, to the benefit of our students" (Christine, email message to author, April 17, 2012).

For insights into how the Vermont library records law is implemented in school libraries, the Vermont School Library Association has a "Confidentiality in School Libraries" brochure available to download at https://docs.google.com/document/d/1em3brHcfMdvrDKgE4xdsCvmB_dPwY3xCwiGMWmQR5uw/edit?hl=en&authkey=CPvzubgC&pli=1#.

lack understanding of or support for privacy rights for minors using school libraries. The Connecticut legislature had an opportunity to create a strong protection for school library media program records but failed to do so. Pennsylvania has proposed legislation that would diminish the rights of minors by allowing parents and guardians to access their minor child's records up to age eighteen. Wisconsin's new law permitting release of surveillance records to a law enforcement agent without a court order is a regression in the rights of patrons to use a library without scrutiny. Unfortunately, state laws are sometimes at odds with the right of privacy for minors affirmed by the library profession. However, admirably the Vermont library community is working together to include protection for school library program patron records in its proposed privacy legislation.

REFERENCES

American Library Association. "State Privacy Laws Regarding Library Records." http://www.ala.org/offices/oif/ifgroups/stateifcchairs/stateifcinaction/stateprivacy (accessed January 14, 2013).

Connecticut General Assembly. 2007. "Substitute Bill 7290." http://www.cga.ct.gov/2007/TOB/H/2007HB-07290-R01-HB.htm [no longer available].

General Assembly of Pennsylvania. 2007. "House Bill 1997, Session 2007." http://www.legis.state.pa.us/cfdocs/billinfo/billinfo.cfm?syear=2007&sind=0&body=H&type=B&BN=1997 (accessed January 14, 2013).

Magi, Trina, email message to author, January 22, 2008.

Vermont, SB 220. 2007. "The Confidentiality of Library Patron Records." [original text as introduced]. http://www.leg.state.vt.us/docs/legdoc.cfm?URL=/docs/2008/bills/intro/S-220.HTM (accessed January 14, 2013).

Wisconsin Legislature. 2007. "Act 34, 43.30 (5) (a) & (b)." http://www.legis.state.wi.us/2007/data/acts/07Act34.pdf (accessed January 14, 2013).

 **Privacy Matters**

The Troubled Student and Privacy

By Helen R. Adams

Originally published in the Privacy Matters column, *School Library Media Activities Monthly*, XXIV (4) (December 2007): 34.

When should a school library media specialist consider violating a student's privacy? Although school library professionals should extend the maximum amount of privacy to students, there may be times when library staff must use common sense rather than American Library Association policy and ethics statements because of a concern for the student's welfare. For example, if a sudden change in personality, dramatic switch in friends, a move toward secrecy or isolation, or a fixation with information on risky or criminal activity is observed, then other actions may be considered. The first step is to talk to the student casually but confidentially. If, after a period of time, the school library professional is still concerned, she or he may seek advice from the school's guidance counselor, who is also bound by a code of confidentiality. The counselor is an excellent choice for a confidant because she or he may already know the child, have obtained similar reports from other sources, and has training and experience on how to proceed in such a situation.

School Counselor Actions

A guidance counselor may look at a student's grades, record of absences, recent disciplinary actions as well as inquire casually among the teachers of the troubled student to see if any changes have been noticed. At times, friends of a student who may be talking about suicide may confide in a teacher, and that information is reported to the counselor. With the collective background information, the counselor will likely choose to speak directly with the student. The school library professional's observations may help in determining what is concerning the student and keep him or her safe. Because of confidentiality, it is unlikely that the library professional will ever learn the result of reported observations but can feel confident that someone with the necessary resources is taking the concerns seriously.

Other Reasons for Infringing on Student Privacy

The principal may be the choice of a confidant if the school library media specialist is concerned that his or her observations may be related to a school safety issue. A principal is responsible for the health and safety of *all* students and staff. If there are indications that the student is actively engaging in potentially dangerous or threatening behavior, the principal may contact the parents and/or the police immediately to protect the well-being of the school community.

When Risk Outweighs Student Privacy

In their daily work, school librarians or library staff may observe or learn about a situation that affects the health and safety of a student. If the information is associated with child abuse, reporting is mandatory; however, there are other instances when the school librarian may feel compelled to share the confidential information with a guidance counselor, principal, social worker, even though doing violates the privacy of the student.

Margaret, a staff member in an elementary library in New York, found herself in just such a circumstance and shared this experience:

> This year a third grade girl asked for books on babysitting. As we were looking through the catalog, she confided that she was very tired because she had been babysitting her three brothers (ages 5, 4 and 4 months) the night before. She couldn't fall asleep because she had heard something and decided to go upstairs to her bedroom with her infant brother. She put him in her bed but was afraid to go to sleep because she thought he might fall out of the bed. I felt comfortable going to the school social worker with this information because I was aware of previous problems in the home. I felt that the situation was incredibly risky on numerous levels and outweighed maintaining the child's privacy (Margaret, online discussion with author, February 17, 2011).

As noted in the column, instances in which a school librarian infringes on a student's privacy will be rare. The librarian must weigh knowledge of the student, the seriousness of the situation, and common sense before seeking assistance from school colleagues who are in a position to obtain more information and have the skills and resources to take appropriate action.

Another instance for violating privacy of school library users may occur if the library media specialist observes indications of possible child abuse. All states have child protection laws which require educators to report suspected maltreatment of children. For example, in Pennsylvania, the Child Protective Services Law (23 Pa. C.S., Chapter 63) establishes definitions of child abuse, who is required to report abuse, and the procedures to be followed (Pennsylvania Department of Public Welfare).

Not the "Information" Police

Aside from the health and safety circumstances outlined above, a school library professional must remember that there are very strong professional policy statements, such as the *Library Bill of Rights* and the *Code of Ethics for the ALA*, that urge library staff to guard the privacy of library users. This is especially true in terms of scrutinizing what a student is reading. In this case, the school library media specialist must accept that she or he is *not* the "information" police. Minors have the right to receive ideas and information from their school's library media center as part of their First Amendment rights, and they should not be subjected to probing inquiry if they are investigating topics which may be personally distasteful to the library media specialist. Only parents have the right to limit or restrict their children's choice of reading—whether in a public or school library setting.

The Children's Internet Protection Act (CIPA) requires that educators monitor students' Internet use. Observing a student looking at a page on bomb-making or guns could elicit several possible reactions. It is possible the student accidentally found the information, or it may be research for a presentation for how easy it is to find weapons-type information on the Internet. The library media specialist should avoid jumping to a false conclusion that a student is planning to build a bomb or use a weapon for criminal purposes.

Stop and Think

Situations in which a school library professional may violate a student's privacy with just cause are rare. Library media specialists should think carefully before taking actions that can compromise a student's privacy because students depend on the discretion of library media program staff. In most instances, the library media specialist should strive to protect student privacy following state library records confidentiality laws, the *Library Bill of Rights*, and the *Code of Ethics of the ALA.*

REFERENCE

Pennsylvania Department of Public Welfare. "Child Abuse Neglect." http://web.archive.org/web/20041012064727/ http://www.dpw.state.pa.us/Child/ChildAbuseNeglect (last accessed April 30, 2012) [no longer available].

Privacy Matters

How Circulation Systems May Impact Student Privacy

By Helen R. Adams

Originally published in the Privacy Matters column, *School Library Media Activities Monthly*, XXIV (6) (February 2008): 36.

When automation systems were first installed, school library media specialists thought only of the convenience and the release from the drudgery of filing checkout cards and typing overdue lists. When an item was checked in, it was believed that the link between the patron and the book or other library resource borrowed was broken; this, however, is erroneous. By checking a book's "copy status," library staff can determine the current borrower and, depending on software configuration, learn who checked it out previously—from the most recent person to a staff-designated number of earlier borrowers. These records remain in the system indefinitely, unless purged. Some library media specialists want this type of information; it allows them to trace recent borrowers if damage is discovered after the item is returned. Conversely, it can also be a privacy issue as it can be used to determine who is reading selected types of books.

Privacy Realities from School Library Media Specialists

None of us imagined how these circulation program features would change and improve to the point of becoming a greater threat to the privacy of school library users. Today's programs allow easy access to data once available only through laborious use of a separate utility program or hand collation. Patron checkout histories, beginning with the first item borrowed by the student through the current time, are now readily available at the click of a mouse. Pat, a middle school library media specialist in Washington agreed to provide information for this article on condition of anonymity. He said that by selecting "checkout history "he is able to view *every title checked out by a student,* its barcode number, and the date of checkout (Pat 2007).

While Pat can disable this feature to protect the circulation history of the student, he is reluctant to do so. He said, "I have had occasion to use this information in conjunction with classroom teachers looking for the truth about what certain students claim they have read versus what they have actually checked out. I do not share the entirety of the list, only sharing the YES or NO on titles in question" (Pat 2007). He sees yet another positive side of the checkout history feature when he states, "I have had students ask me what they checked out in the past. One in particular comes to mind. She is a migrant student and reads voraciously. When she found out she had checked out 52 books in one year, she crowed about it to her friends and bragged about how well she was doing. To me, that is worth it" (Pat 2007).

According to Gwen, a middle school library media specialist in Virginia, who also agreed to provide information for this article under condition of anonymity, students are able to access their own circulation records from any Internet accessible computer (Gwen 2007). This means they can learn what items are checked out, when they are due, and put others on reserve. Are there any privacy concerns associated with this new freedom for students? In some schools such as Gwen's, patron library numbers are the same as student lunch numbers. Although this may make it easier for students to remember, it also means that the number has a greater opportunity to be learned by others. To Gwen's knowledge, students have not shared their patron library numbers or played tricks on each other by checking out "interesting" items to one another (Gwen 2007).

Protecting Student Circulation Records

Why should the advances in automation systems concern school library professionals? The *Code of Ethics of the American Library Association* advocates in Article III that school library staff protect the privacy of each user's choice of library resources and keep confidential any records associated with that use, including those retained in a library automation system (ALA 2008). School library media specialists must take steps to ensure that the readily available information about student patrons' use of library resources is protected from teacher and administrator inquiries, parent and student volunteers, and students who may be at the circulation computer involved in self-checkout of their library materials.

There are a number of ways school library media specialists can protect student circulation records including:

- Develop a Privacy Policy that states who has access to library patron records and the circumstances under which records may be released.

- Use a password to protect circulation records with differing levels of access "rights" assigned to students, volunteers, and library staff (Gwen 2007).

- Make a conscious effort to purge circulation records on a regular basis. Note: For specifics read the Privacy Matters column on "Retaining School Library Records." [The column is included in this chapter.]

- Teach ALL students to respect the confidentiality of library records—their own and those of others.

Additionally, Pat, the media specialist from Washington, trains student assistants about library privacy and provides each with a brochure, which includes guidelines for being a volunteer (Pat 2007). Key points relating to the confidentiality of library records include:

- "Student aides are not to use the circulation program to look at other students' information, either personal or academic.

- Library aides will not give out information about other students' library circulations to anyone" (Pat 2007).

If we are serious about students' privacy when they use the school library media center and its resources, we must consider how the automation system and each upgrade may affect the confidentiality of library records, and take proactive measures to protect them. Our students are depending on us!

REFERENCES

American Library Association. 2008. *Code of Ethics of the American Library Association.* Article III. http://www.ala.org/advocacy/proethics/codeofethics/codeethics (accessed January 14, 2013).

Gwen, email message to author, October 4, 2007.

Pat, email message to author, October 2, 2007.

Pat. 2007. "Guidelines for Middle School Library Aides" Brochure.

Privacy Matters

More Privacy Concerns about Technology Use in the Library Media Center

By Helen R. Adams

Originally published in Privacy Matters column, *School Library Media Activities Monthly*, XXIV (8) (April 2008): 36.

The previous column described the potential impact of library automation systems on student privacy; however, there are additional technologies currently used in library media centers or on their way. Consequently, library media specialists must also consider these new technologies and their possible effects on the privacy of students.

Radio Frequency Identification

Radio Frequency Identification (RFID) is a technology installed in many libraries that uses radio waves to recognize individual library resources (Adams 2005, 128). The technology combines the automation of library circulation, inventory management, and security for resources in one self-adhesive tag. The RFID tag is a small, paper-thin label that can be applied to a library book or other item allowing check out of multiple items simultaneously, self-checkout by patrons, security for items from theft, and more efficient management of the inventory process. One of the major differences between barcodes and RFID tags is that they do not require direct contact or line-of-sight scanning (SearchNetworking 2002).

RFID is being implemented in public and academic libraries; however, the technology is slower in coming to school libraries. Because of its cost, major school library automation vendors have been discussing RFID but have not put its development on the fast track. According to the *School Library Journal* and San Jose State University 2006 Automation Survey, over 50 percent of school library professionals completing the survey were not interested in the RFID technology. One interpretation may be that respondents were not familiar with the technology (Fuller 2006). When the cost of RFID technology drops, however, more schools may move from traditional barcodes and electromagnetic theft detection systems to RFID technology.

Due to the privacy concerns expressed over the possible misuse of RFID to collect information about patrons' use of library materials, the

> **RFID Update**
>
> Although numerous public and academic libraries have installed RFID technology, the adoption rate in public schools is very small. It is likely that the financial situation of many districts has focused technology funds for instructional purposes, rather than updating library automation practices/software to include RFID.
>
> There are still privacy concerns with the use of RFID technology, and they are outlined in an article by Deborah Caldwell-Stone, the deputy director of the American Library Association (ALA) Office for Intellectual Freedom, in a *Library Technology Reports* issue devoted to privacy and freedom of information. It is interesting to note that Caldwell-Stone documents that there are only thirteen states with laws governing the use of RFID in documents (such as drivers' licenses) and in human implantation (Caldwell-Stone, Deborah. 2010. "Chapter 6: RFID in Libraries." *Library Technology Reports* 46, no. 8: 7).

ALA Council, in 2005, approved the "Resolution on Radio Frequency Identification (RFID) Technology and Privacy Principles" (http://www.ala.org/offices/oif/statementspols/ifresolutions/rfidresolution). In June 2006, in an effort to assist libraries during implementation of the technology and to protect patron privacy, the ALA Intellectual Freedom Committee approved the "RFID in Libraries: Privacy and Confidentiality Guidelines" (http://www.ala.org/offices/oif/statementspols/otherpolicies/rfidguidelines). ALA continues to monitor RFID technology and its implications on patron privacy.

Biometrics in Schools

Biometric accessory technology is still being implemented in schools for library circulation, school bus access, and cafeteria meal sale control; however, the use of biometrics in general has been controversial with opponents citing privacy infringements and concerns about misuse of the information. Proponents point out the efficiency of using biometric technology for the intended purposes; however, Arizona, Illinois, Iowa, Louisiana, and Michigan have enacted laws regulating the collection of biometric information from minor students (Mizio, Ellen. 2011."The Use of Biometric Technology in K–12 Schools." http://www.ncstl.org/evident/The%20Use%20of%20Biometric%20Technology%20in%20K-12%20Schools-MIZIO [accessed January 14, 2013]).

Educational Biometric Technology, the company cited in the column, is still selling biometric accessory technology to schools. Its website indicates that some of the advantages for use with school library circulation systems are quick, accurate identification of users, fast recognition of the fingerprint, and no library cards or identification codes. The hardware and software also interface easily with other systems. More information on products and their use is available at http://fingerid.net/ (Educational Biometric Technology. "Overview." http://www.fingerid.net/overview [accessed January 14, 2013]).

Biometrics

At the AASL Conference in Reno in October 2007, there were demonstrations of how biometric technology may be used to identify library patrons in automation programs for the purpose of checking out materials. The website, SearchSecurity, states that biometrics "refers to technologies that measure and analyze human body characteristics, such as fingerprints, eye retinas and irises, voice patterns, facial patterns and hand measurements, for authentication purposes" (SearchSecurity 1998). In the case of library automation, the biometric technology involved is the Universal Finger Identification System (UFID). The system takes measurements of an individual's finger, uses software to identify specific data as "match points," converts and stores the information as a numeric value in a database, and uses the "match points" biometric data for comparison when a live, human finger touches the finger reader/scanner at a circulation desk (SearchSecurity 1998).

Are there privacy issues involved? According to Bob Engen, President of Educational Biometric Technology, actual fingerprints are not stored, only the measurements of the fingerprint; therefore, an individual's fingerprint cannot be generated from the data stored (Wieneke 2007).

Surveillance Cameras

Since the tragedy at Columbine High School in 1999 and more recent incidents of school violence, administrators have been installing surveillance cameras in an effort to improve security for students and staff. In many schools, cameras record activity in entrances, hallways, classrooms, the cafeteria, the library, computer labs, parking lots, the perimeter of the facility, and school buses. The general consensus is that the locations selected for security cameras are limited to public spaces where school staff and students *have no reasonable expectation of privacy* (Adams 2005, 130).

Although the surveillance cameras may provide administrators, faculty, students, and parents with a sense of relief, when placed in a library, they *may infringe* on the expectation of privacy for patrons. Whether there is intrusion on patrons' privacy depends on camera placement and the clarity of the recorded image. Cameras directed at entrances/exits, general seating areas, or computers may only record students and staff entering, leaving, and working, not the specific materials which are being used such as documents or websites. To protect the privacy of students, the school library professional should request that a camera not be aimed at the circulation area(s).

As noted frequently in this column, Article III of the *Code of Ethics for the American Library Association* advocates that school library professionals protect the privacy of library users. The role of the school library media specialist with regard to the use of *any* technology in the library media center is to assess its impact on patron privacy, take proactive measures, and advocate for the privacy of students and staff.

Surveillance in Schools

Schools continue to install and upgrade surveillance systems in school facilities and on school grounds. Joel VerDuin, director of technology and media services for the Wausau School District (Wisconsin) explains their purpose: "Columbine (High School) and subsequent school violence raised the hype-factor of camera systems, and we seemed to go on a spending spree as dollars from various sources became available for camera systems post-Columbine. Once installed and used, fad or hype turned into a useful post-event tool. I believe our school principals would not trade them in for the world as footage has retroactively allowed for schools to find evidence in issues of vandalism, harassment, fraudulent 911 calls, fights, and theft. The number of times we go back to view video footage is staggering" (VerDuin, Joel. Email message to author, December 27, 2010).

At one time, official surveillance technology in schools was limited to locations where there was no expectation of privacy by students or staff; however, with the sanctioned use of student smart phones in schools as part of the "bring your own device" (BYOD) trend, there is little, if any, privacy for students or staff. Phone cameras are used for fun, mischief, and malice, with resulting photos posted on social media sites or passed around by students with no regard for privacy of their peers. As a result, it is doubly important for school librarians to teach students about personal privacy and the need to respect the privacy of others both in a library context and online.

REFERENCES

Adams, Helen R., Robert Bocher, Carol Gordon, and Elizabeth Barry-Kessler. 2005. *Privacy in the 21st Century: Issues for Public, School, and Academic Libraries.* Westport, Connecticut: Libraries Unlimited.

American Library Association. Office for Intellectual Freedom. 2006. *Intellectual Freedom Manual.* 7th ed. Chicago: Illinois. American Library Association.

Fuller, Daniel. 2006. "School Library Journal & San Jose State University 2006 Automation Survey." October 1, 2006. *School Library Journal.* http://www.schoollibraryjournal.com/article/CA6376081.html (accessed January 14, 2013).

SearchNetworking. 2002. "RFID Definition." http://searchnetworking.techtarget.com/sDefinition/0,,sid7_gci805987,00.html (accessed January 14, 2013).

SearchSecurity. "Biometrics Definitions." http://searchsecurity.techtarget.com/sDefinition/0,,sid14_gci211666,00.html (accessed January 14, 2013).

Wieneke, Nancy. 2007. "Finger ID System to Facilitate School Food Service." January 18, 2007. *Clintonville Tribune-Gazette.* http://www.fingerid.net/clintonv.pdf (accessed January 14, 2013).

Privacy Matters

Protecting the Privacy of Student Patrons

By Helen R. Adams

Originally published in the Privacy Matters column, *School Library Media Activities Monthly*, XXIII (4) (December 2006): 37.

<table>
<tr><td>

Two Policies or One?

When this column was written in 2006, having two policies (one to direct the actions of staff and the other focused on helping student and adult users understand their privacy rights in a school library) seemed like an appropriate choice. Today, a single school library privacy policy can accomplish the same purposes if all the elements described in the column for both policies are included.

</td></tr>
</table>

What single action can a school library media specialist (SLMS) take to protect the privacy of student patrons considering the variation in state library records laws and the uncertainty over the application of the Family Educational Rights and Privacy Act (FERPA) to school library records? The answer is to create two separate policies, a "Confidentiality of School Library Records Policy" and a "School Library Privacy Policy." Two policies are needed because the purpose of each policy differs. A confidentiality of library records policy is aimed at directing the actions of library professional and support staff, student assistants, and adult library program volunteers with the goal of maintaining confidentiality for all types of patron records. A privacy policy, on the other hand, describes to patrons how library staff will protect and ensure privacy in the school library.

Elements of a School Library Records Policy for Staff

What should be included in a "Confidentiality of School Library Records Policy?" The following topics would address the full scope of such a policy: 1) the right of patrons to enjoy privacy while using any library service or resource; 2) reference to relevant state or federal library records laws relating to the release of library records containing personally identifiable information about patrons and their use of library resources and services; 3) rationale for maintaining library program records; 4) the creation of rules and procedures to ensure confidentiality of patron records, secure the data, and assure their integrity; and 5) training of all library staff. In addition to the policy language, it is important to attach related documents from professional associations which provide reinforcement and rationale for local policy.

The American Library Association (ALA) has two policy statements that would be useful as supporting documents: "Confidentiality of Library Records" (http://www.ala.org/Template.cfm?Section=otherpolicies&Template=/ContentManagement/ContentDisplay.cfm&ContentID=13084) and "Confidentiality of Personally Identifiable Information about Library Users" (http://www.ala.org/offices/oif/statementspols/otherpolicies/policyconcerning). These policies state clearly the responsibilities of library staff in maintaining the confidentiality of patron personally identifiable information (PII) and records related to usage of library resources both within and outside a school library.

Creating a School Library Privacy Policy for Patrons

Developing a privacy policy for the school library relies on many of the same intellectual freedom concepts, laws, and policy statements. Basic considerations to address in a school library privacy policy include: 1) a definition of privacy and why it is crucial to student library patrons; 2) a notice of dedication by library staff to protecting the privacy of patrons and the confidentiality of their library records; 3) a reference to the state's library record confidentiality law, to whom and under what circumstances library records may be legally released; 4) a description of the type of the PII collected about patrons and how library staff use the information, how they secure the data, and if it is purged when no longer needed; 5) when and how students may access their own library circulation records; 6) a statement advising students of their right to privacy when using a school library; 7) recourse for a student patron if he/she feels personal privacy has been violated in the library; and 8) provision of training for students and staff on protecting personal privacy. Supporting documents for a privacy policy include ALA's "Privacy: An Interpretation of the Library Bill of Rights" and the two ALA policy statements described above ("Confidentiality of Library Records" and "Confidentiality of Personally Identifiable Information about Library Users").

Resources are available to help in the development of both policies. Sample privacy and confidentiality policies may be found in *Privacy in the 21st Century: Issues for Public, School, and Academic Libraries* by Helen R. Adams, et al (Libraries Unlimited, 2005). The American Library Association includes a sample privacy policy online as part of its Privacy Tool Kit, but the language is more general and better suited to public libraries (http://www.ala.org/offices/oif/iftoolkits/toolkitsprivacy/privacy). [Author note: Created in 2005, ALA's Privacy Tool Kit is currently being revised by a subcommittee of the ALA Intellectual Freedom Committee.]

Update on Creating a School Library Privacy Policy

As explained earlier in this chapter, school library circulation records and other written library records that identify individual students are also considered *education records* as defined under the FERPA. Because FERPA was never intended to shield library records, guidance on how the FERPA impacts the confidentiality of students' library records should be included in a school library privacy policy. Additionally, if a state's library records law is protective of minors' privacy, its provisions should be added to the policy and cited as state law (ALA. 2012. "Questions and Answers on Privacy and Confidentiality." January 23, 2012. http://www.ala.org/advocacy/intfreedom/librarybill/interpretations/qa-privacy [accessed January 15, 2013]). The complicated legal nature of protecting minors' privacy in school libraries (involving both federal and state laws) necessitates that administrators seek the advice of district legal counsel when drafting a school library privacy policy.

Because the library profession supports extending privacy to minors, the policy should also include reference to ALA documents including, Article II of the *Code of Ethics of the American Library Association*, "Privacy: An Interpretation of the Library Bill of Rights," and AASL's "Position Statement on the Confidentiality of Library Records." These three documents provide a rationale for school librarians supporting the privacy of their student patrons.

Updated Resource for Writing a Privacy Policy

In 2012, Theresa Chmara, Freedom to Read Foundation legal counsel, wrote a comprehensive article, "Privacy and E-Books," in which she explained the importance of a privacy policy and detailed the connection between library privacy and students' First Amendment right to receive information in a library. She also outlined her recommendations for the elements a school library privacy policy should contain, including considerations for protecting records relating to the circulation of e-books (Chmara, Theresa. 2012. "Privacy and E-Books." *Knowledge Quest* 40 no. 3: 62–65).

Educating the School Community about Student Library Privacy

When the school library privacy policy has been approved by the board of education, it should be distributed and introduced to school staff, students, and parents. In each case, the librarian should explain the rationale for the policy, review its provisions, and answer questions. When administrators, teachers, support staff, students, and parents are knowledgeable about minors' privacy in school libraries, the school librarian has additional allies in ensuring that students are not dissuaded from seeking information or checking out materials fearing that their inquiries will become known or questioned.

It is wise to have library policies formally adopted by the board of education or other governing body. Formal approval ensures that the policy will be official and further protects patrons and directs library staff. Additionally, because state library records laws differ in each state and not all state library records laws protect school library patron records from disclosure, the district's school library privacy policy should address how school library patron records will be protected if state law is silent.

Privacy Matters

Retaining School Library Records

By Helen R. Adams

Originally published in the Privacy Matters column, *School Library Media Activities Monthly*, XXIII (5) (January 2007): 33.

Our topic this month is record retention in school libraries—what should you keep and for how long? Are you a saver? Many of us are, but this may not be a good trait when it comes to keeping library records which include personally identifiable information about patrons. The purpose of library records is to manage library resources efficiently. However, after materials are returned and statistical data such as how many books were circulated during a school year has been obtained, the raw information which connects a user to an item or service should be erased, shredded, or expunged.

What Is Considered a Library Record?

Library records may include but are not be limited to circulation records, interlibrary loan records, public access computer/Internet sign-up lists or automated logins, temporary files, cookies, and use records created during Internet searching, reference interviews and email queries, and server logs. Library media and technology staff should develop a schedule and specific guidelines to destroy nonessential personally identifying data or files of library records that are no longer needed.

Two Concepts to Protect Library Records

There are two important concepts regarding library records. The first is that library records should be kept for as long as they are needed and then destroyed. The shortest possible retention of records helps ensure patron privacy. The second important concept is to retain minimal library records. After all, you cannot produce those library records that are no longer available, nor can those records be vulnerable to unauthorized disclosure.

Required Records Retention

Retention periods for records are a matter of local policy unless dictated by state or

Data Privacy Day

Annually on January 28, organizations and individuals in the United States, Canada, and the forty countries comprising the Council of Europe celebrate the signing of the "Convention for the Protection of Individuals with regard to Automatic Processing of Personal Data," known by the short title "Convention 108" (http://conventions.coe.int/treaty/en/treaties/html/108.htm). Signed in Strasbourg, France, on January 28, 1981, by members of the Council of Europe, "Convention 108" was the first international treaty to acknowledge a person's right to data privacy and the protection of personal information. In the United States, one of the goals of "Convention 108" is to educate parents, children, and young adults about the privacy of their information on social networking sites, when using smartphones, and during online gaming (National Cyber Security Alliance.

"About" [Data Privacy Day]. http://www.staysafeonline
.org/data-privacy-day/about [accessed January 15, 2013]).

Resources for celebrating Data Privacy Day include:

- **StaySafeOnline** http://staysafeonline.org/teach-on
line-safety/ (lesson plans and classroom materials for
teaching students about their privacy online).

- **Privacyrevolution.org** http://www.privacyrevolution
.org (news articles, activities, logos, information connecting data privacy to libraries).

- **Demand Your dotRights** http://www.dotrights.org/
home (not formally connected to Data Privacy Day, the
ACLU of Northern California-sponsored site provides
information and advocacy on keeping control of personal data).

Circulation Systems and Records Retention Decisions

Kathy, a school librarian in a Midwest city of slightly
over 40,000, is responsible for overseeing four school
libraries: three middle schools and a high school. She
works in each library one day per week, and on Fridays
she is at the district office handling the selection, budget-
ing, and management for the libraries. As the single library professional administering multiple libraries, Kathy
is concerned about library records retention and has
given thought to protecting students' circulation records.

We have the Alexandria Library System, and
each school has the ability to keep patron
histories or turn that feature off. I turned it
off in all [schools] but the high school, because its library secretary has relied upon it
for years to provide readers' advisory and to
assign responsibility for book damage. This is
my first year at the high school library, and I
decided to let it remain as is for now.

Unfortunately I have been unable to turn
off the history from the *item* records. Each
item displays the names of the last three circulations, and the company has told me this
function cannot be turned off. This information is available to many adults in my building because numerous persons are trained in
checking out materials due to short staffing
in the school library. Unless shown, however,
I doubt if anyone would realize they could

federal law, state records retention schedules,
or contracts. Before creating a school library
records retention policy, the school librarian
must be aware that most states have a record
retention schedule for school districts. This
schedule lists the records that districts must
retain and the length of retention. Although
school library records may not be specifically
mentioned, the state document will give an
overview of the types of records that must be
retained and may provide some useful insights
for developing a library records retention
policy. If the type of library record is not specifically noted and there is no broad language
that may include the record, school library staff
may presumably dispose of the information.

Unintended Consequences

Unexpected retention of data may produce a threat to the confidentiality of patron
library records. School librarians may not be
aware that many circulation systems can be
configured to retain additional book checkout history on previous borrowers of a library
resource. This feature allows staff to learn the
names of the last one or more persons to check
out a particular book. While it may not be easy
to obtain the information, it can be done. Library automation vendors state it is not their
place to determine if checkout history data
should be retained; this is a local decision.
Therefore, it is very important that library media specialists be knowledgeable about how
their circulation systems operate and what
types of confidential data may be retrievable.

The Value of a Library Records Retention Policy

In a previous column, the case was made
for creating two policies—"Confidentiality of
School Library Records Policy" and a "School
Library Privacy Policy." [Note: This is a reference to the "Protecting the Privacy of Student
Patrons" reading in this chapter. It immediately
precedes this column.] Creating a "School Library Records Retention Policy" would also be
useful to protect the privacy of library patrons

and the confidentiality of their library records. According to Deborah Caldwell-Stone, deputy director of the American Library Association's Office for Intellectual Freedom, a records retention policy is crucial for two reasons. First, it is a reminder to ensure that records slated to be purged are eliminated; and second, the policy's text provides the rationale for why a record is no longer available (Adams 2005, 112–113). Items to be included in a retention policy include the concept of destruction of unnecessary records on a regular basis, record disposal will follow local school policy as well as state and federal laws, and guidelines for record removal should be provided for each type of record. A sample "School Library Media Program Records Retention Policy" with guidelines for record retention may be found in the book, *Privacy in the 21st Century: Issues for Public, School, and Academic Libraries* (2005, 230–233).

access this information. I did witness a secretary showing someone that feature and voiced my concerns about using that history to identify users. Nonetheless, I am satisfied with keeping a limited history. It is often useful when books are damaged or some other confusion occurs. All patron files are purged each July unless the patron has outstanding fines or materials.

Kathy mentioned another feature of her district's library automation system: users may keep their own circulation histories password-protected. "I did instruct all students (about this feature) in grades 6–9. Printed instructions were made available to other students and staff," Kathy explained. "I do not think very many make use of this feature, but if they changed the generic password as I instructed, others would not be able to access it through the public catalog. I am planning to do a more thorough training next year" (Kathy, email message to author, April 15, 2012).

It is very important to be prepared for a record request. If the library does not hold or no longer retains the record or information requested, the matter ends there. If records exist, library staff should never destroy the record after receiving a records request. Library staff and administrators, in conjunction with district legal counsel, will determine the proper course of action.

REFERENCE

Adams, Helen R., Robert Bocher, Carol Gordon, and Elizabeth Barry-Kessler. 2005. *Privacy in the 21st Century: Issues for Public, School, and Academic Libraries.* Westport, Connecticut: Libraries Unlimited.

 **Privacy Matters**

Privacy Checklist: Evaluating Privacy in Your School Library Media Program

By Helen R. Adams

Originally published in the Privacy Matters column, *School Library Media Activities Monthly*, XXV (7) (March 2009): 55.

Situations in which students' privacy is either disregarded or protected occur every day in school library media centers. The difference between the two outcomes depends on whether the school library media specialist accepts privacy as one of the core values of librarianship and has the moral courage to stand up for that principle. As noted many times in this column, Article III of the *Code of Ethics of the American Library Association* directs school librarians to protect the privacy of students using the school library and to maintain the confidentiality of their library use records (ALA 2008). Also referred to frequently, the American Association of School Librarians (AASL) "Position on the Confidentiality of Library Records" declares the *age* of the patron is *not* considered in extending and protecting privacy. Minors are considered to have the same privacy rights as adult library users (AASL). However, actions of administrators, teachers, students, parents, *and the school library professional* can nibble away at the privacy of minors using school libraries.

Rate the Status of Your Students' Library Privacy

As a library media specialist, have you taken action to protect students' privacy? Some of the items listed below may be decided at a district level; however, all school library media specialists should be aware of the concern. To determine the status of students' privacy in *your* school library, complete the privacy checklist in this column.

If you answered "not yet" or are uncertain about any of these best practices related to privacy in school library media programs, review ALA's "Privacy: An Interpretation of the Library Bill of Rights." The statement reminds library media professionals of their obligation to extend privacy to library users by assisting them, not scrutinizing their use of library resources (ALA 2002). Consider that students will only feel comfortable to research topics and make personal reading choices if they are confident that their use of library resources will be kept confidential by library staff. The right of privacy for minors may not be an easy principle to defend; however, whether state library laws shield or fail to protect student library records, library media specialists have the most knowledge of library records law and intellectual freedom concepts and bear the greatest responsibility to protect the privacy of their student patrons.

School Library Program Privacy Checklist

I have . . .	Met	Not Yet or District Level Decision	Next Steps
✓ Educated myself about state and federal laws affecting minors' privacy in schools and libraries and reviewed American Library Association policy statements related to privacy and personally identifiable information (PII) about patrons.			
✓ Analyzed my state's library records law and understand how it applies to student library records.			
✓ Inquired how the Family Educational Rights and Privacy Act (FERPA) applies to local school library records.			
✓ Developed with other stakeholders a privacy policy that includes: what PII is collected, who may access library patron records, the circumstances under which minors' records may be released legally, FERPA guidelines, state library record law protections where applicable, and extends the maximum privacy protections possible. The draft was reviewed by the school district's legal counsel, and administrators sought formal approval of the policy by the school board or institution's governing body.			
✓ Posted the library's privacy policy for patrons to read.			
✓ Supported library procedures granting the maximum privacy possible to students regardless of age.			
✓ Protected circulation records with passwords and provided different levels of access for students, volunteers, and library staff.			
✓ Configured automation software to delete students' circulation history.			
✓ Created a records retention policy that protects students' privacy by retaining library user records for the shortest period possible and destroys records when they are no longer needed.			
✓ Retained as few student library records as possible and purged library records identifying individual students' use of resources and services on a regular basis.			
✓ Trained library staff, volunteers, and student assistants about the confidentiality of all library records, instructing them not to examine circulation records of others.			
✓ Proactively educated administrators and teachers about the confidentiality of student library records.			
✓ Taught students to respect the confidentiality of library records—their own and those of others.			
✓ Informed students of overdue materials in a manner that respects their privacy.			

(*continued*)

School Library Program Privacy Checklist (*continued*)

I have . . .	Met	Not Yet or District Level Decision	Next Steps
✓ Protected students' interlibrary loan and reserve requests from the scrutiny of non-library staff.			
✓ Modeled best practice by making sure that conversations with students about materials being checked out or used in the library media center are confidential.			
✓ Guarded information gained through student use of resources and services by not divulging it indiscriminately to faculty, administrators, or others.			
✓ Refrained from affixing labels denoting a book's reading level or leveling a collection to avoid having students learn the reading levels of their peers.			
✓ Supported incorporating privacy into the district's acceptable use policy (AUP).			
✓ Included information about protecting one's privacy online as part of instruction on Internet safety.			
✓ Encouraged students to realize that citizens have privacy rights under the 4th and 5th Amendments, state, and federal laws.			
✓ Celebrated Choose Privacy Week and Data Privacy Day to raise awareness about privacy.			
✓ Reached out to parents by communicating library policy as it relates to student privacy and provided information about protecting minors' privacy online.			
✓ Demonstrated personal judgment when violating a student's privacy by speaking to a counselor or principal out of concern for a student's welfare.			
✓ Counseled that surveillance camera(s) not be aimed at the circulation desk or be intrusive in recording actions of persons using the school library.			
✓ Discussed privacy concerns with vendors of any technology currently owned or under consideration for purchase and requested that they include privacy protections in future software changes.			

The checklist was originally published in *School Library Media Activities Monthly* vol. XXV, No. 7 (March 2009). It was revised in July 2012 to reflect new information.

REFERENCES

American Association of School Librarians. "Position Statement on the Confidentiality of Library Records." http://www.ala.org/aasl/aaslissues/positionstatements/conflibrecds (accessed January 15, 2013).

American Library Association. 2008. *Code of Ethics of the American Library Association.* http://www.ala.org/advocacy/proethics/codeofethics/codeethics (accessed January 15, 2013).

American Library Association. 2002. "Privacy: An Interpretation of the Library Bill of Rights." http://www.ala.org/advocacy/intfreedom/librarybill/interpretations/privacy (accessed January 15, 2013).

Key Ideas Summary

Readings in this chapter focus on protecting the privacy of students using school libraries and the confidentiality of their library use records. Major ideas include:

- *Privacy* in a library context refers to patrons being free to read and research without having their interests monitored. Its twin concept, *confidentiality*, is achieved when library staff have information about a library patron's use of library resources or personal interests and do not divulge that information.

- Students using a school library should have two expectations of privacy guaranteed: 1) the right to read and borrow from the library collection free from surveillance; and 2) the right to search for information and have the subject of their research remain confidential.

- Major ALA policy statements, including the *Library Bill of Rights* interpretations and the ALA *Code of Ethics*, do not differentiate between minors and adult library users except to speak forcefully for the rights of youth. The AASL "Position Statement on the Confidentiality of Library Records" affirms that *age* does not make a difference in the privacy granted to children and young adult library users.

- Young children have little concept of personal privacy, and the school librarian should use common situations to teach them about privacy in the library.

- Having established trust about library privacy with students when they are young, the school librarian may be one of the persons to whom preteen and teenage library users turn for assistance when seeking information on sensitive personal topics.

- Librarians honor students' trust and demonstrate professional ethics by providing scrutiny free, confidential access to information.

- State legislatures continue to propose legislation impacting the confidentiality of library records, including bills that may not support the right of privacy in libraries for minors.

- Although a school librarian may feel compelled to violate a student's privacy in rare situations, there can be just cause if the library professional observes changes that cause concern for the student's personal welfare or the safety of others.

- The school counselor is a logical choice as a confidant for student personal welfare issues, and the principal should be approached with school safety concerns.

- Suspected child abuse must be reported by educators, including school librarians, as required by state law.

- Unless configured to delete the connection between the borrower and the item borrowed, school library circulation systems will retain students' borrowing history, thereby leaving open the possibility of compromising the confidentiality of users' records.

- Protect circulation records by training library staff, including student assistants and adult volunteers, to respect the privacy of library users and the confidentiality of their library records.

- Technologies such as Radio Frequency Identification (RFID), biometrics, and surveillance cameras all have specific issues affecting the privacy of library users. School librarians must carefully assess the impact of any new technology on the privacy of patrons before installation and take steps to ameliorate the concerns.

- A school library privacy policy should describe students' privacy rights in a school library, how their library records are shielded, and when/to whom their records may be divulged legally.

- Creating a school board approved privacy policy has three major benefits: 1) protecting the privacy of student library users and the confidentiality of their library records; 2) providing guidance to the school librarian about release of student library records, and 3) serving as a document for educating administrators, faculty and staff, students, and parents about minors' privacy in a school library.

- Because of the complicated relationship between state library records law and the Family Educational Rights and Privacy Act (FERPA) related to minors' records in school libraries, administrators should seek district legal counsel's advice when drafting a library privacy policy.

- The two primary recommendations to protect the confidentiality of library records are: 1) keep records until they are not needed and then expunge them; and 2) retain minimal records.

- A library records retention policy should include the rationale for the destruction of unnecessary records, a statement that district policy and state/federal laws will be followed in record expunging, and guidelines for the purging of each type of record.

- School librarians can use the "School Library Program Privacy Checklist" in this chapter to gauge their library's protection of students' privacy and the confidentiality of minors' library records.

Resource Roundup:
School Library Privacy

- **American Library Association. 2005. "Privacy Tool Kit." http://www.ala.org/offices/oif/iftoolkits/toolkitsprivacy/default**

  Although older and aimed primarily at protecting patrons' privacy in public libraries, the toolkit contains information useful to school librarians, including background information on privacy, references to ALA's privacy documents, federal and state privacy laws, and recommendations on developing a privacy policy. The Privacy Subcommittee of the ALA Intellectual Freedom Committee is currently updating the document.

- **American Library Association. Intellectual Freedom Committee. 2012. "Questions and Answers on Privacy and Confidentiality." January 23, 2012. http://www.ala.org/advocacy/intfreedom/librarybill/interpretations/qa-privacy**

  Recently revised, the lengthy document has an expanded section on minors' privacy rights in school and public libraries. Of particular interest is the description of how the Family Educational Rights and Privacy Act (FERPA) affects school library records. The Q & A advocates for a school library privacy policy, with a brief explanation of what should be included.

- **American Library Association. Office for Intellectual Freedom. "State Privacy Laws Regarding Library Records." http://www.ala.org/offices/oif/ifgroups/stateifcchairs/stateifcinaction/stateprivacy/**

  Forty-eight states and the District of Columbia have individual laws on the confidentiality of library records, and the ALA maintains the current text of each available to download. Hawaii and Kentucky do not have specific statutes protecting the confidentiality of library records, but their attorneys general have written opinions supporting the confidentiality of these records (posted on this site).

- **American Library Association. Office for Intellectual Freedom. 2009. *Choose Privacy Week Resource Guide.* Chicago, Illinois: American Library Association.**

  This informative guide includes background information on the importance of privacy and provides programming ideas for all types of libraries to promote an understanding of privacy issues and how to protect one's personal privacy.

- **American Library Association. Privacyrevolution.org http://privacyrevolution.org/**

  This is ALA's official website for its privacy initiatives, including Choose Privacy Week (celebrated annually during the first week in May). Resources include videos, lesson plans, ideas for promoting Americans' privacy, and links to ALA Store posters and other privacy-related merchandise.

- **Chmara, Theresa. 2012. "Privacy and E-Books."** *Knowledge Quest* **40 no. 3: 62–65.**

  Although the article includes information on privacy issues related to e-books, one of the key elements is Chmara's explanation of the link between students' First Amendment right to read and receive information in a school library and the importance of meeting students' expectations of privacy in school libraries. She also details what should be included in a school library privacy policy.

- **U.S. Department of Education. Family Policy Compliance Office (FPCO).**
  http://www2.ed.gov/policy/gen/guid/fpco/index.html

  FCPO oversees the implementation of and compliance with FERPA and provides guidance to school employees, parents, and students. This site provides useful documents such as "Guidance for Parents" and a Q & A to assist families and schools in understanding FERPA's provisions.

Discussion Questions

- Discuss whether students using your school's library have privacy when checking out materials, reading magazines, requesting materials on interlibrary loan, asking reference questions, and using the Internet.

- From your observations in your school library (elementary, middle school, or high school), describe ways in which students' privacy is breached or infringed upon.

- Does the age of a student make any difference to you in extending privacy rights in circulation of resources, seeking information, or in protecting the confidentiality of their library records? Provide the rationale for your answer.

- Do you (or does your school's librarian) have any special practices in place to protect students' library privacy?

- Reflect on an experience from your teaching or library career when you may have observed or had confided to you information that constitutes a threat to a student's welfare. What action, if any, did you take? Was the student's privacy considered in your decision?

- Outline the incremental steps and the information you would share with a principal to persuade him or her to begin the process of drafting a privacy policy.

- List and describe the specific types of information you would include in a school library privacy policy and the rationale for incorporating each.

- Circulation systems will retain student checkout history from the first day the system is used. Describe one situation in which you may want to keep the circulation records of all students and one circumstance in which minimal records are preferable.

- As a school librarian, educator colleague, or general observer, complete the "School Library Program Privacy Checklist" for your school library and discuss the first two steps you would take to improve students' library privacy.

- Crystallize your thoughts about minors' privacy rights in school libraries. Where do you stand in the ethical dilemma between the ALA and AASL statements on extending maximum privacy to students using library resources and the reality of state and federal law provisions? Share your position with the group.

Chapter 7

The Intellectual Freedom Community

Including the Columns

"Are You Part of the Intellectual Freedom Community?"

"Who Are Our Friends? The Community of the Book"

"The American Civil Liberties Union: Another Ally for School Librarians"

"Happy Birthday to the Freedom to Read Foundation: 40 Years of Protecting Library User's Access to Information"

"Libraries and Intellectual Freedom in Developing Countries"

Chapter 7

The Intellectual Freedom Community

INTRODUCTION

School librarians usually work as the single library professional in their schools. Because of the fiscal crises that schools across the country face, school librarians increasingly find themselves becoming the "solo" librarian in their districts. There is no need, however, to feel alone and isolated. School librarians have a huge support network available for assistance during a book challenge, for advice in decision-making, for job seeking leads, and, of course, for personal collegiality. Formal organizations—regional and state library associations; national professional, trade, and advocacy organizations; and international library organizations—all offer librarians support to promote access to information and defend against censorship.

The Intellectual Freedom Community and You

The first column of this chapter, "Are You Part of the Intellectual Freedom Community?" outlines the far-reaching library network that supports the profession's core value of *intellectual freedom*. The community begins informally at the local level but widens to embody formal regional, state-level, national, and even international organized communities (professional associations) of school, public, academic, and special librarians who advocate for the universal belief of unrestricted access to information and patron privacy. This column emphasizes the need for school librarians to participate in their "communities" such as the American Library Association (ALA) and the American Association of School Librarians (AASL) in order to keep a finger on the national pulse of intellectual freedom. School librarians need this information to be effective protectors of their students' information-seeking and privacy rights.

Finding Our Friends

Outside the well-known state and national library associations, there is a community of authors, publishers, and booksellers that is also interested in intellectual freedom and fights against censorship. The second column, "Who Are Our Friends? The Community of the Book," discusses the "book" community's organizations including the American Booksellers Foundation for Free Expression (ABFFE), the PEN American Center, and the Association of American Publishers (AAP). Judith Platt, director of AAP's Freedom to Read Committee, describes in a lengthy interview her organization's active support for intellectual freedom in school libraries, in classrooms, and online. She also introduces readers to three other networks of pro-free speech advocates: the Media Coalition, the National Coalition Against Censorship, and the Free Expression Network (all described in greater detail in the Resource Roundup at the end of the chapter).

The ACLU

"The American Civil Liberties Union: Another Ally for School Librarians'" highlights a potential partner for school librarians in defense of free speech. The column describes the advocacy, anti-censorship, and legal efforts of the American Civil Liberties Union (ACLU) to defend library users' First Amendment free speech rights whether in print or online. The reading recounts the ACLU's lawsuit against a school district in Tennessee after a high school librarian was unable to end the filtering of pro-gay, lesbian, bisexual, and transgender (GLBT) websites in the school. Eventually, the ACLU's experience with *Franks v. Metropolitan Board of Public Education* led to its national "Don't Filter Me" campaign to end viewpoint discrimination of GLBT websites in K–12 schools.

The Freedom to Read Foundation

Are you familiar with the Freedom to Read Foundation (FTRF)? The fourth reading, "Happy Birthday to the Freedom to Read Foundation: 40 Years of Protecting Library User's Access to Information," introduces an organization that protects the First Amendment freedom of speech rights of all library users through its legal actions. Although a separate organization, the FTRF is the *litigious* partner of the ALA, participating in lawsuits and fiscally supporting others engaged in First Amendment litigation. The column describes FTRF's numerous historical efforts on behalf of minors' free speech rights in school libraries, illustrating how FTRF membership benefits its members and access to information in libraries.

Global Intellectual Freedom

The final column in Chapter 7, "Libraries and Intellectual Freedom in Developing Countries," is based on an interview with longtime global intellectual freedom advocate and the director of the ALA Office for Intellectual Freedom (OIF) and the FTRF, Barbara Jones. Barbara introduces the International Federation of Library Associations and Institutions (IFLA), the worldwide organization of library associations that protects intellectual freedom and freedom of expression around the world, and its Committee on Freedom of Access to Information and Freedom of Expression (FAIFE), which is comparable to ALA's Intellectual Freedom Committee in the United States. Using stories of FAIFE's influence in Nigeria, Barbara explains the link between libraries and "social justice" in underdeveloped countries.

Reflections on Being Part of the Intellectual Freedom Community

To be effective as an advocate and protector of students' intellectual freedom, a school librarian must be aware of trends and threats to such principles as access to information, selection of materials from multiple perspectives, and privacy and confidentiality in school libraries. Current information is gleaned from professional contacts in the far-reaching local, regional, statewide, national, and international intellectual freedom communities. Robust communities, however, also require members to be active contributors by serving on committees, collaborating on documents, and adding to discussions that strengthen these groups. The Internet, electronic communication, and Web 2.0 tools give *every school librarian* the opportunity to be an active participant in the full spectrum of the intellectual freedom community. Use the information and resources in this chapter to join an intellectual freedom community. Your students are counting on you to defend their rights!

IF Matters: Intellectual Freedom @ your library®

Are You Part of the Intellectual Freedom Community?

By Helen R. Adams

Originally published in the IF Matters: Intellectual Freedom @ your library® column, *School Library Media Activities Monthly*, XXV (9) (May 2009): 54.

The word *community* has various meanings, and in one context the term is defined as "A group of people having common interests" (Free Dictionary). Persons within the library profession can be considered the intellectual freedom community when referring to their shared belief in access to information and privacy for library users.

These intellectual freedom communities can be subdivided into local, statewide, national, and even international communities. The **global intellectual freedom library community** is represented by the International Federation of Library Associations and Institutions (IFLA). Founded in 1937, it is a worldwide library organization with members in 150 countries (IFLA About). Within IFLA, the Free Access to Information and Freedom of Expression Committee (FAIFE) is the watchdog group that advocates for intellectual freedom worldwide and provides guidance and educational programs for librarians in developing and established countries (IFLA Committee).

The **American intellectual freedom community** revolves around the American Library Association (ALA) and its divisions such as the American Association of School Librarians (AASL), and separate but related organizations, such as the Freedom to Read Foundation. Members of the ALA, AASL, and FTRF support the national intellectual freedom community through their dues and have opportunities to participate directly in the community.

Intellectual freedom is one of the ALA's core values, and the association protects the First Amendment

> ### The Origin of Global Intellectual Freedom
>
> One of the sources for intellectual freedom in the United States is the First Amendment to the U.S. Constitution. Internationally, support for intellectual freedom is found in the United Nations' document, "Universal Declaration of Human Rights," approved in 1948. Most specifically, principles related to intellectual freedom are found in Article 2 (equality to all rights without discrimination based on race, gender, religion, nationality, or political opinions), Article 12 (right of privacy), Article 19 (freedom of expression and right to seek and receive information), and Article 26 (right to a free education, with a minimum of an elementary education) (United Nations. 1948. "Universal Declaration of Human Rights." December 10, 1948. http://un.org/Overview/rights.html#a19 [accessed January 15, 2013]).

free speech rights of library users, assuring them the right to read and access information (ALA). The ALA Office for Intellectual Freedom (OIF) staff reach out to members and non-members by providing support during actual or potential challenges to books, Internet resources, magazines, and other library materials. (Members and non-members can call this number for help: 800-545-2433, ext. 4220.) The OIF also offers extensive online resources ranging from dealing with the media to promoting Banned Books Week (http://www.ala.org/ala/aboutala/offices/oif/index.cfm).

As a division of ALA, AASL supports minors' First Amendment rights to receive information in a school library media program. Its Intellectual Freedom Committee plans professional development opportunities for the annual ALA Conference and the biennial AASL Conference. Online resources related to materials selection, censorship, privacy, filtering, and ethics are posted in the AASL "Essential Links: Resources for School Library Media Program Development" wiki (http://aasl.ala.org/essentiallinks/index.php?title=Directory). "What is Intellectual Freedom?" a brochure promoting intellectual freedom in school library media programs, can be downloaded from the wiki.

The Freedom to Read Foundation (FTRF) serves as the "First Amendment legal defense arm of the American Library Association" (Freedom to Read). Throughout its history, the FTRF has joined legal battles to protect the First Amendment rights of library patrons including those of minors in *Board of Education, Island Trees Union Free School District v. Pico* (1982) and *Counts v. Cedarville School District* (2003). Membership in the FTRF supports the legal fight against censorship and advocates for maintaining the rights of citizens of all ages to use a library freely.

Members of state school library and technology associations form a **statewide intellectual freedom community** and promote intellectual freedom in a variety of ways. Associations publish sample policies and best practices manuals, promote the ongoing education of members on intellectual freedom topics, and provide collegial support for those who face challenges. Being a member of a state library association can reduce the feeling of isolation and provide networking opportunities for personal exploration of dilemmas relating to selection and access to resources in a library media program.

School library media specialists are the most well-informed persons in schools about intellectual freedom, access to information for students, and minors' First Amendment rights. This knowledge comes with a responsibility to help establish a **local intellectual freedom community** including colleagues, students, parents, public library staff, and like-minded community members. Reaching out to students is especially important because in the AASL *Standards for the 21st-Century Learner*, Standard 3, states it is the responsibility of learners to "Respect the principles of intellectual freedom" (AASL 2007).

The intellectual freedom community stretches globally from the local school to library associations and to individual librarians around the world. To be a leader, school library professionals must stay informed and alert to the local, state, national, and international "climate" for intellectual freedom. The more knowledgeable and "connected" to the full spectrum of the intellectual freedom community, the more effective school library personnel will be in protecting and advocating for the rights of students.

REFERENCES

American Association of School Librarians. 2007. *Standards for the 21st-Century Learner.* http://www.ala.org/aasl/sites/ala.org.aasl/files/content/guidelinesandstandards/learningstandards/AASL_LearningStandards.pdf (accessed January 15, 2013).

American Library Association. "Key Action Areas." http://www.ala.org/aboutala/missionhistory/keyactionareas (accessed January 15, 2013).

Freedom to Read Foundation. "Free People Read Freely" [brochure]. http://www.ala.org/ groups/sites/ala.org.groups/files/content/affiliates/relatedgroups/freedomtoread foundation/ftrforg/joinftrf/FTRF%20brochure_FINAL.pdf (accessed July 6, 2012). [Author's note: In August 2012, the FTRF website resources moved to http://www.ftrf.org/.]

International Federation of Library Associations and Institutions. "About IFLA." http://www .ifla.org/III/index.htm/ (accessed January 15, 2013).

International Federation of Library Associations and Institutions. "IFLA Committee on Free Access to Information and Freedom of Expression (FAIFE)." http://www.ifla.org/faife/ index.htm/ (accessed January 15, 2013).

The Free Dictionary. "Community." http://www.thefreedictionary.com/community/ (accessed January 15, 2013).

IF Matters: Intellectual Freedom @ your library®

Who Are Our Friends? The Community of the Book

By Helen R. Adams

Originally published in the IF Matters: Intellectual Freedom @ your library® column, *School Library Monthly*, XXVII (2) (November 2010): 52.

School librarians rely on personal friends and professional colleagues for advice and assistance during times of trouble. Associations, however, can also be "friends" when members collectively use their voices to fight censorship and promote the right to read. Previous columns in *School Library Monthly* described the anti-censorship efforts by the American Library Association (ALA) and the Freedom to Read Foundation (FTRF). School librarians, though, may be less aware of the pro-First Amendment activities of organizations related to the publishing industry.

Knowing the Players

Authors, publishers, and booksellers have a stake in ensuring the right to read, and associations representing their interests act to educate, advocate, and defend against censorship. Pro-free speech organizations from the publishing and bookselling world include:

The American Booksellers Foundation for Free Expression (ABFFE) uses the tag line the "bookseller's voice in the fight against censorship" (ABFFE). The organization participates in legal challenges involving First Amendment rights and collaborates with other free speech groups. Since 2007, its Kids Right to Read Project has resisted challenges to 250 books in 31 states (ABFFE). ABFFE co-sponsors the kidSPEAK website that encourages students to learn about their right to free expression (http://www.kidspeakonline.org/). The site includes news about free speech, tips for protecting the right of free expression and a "What's Your Censorship IQ?" quiz (kidSPEAK).

The PEN American Center is the United States branch of an international literary and human rights organization that opposes censorship. According to children's book author, Susannah Reich, PEN's Children's/Young Adult Book Authors Committee "offers ongoing support to writers and librarians whose books have been banned or challenged" (Reich 2010).

The Association of American Publishers (AAP) is the major trade organization for publishers of all sizes in the United States. Activities of its Freedom to Read Committee are described by its director Judith Platt later in this column.

> ### Anniversary for the PEN American Center
>
> In 2012, the PEN American Center celebrated its ninetieth year of promoting worldwide advocacy for free expression in literature and supporting authors whose lives are imperiled because of their written ideas. Its website lists names of authors whose work has been censored or attacked, as well as a historical timeline of its efforts (PEN American Center. Defending Writers. http://www.pen.org/lp-defending-writers%20 [accessed January 15, 2013]).

AAP: Protecting Minors' Freedom to Read

To learn more about the defense of intellectual freedom in school libraries by one of the three associations listed above, I interviewed Judith Platt, Director of the Association of American Publishers' Freedom to Read Committee. The Committee is involved in efforts to protect minors' freedom to read, and Judith described some of its most recent and historical advocacy efforts in detail.

One of the [Freedom to Read] Committee's primary concerns is to protect the rights of young people to read a wide variety of books of their own choosing and to resist attempts to remove or limit access to books in school libraries and on classroom reading lists. Over the past year AAP has been involved in successfully resisting attempts to remove Toni Morrison's *Song of Solomon* from AP English classes in Indianapolis and Judy Blume's *Forever* from a school library in Florida as well as protesting attempts to remove gay and lesbian-themed books from high school library shelves in New Jersey.

Most recently we are concerned about the growing popularity of book rating systems—in particular those of an organization called Common Sense Media (CSM)—that are waving red flags about "difficult" (sensitive) subject matter in the books being read by young people. Despite CSM's protestations that they are "about information not censorship," these rating systems are often the tools that facilitate the removal of controversial books from school library shelves. The AAP Freedom to Read Committee is part of a coalition of book and free speech groups working together to raise awareness of the dangers inherent in segregating books by "age appropriateness" and subjecting them to "filters" that determine sexual content, violence, profanity and other criteria that are bound to raise warning flags for risk-averse educators and worried parents. In the hope of opening a dialogue, AAP met at ALA headquarters in Chicago in late May (2010) with representatives of Common Sense Media to express our concerns.

AAP actively participates, as a plaintiff or friend-of-the-court, in important First Amendment free speech cases. The determination to enter a case is made by the Freedom to Read Committee, whose members are senior editors and in-house legal counsel from AAP publishing houses. The Association of American Publishers:

- was one of the earliest organizations to join ALA as a plaintiff in the challenge to the Communications Decency Act,
- led the *amicus* effort in the COPA (Child Online Protection Act) challenge,
- took the lead in providing *amicus* support for ALA in CIPA (*United States v. American Library Association* (2003). [Note: *Amicus Curiae*: "Latin term meaning 'friend of the court'. The name for a brief filed with the court by someone who is not a party to the case" (Tech Law Journal).]
- was an *amicus* in the successful court challenge to the removal of the *Harry Potter* books from schools in Arkansas (*Counts v. Cedarville School District* [2003]), and
- has been a plaintiff in virtually all of the cases coordinated by Media Coalition that successfully challenged state statutes attempting to ban harmful-to-minors material from the Internet. (Platt 2010)

The "Community of the Book"

According to Judith Platt, the Freedom to Read Committee is one of AAP's "core" committees, and she went on to describe its endeavors.

> The Committee works on behalf of the book publishing industry to protect the free marketplace of ideas, serving as the industry's watchdog and early warning system on issues such as libel, privacy, school and library censorship, the right of journalists and authors to protect confidential sources, and Internet censorship.

> The [Freedom to Read] Committee coordinates AAP participation in First Amendment court cases, sponsors educational programs, and works with like-minded organizations . . . Our work is almost always carried out in concert with allied groups. We have especially close ties to the ALA Office for Intellectual Freedom, the American Booksellers Foundation for Free Expression, and the PEN American Center. I share Judith Krug's abiding faith in the power of the "community of the book." [Author's note: Judith Krug was the executive director of the ALA Office for Intellectual Freedom from 1967 until her death in 2009.] Judith was convinced, as I am, that when librarians, publishers, booksellers, and authors stand together in defense of intellectual freedom, we are unstoppable.

> Information on library challenges and other intellectual freedom issues is shared widely among the 'book community' organizations. Our information network also covers the wider free speech community, including the Media Coalition, the National Coalition Against Censorship, and an umbrella group called the Free Expression Network. (Platt 2010)

Websites for the "Community of the Book" Organizations

Association of American Publishers
http://www.publishers.org/

American Booksellers Foundation for Free Expression
http://www.abffe.com/

PEN American Center
http://www.pen.org/

Media Coalition
http://www.mediacoalition.org

National Coalition Against Censorship
http://www.ncac.org/

Free Expression Network
http://www.freeexpression.org/

[Note: Information on the three organizations (Media Coalition, the National Coalition Against Censorship, and the Free Expression Network) referred to by Judith Platt is available in the Resources Roundup section at the end of this chapter.]

Judith Platt ended her interview by stating, "We would like school librarians to be aware of the AAP Freedom to Read Committee as an intellectual freedom resource and as an ally. In addition, AAP member publishers are enthusiastic supporters of Banned Books Week, creating graphics, teaching guides and other materials available to school librarians" (Platt 2010).

With this new knowledge, school librarians should consider "friending" associations (such as those described in this column) who are members of the "community of the book." Librarians can reach out to them as partners in the fight against censorship.

REFERENCES

American Booksellers Foundation for Free Expression. "About Kids' Right to Read Project." http://www.abffe.org/?page=KRRP (accessed January 15, 2013).

kidSPEAK. http://www.kidspeakonline.org (accessed January 15, 2013).

Platt, Judith, email interview with author, July 21, 2010.

Reich, Susannah, email message to Sarah Hoffman, July 28, 2010.

Tech Law Journal. "*Amicus Curiae*." http://www.techlawjournal.com/glossary/legal/amicus.htm (accessed January 15, 2013).

IF Matters @ your library

The American Civil Liberties Union: Another Ally for School Librarians

By Helen R. Adams

Originally published in the IF Matters @ your library column, *School Library Monthly*, XXVIII (4) (January 2012): 27–28.

Even though school librarians traditionally think of the ALA Office for Intellectual Freedom for support during book challenges, library privacy, and filtering issues, the ACLU has also proven to be another strong ally in these cases. Hedy Weinberg, Executive Director of ACLU-Tennessee, maintains, "I have long believed that librarians are some of our best allies and certainly the best messenger on freedom of speech issues" (Weinberg 2011).

The ACLU, founded in 1920, is a national organization that protects individuals' First Amendment rights, supports due process and equal protection under the law, and defends personal privacy. The organization has staffed chapters in fifty states, and legal advice is provided by ACLU staff and volunteer lawyers (ACLU).

The ACLU and K–12 Internet Filtering

During student research, Tennessee high school librarian, Karyn Storts-Brinks, noticed that nationally acclaimed and informative lesbian, gay, bisexual, and transgender (LGBT) websites were blocked but sites that were anti-LGBT were not. She recounts, "I had spent nearly 2 years grappling with various departments and individuals in the district with no results. Finally I contacted the ACLU in Tennessee and received a phone call from Tricia (Herzfeld, ACLU legal counsel). I could NOT have experienced anywhere near the results achieved by the ACLU on my own. Once they were involved, events progressed VERY quickly" (Storts-Brinks 2011). Eventually Karyn and several students became plaintiffs in the *Franks v. Metropolitan Board of Public Education* lawsuit filed on their behalf by the ACLU (http://www.aclu.org/lgbt-rights_hiv-aids/franks-v-metropolitan-board-public-education-case-profile). Settled out of court, the legal action resulted in unblocking of pro-LGBT sites and restoring of students' access to information.

Missouri Filtering Lawsuit Settled

The ACLU won its lawsuit (*PFLAG, Inc. v. Camdenton R-III School District*) against the Camdenton R-III School District when the judge issued a preliminary injunction in February 2012 against the Missouri district ordering it to stop using the discriminatory filter. In March 2012, the district and the ACLU reached an agreement that required the district

---

According to Chris Hampton of the ACLU Lesbian Gay Bisexual Transgender and AIDS Project, "Our experience with the *Franks v. Metropolitan Board of Public Education* case against two Tennessee school districts, whose web filtering software discriminated on the basis of viewpoint, made us realize that this problem was probably widespread. The 'Don't Filter Me' national campaign was launched in February of 2011 to encourage students at public schools to check their school web filtering software and inform us if their school was blocking access to LGBT-positive information while allowing access to anti-LGBT information" (Hampton 2011). The ACLU received completed survey forms from students reporting both blocking of pro-LGBT sites and noting the sites were accessible. After follow-up with the students or submitting state open records requests about district filtering practices, the ACLU contacted schools, and most adjusted their filters to be non-viewpoint discriminatory. In one exception, as reported by Suzanne Ito on August 15, 2011 on the Blog of Rights, the ACLU filed a lawsuit against the Camdenton R-III School District (Missouri) that continued to filter constitutionally protected LGBT websites (Ito 2011). The ACLU has also been working successfully with filtering companies implicated by student reporting to change their software (Hampton 2011).

> to stop its discriminatory filtering of pro-LGBT non-sexual websites, pay court costs and legal fees, and agree to have its filters monitored for eighteen months. On April 6, 2012, the judge issued a "Consent Judgment" finalizing the terms of the agreement and ending the litigation (ACLU. 2012. "PFLAG, Inc. v. Camdenton R-III School District." April 6, 2012. http://www.aclu.org/lgbt-rights/pflag-v-camdenton-r-iii-school-district [accessed January 15, 2013]).

Battle in Belleville

In 2010, Stacy Harbaugh, Wisconsin ACLU community advocate, provided assistance to a group of parents and students who were fighting the removal of *Staying Fat for Sarah Brynes* (Harper Collins 1993) from the ninth grade English curriculum based on the complaint of one parent. "My work with the Belleville parents was very informal. It was mostly discussions about what to expect in the process, how to organize supporters, and what would be effective to say to the school board" (Harbaugh 2011). Kelly Forman, one of the Belleville parents fighting withdrawal of the book, explains, "I was concerned about the book's removal because it covered a lot issues that young adults encounter—religious differences, abortion, bullying, friendship." She went on to praise ACLU staff efforts saying, "Stacy asked us what message we wanted to convey to the school board and helped us organize in a way that I don't believe we could've done without her" (Forman 2011).

When seemingly unresolvable local school library issues occur, school librarians should consider seeking help not only from the ALA but also from the ACLU, another natural ally. Librarians should check out the national ACLU website (http://www.aclu.org) or contact the closest state ACLU affiliate (http://www.aclu.org/affiliates).

REFERENCES

ACLU. "About ACLU." http://www.aclu.org/about-aclu-0/ (accessed January 15, 2013).

Forman, Kelly, email message to author, August 17, 2011.

Hampton, Chris, email message to author, August 19, 2011.

Harbaugh, Stacy, email message to author, July 21, 2011.

Ito, Suzanne. 2011. "ACLU Sues Missouri School District for Illegally Censoring LGBT Websites." August 15, 2011. Blog of Rights. http://www.aclu.org/blog/free-speech-lgbt-rights-religion-belief-reproductive-freedom/aclu-sues-missouri-school-district (accessed January 15, 2013).

Storts-Brinks, Karyn, email message to author, July 25, 2011.

Weinberg, Hedy, email message to author, July 26, 2011.

IF Matters: Intellectual Freedom @ your library®

Happy Birthday to the Freedom to Read Foundation: 40 Years of Protecting Library Users' Access to Information

By Helen R. Adams

Originally published in the IF Matters: Intellectual Freedom @ your library® column, *School Library Monthly*, XXVI (2) (October 2009): 46–47.

The Freedom to Read Foundation (FTRF) was established in 1969 and celebrates its 40th birthday in 2009. Its charter sets down four purposes clearly aligned with libraries:

- Promoting and protecting the freedom of speech and of the press;
- Protecting the public's right of access to information and materials stored in the nation's libraries;
- Safeguarding libraries' right to disseminate all materials contained in their collections; and
- Supporting libraries and librarians in their defense of First Amendment rights by supplying them with legal counsel or the means to secure it (ALA http://www.ala.org/ala/mgrps/affiliates/relatedgroups/freedomtoreadfoundation/aboutftrf/aboutftrf.cfm).

Strength through Collaboration

The FTRF is a separate entity from the American Library Association (ALA); however, it supports the work of the ALA Office for Intellectual Freedom (OIF). The OIF offers advice and support in challenges to library books, magazines and other resources as well as on Internet access issues; and the FTRF's activities complement that work in the legal arena. The director of the OIF traditionally has also served as executive director of the FTRF; however, the Foundation has its own general legal counsel. The organization is governed by a board of trustees elected by its members. To emphasize the close connection between the ALA and the FTRF, the ALA president and president-elect, the ALA Intellectual Freedom Committee chairperson, and the ALA executive director are ex-officio members of the board of trustees.

Importance to All Libraries

The FTRF is important to *all* libraries and librarians because of its two main activities:

- FTRF takes direct legal action or files *amicus briefs* (friend of the court supporting documents) in cases championing the First Amendment and freedom of speech related to libraries and librarians and
- FTRF supplies financial grants to those engaged in freedom of speech First Amendment litigation that impacts libraries, librarians, and users (ALA http://www.ala.org/ala/mgrps/affiliates/relatedgroups/freedomtoreadfoundation/aboutftrf/aboutftrf.cfm).

The FTRF also supports freedom of speech as it applies to library users through letters of protest. For example, in March 2009, the Foundation and several other like-minded organizations sent a joint letter to the Topeka and Shawnee County Public Library (Kansas) board of trustees objecting to their vote to remove several books from open shelving in the health section of the library to an area inaccessible to minors (American Booksellers Foundation for Free Expression 2009).

Legal Impact

The FTRF has been involved in numerous court cases that have an impact on minors' First Amendment free speech rights in school libraries and has also provided financial grants to support the legal costs of those involved in relevant litigation. In *Todd v. Rochester Community Schools* (1971) the Foundation took its first action to oppose removal of library materials by giving a grant to the school district to assist with its legal costs when appealing a state trial court decision to remove the book *Slaughterhouse-Five* from its classrooms and school library (ALA, FTRF Time Line 1969–1979). Other prominent cases in which the Freedom to Read Foundation supported minors' First Amendment rights in school libraries include:

- *ACLU of Florida v. Miami-Dade School Board* (2006) The issue: a Florida school board removed *Vamos a Cuba* from elementary libraries based on alleged inaccuracies and its too positive portrayal of contemporary Cuban life.
- *Counts v. Cedarville School District* (2003) The issue: an Arkansas school board removed *Harry Potter* books from open library shelves and required students to have written parental permission to borrow them.
- *Case v. Unified School District No. 233* (1994) The issue: a Kansas school board removed a lesbian-themed novel, *Annie on My Mind,* from middle and high school libraries because of personal disagreement with ideas in the book.
- *Pico v. Board of Education, Island Trees Union Free School District No. 26* (1978–1982) The issue: a New York school board removed nine books from its school library based on disapproval of the ideas they contained (ALA http://www.ala.org/groups/affiliates/relatedgroups/freedomtoreadfoundation/ftrfinaction/timeline/timeline).

The Foundation's semi-annual reports to the ALA Council present an overview of its ongoing litigation to defend adult and minors' First Amendment rights in libraries (http://www.ala.org/groups/affiliates/relatedgroups/freedomtoreadfoundation/ftrfinaction/reportstocouncil/reportscouncil/). In recent years, for example, the Foundation has supported litigation related to the right of privacy of library users and opposing provisions of the USA PATRIOT Act affecting libraries.

Many divisions and other groups within the ALA appoint a representative to the Freedom to Read Foundation. Roger Ashley, a retired school librarian from Michigan, is the representative of the American Association of School Librarians (AASL). In an email to the author of this column he explains the importance of the Foundation to school libraries in this way:

> The Freedom to Read Foundation is a hidden value for AASL members. Many of the [legal] cases it supports are related either directly or indirectly to school media center issues. It is the legal support system for school media specialists and librarians of all types who find themselves facing huge expenses in legal matters. It represents libraries and librarians at the federal courts including the U. S. Supreme Court. The

Foundation is the voice to the American court system in defending the rights of citizens to access, read, and debate intellectual freedom issues. It raises thousands of dollars for the defense of having "the Freedom to Read." (Ashley 2009)

Happy Birthday

Say Happy Birthday to the Freedom to Read Foundation, and celebrate its 40th year by becoming a member. The cost of a personal membership in the Freedom to Read Foundation is thirty-five dollars, and that amount helps ensure the continued legal defense of library users' First Amendment free speech rights, especially those of minors. The Foundation's efforts are funded solely by membership dues and fund raising efforts; it is not financed by large corporate or private donations, thus allowing the Foundation to act independently. Information on membership benefits can be found at http://www.ftrf.org/. Members receive the *Freedom to Read Foundation News*, a quarterly publication that includes information on censorship trends, current court cases, and other issues of interest to school librarians. Joining the Freedom to Read Foundation may be the best thirty-five dollars ever spent!

REFERENCES

American Booksellers Foundation for Free Expression. 2009. "Letter to the Topeka and Shawnee County Public Library Board of Trustees Opposing Restrictions on *The Joy of Sex* and three other titles." March 4, 2009. http://web.archive.org/web/20090601184626/http://www.abffe.com/topekalibrary-letter.htm (accessed January 15, 2013).

American Library Association. "About the Freedom to Read Foundation." http://www.ala.org/ala/mgrps/affiliates/relatedgroups/freedomtoreadfoundation/aboutftrf/aboutftrf.cfm (accessed January 15, 2013).

American Library Association. "Freedom to Read Foundation Time Line." http://www.ala.org/groups/affiliates/relatedgroups/freedomtoreadfoundation/ftrfinaction/timeline/time line (accessed January 15, 2013).

Ashley, Roger, email message to author, May 10, 2009.

IF Matters: Intellectual Freedom @ your library®

Libraries and Intellectual Freedom in Developing Countries

By Helen R. Adams

Originally published in the IF Matters: Intellectual Freedom @ your library®, *School Library Monthly*, XXVII (10) (June 2010): 47–48.

The devastating earthquake in Haiti in January 2010 and the response of the library community reminded us that we are a global society. Beyond the reports of libraries and priceless collections that have been damaged or destroyed, the situation in Haiti caused me to wonder about intellectual freedom there and in other developing countries. For answers, I contacted Barbara Jones, the new executive director of both the American Library Association's Office for Intellectual Freedom and the Freedom to Read Foundation. Jones is well known internationally for her work as a trainer and consultant for the Committee on Freedom of Access to Information and Freedom of Expression (FAIFE), a group within the International Federation of Library Associations and Institutions (IFLA). IFLA is dedicated to protecting intellectual freedom and the freedom of expression worldwide.

> **Contact Information**
>
> Barbara Jones, Executive Director
>
> ALA Office for Intellectual Freedom
>
> 800-545-2433, Ext. 4222
>
> bjones@ala.org

Global Intellectual Freedom Documents

According to Jones, the FAIFE Committee and librarians in developing countries rely on the United Nations' "Declaration of Human Rights" as a basis for working toward basic human rights such as access to information in libraries. Article 19 of the Declaration states:

> Everyone has the right to freedom of opinion and expression; this right includes freedom to hold opinions without interference and to seek, receive and impart information and ideas through any media and regardless of frontiers. (United Nations 1948)

The FAIFE Committee also produces its own intellectual freedom documents including the "Internet Manifesto," that asserts principles familiar to American librarians including:

- "Freedom of access to information, regardless of medium and frontiers, is a central responsibility of the library and information profession.
- The provision of unhindered access to the Internet by libraries and information services supports communities and individuals to attain freedom, prosperity and development" (IFLA 2002).

Do documents such as the "Internet Manifesto" make a difference in countries where citizens struggle with poverty and lack of access to accurate information? The answer is YES! In March 2009, FAIFE used the "Internet Manifesto" at a train-the-trainer workshop to help Peruvian librarians prepare to present their own workshops throughout their country. Two trainers used a very creative way to bring information about the Internet as a source of information to villages along the Amazon River. They employed a group of actors to read the Manifesto to local residents (IFLA 2009).

Social Justice as a Library Mission

The mission of libraries in developing countries is frequently aligned with "social justice." *Social justice* is defined as "Fair and proper administration of laws conforming to the natural law that all persons, irrespective of ethnic origin, gender, possessions, race, religion, etc. should be treated equally and without prejudice" (Business Dictionary). According to Jones in an email interview with me, "Most other countries see social justice as tied very closely to intellectual freedom—more so than we have done in ALA. . . . It is very natural at FAIFE to see, for example, how providing access to HIV/AIDS information is part of access, which is part of intellectual freedom. Overseas there is much more attention paid to the way poverty provides a barrier to access" (Jones 2010).

Barbara Jones shared two stories about how libraries have used intellectual freedom principles such as those expressed in the United Nations' "Declaration of Human Rights" to take action. For example, "The HIV/AIDS curriculum [training materials] developed by FAIFE is being taught by librarians in Nigeria, in cooperation with the University of Ibadan [Nigeria] which, by sheer luck, has a relationship with Northwestern University [Illinois]. So we have been able to add strength to strength by forging coalitions. This curriculum is being taught in villages, where storytelling, music, and street drama are used to convey the message to those who can't read" (Jones 2010).

As a result of the focus on social justice, Barbara states, "There is no question that librarians in developing countries can make a difference. The thing that struck me first and foremost in ALL of the developing world is—libraries are about SERVICE. They care deeply about how libraries can bring people out of poverty. A group of Nigerian librarians actually decided that if they were going to teach about HIV, they ought to be tested themselves. They walked down to the clinic, hand in hand, and were tested. It was a real act of courage for some of them, and they told me that they did it to set an example for their children. Another group of librarians discovered that the local clinic was spreading rumors about who had AIDS. So the librarians learned how to give the blood tests AT THE LIBRARY, and they got lots of customers because the library users knew about the privacy ethics" (Jones 2010).

School Libraries Manifesto

The United Nations Educational Scientific and Cultural Organization (UNESCO) and IFLA created a "School Libraries Manifesto" in 1999 to promote school libraries for elementary and secondary students in developing countries (http://archive.ifla.org/VII/s11/pubs/manifest.htm). Although the mission statement would describe well-managed American

School Libraries in Developing Countries

On the topic of school libraries, Barbara Jones related, "School librarians have attended many of our [FAIFE training] sessions—in Ecuador, Costa Rica, the Philippines, and Nigeria. But we need to do more. There is a 'School Libraries Manifesto' crafted by the UN and by IFLA (http://archive.ifla.org/VII/s11/pubs/manifest.htm), but most librarians aren't even close to meeting the goals.

Librarians in the developing world are incredibly interested in children's library use, but it has not been emphasized until recently" (Jones 2010).

Barbara Jones went on to describe, "I have not seen many school libraries [in underdeveloped countries] because they don't exist. One of my friends in Yola, Nigeria, has started the KARITU Foundation to help create a reading culture among children in the Yola region. Private groups are doing most of this work. I was with Martha when we drove out to a village with books (These are brand new books, by the way, not hand-me-downs.), and children were chasing the car to get first chance at the books. But their schools offer nothing of the sort" (Jones 2010).

Final Thoughts

After this brief introduction to intellectual freedom in developing countries, let's focus on Haiti again. According to ALA's International Relations Office, the Association will post information on the damage to libraries and will coordinate its relief and reconstruction work with three groups including the U.S. Committee of the Blue Shield http://www.uscbs.org/, IFLA http://www.ifla.org/, and UNESCO http://www.unesco.org/new/en/. Donations can be made by check or credit card at http://www.ala.org/ala/aboutala/offices/iro/iroactivities/haitirelieffund.cfm/ (ALA 2010).

REFERENCES

American Library Association. 2010. "Haiti Library Relief." http://www.ala.org/ala/aboutala/offices/iro/iroactivities/haitirelieffund.cfm (accessed January 15, 2013).

Business Dictionary.com. "Social Justice." http://www.businessdictionary.com/definition/social-justice.html (accessed January 15, 2013).

International Federation of Library Associations and Institutions. 2002. "IFLA Internet Manifesto." March 27, 2002. http://www.ifla.org/en/publications/the-ifla-internet-manifesto (accessed January 15, 2013).

K–12 school libraries, there is a global touch because of the reference to providing access to information and services in accord with the "United Nations Universal Declaration of Human Rights." The Manifesto lays out goals for the school library program and addresses funding, staff, library management, and implementation. To help librarians implement the Manifesto, the IFLA/UNESCO "School Library Guidelines" were published in 2002 (IFLA and UNESCO. 1999. "School Library Manifesto." http://archive.ifla.org/VII/s11/pubs/manifest.htm [accessed January 15, 2013]).

ALA's International Disaster Relief for Libraries

ALA's international relief efforts are managed by its International Relations Office (IRO). According to IRO director Michael Dowling, "By spring 2012, ALA had raised $60,000 to help reconstruct three libraries in Haiti. Thanks to these funds, one library is already back in operation, one is rebuilding on newly purchased land, and one is moving into a temporary facility until a new library can be built. School librarians, such as Deborah Lazar at New Trier High School in Northfield (IL) and Katherine Nelson of Carleton Washburne School in Winnetka (IL), have championed the cause through Read-A-Thons and T-shirt sales to mobilize their students and their communities. Even students themselves have led fundraising efforts, such as the Ramstein (Germany) American Middle School Junior Librarians. We're grateful for all the support from librarians, students, and others to help rebuild these libraries in Haiti, and elsewhere." Dowling continued, "These efforts have raised awareness, spurred engagement, and connected cultures" (Dowling, Michael, email message to author, April 16, 2012).

In addition to its disaster relief work in Haiti, the ALA IRO has also been overseeing assistance to Chilean libraries destroyed in devastating earthquakes in 2010 and supporting rebuilding of Japanese libraries decimated by the 2011 earthquake and subsequent tsunami (American Library Association. International Relations Office. "Initiatives, Projects, and Highlights." http://www.ala.org/offices/iro [accessed January 15, 2013]).

International Federation of Library Associations and Institutions. 2009. "IFLA Internet Workshop in Cusco, Peru- Assessing the Impact." November 13, 2009. http://www.ifla.org/en/news/ ifla-internet-workshop-in-cusco-peru-assessing-the-impact (accessed January 15, 2013).

Jones, Barbara, email message to author, January 25, 2010.

United Nations. 1948. "Universal Declaration of Human Rights." December 10, 1948. http:// www.un.org/en/documents/udhr/ (accessed January 15, 2013).

Key Ideas Summary

Readings in this chapter focus on the local, regional, statewide, national, and international "intellectual freedom communities." Major ideas include:

- The full spectrum "intellectual freedom community" ranges from informal local groups of individuals dedicated to protecting libraries against censorship to well-organized state and national library and First Amendment advocacy associations to strong multinational organizations such as the International Federation of Library Associations and Institutions (IFLA).

- ALA and, its school library division AASL, are the primary national library associations that vigorously protect school library users' right of free speech under the First Amendment, which has been interpreted by American courts to include the right to read, view, and listen to the expression of others.

- Associations representing publishers, booksellers, and authors have a stake in protecting authors' works, libraries, and library patrons against censorship attacks. These organizations include the American Booksellers Foundation for Free Expression (ABFFE), the PEN American Center, and the Association of American Publishers (AAP).

- ABFFE cosponsors kidSPEAK, a website that helps students learn about their First Amendment right of free speech, what censorship means, how to defend against censorship, and their allies in the fight (http://www.kidspeakonline.org).

- Founded in 1920, the American Civil Liberties Union (ACLU) is another pro–First Amendment rights organization that defends Americans' free speech rights through litigation and education.

- Based on its experience in the Tennessee lawsuit *Franks v. Metropolitan Board of Public Education*, the ACLU began its national "Don't Filter Me" project to test whether schools' Internet filters block pro-LGBT non-sexual websites but do not block anti-LGBT sites. The result has been positive, with filtering companies adjusting their software to avoid viewpoint discriminatory filtering of positive LGBT websites. With one exception, school districts contacted by the ACLU about their filtering practices related to pro-LGBT educational websites adjusted their filters to unblock the sites. The non-cooperating Missouri school district was sued by the ACLU (*PFLAG, Inc. v. Camdenton R-III School District)* and lost the case.

- Since 1969, the Freedom to Read Foundation (FTRF) has protected the public's First Amendment right to access information in American libraries through participating in litigation and by giving financial grants to others to support their freedom of speech legal battles. Its website is http://www.ftrf.org/.

- FTRF has been involved in four landmark legal cases that supported minors' rights in school libraries: 1) *Pico v. Board of Education, Island Trees Union Free School District No. 26* (1978–1982); 2) *Case v. Unified School District No. 233* (1994); 3) *Counts v. Cedarville School District* (2003); and 4) *ACLU of Florida v. Miami-Dade School Board* (2006). Details of these First Amendment legal decisions are available on the ALA Office for Intellectual Freedom (OIF) website (http://www.ala.org/offices/oif/firstamendment/courtcases/courtcases).

- The International Federation of Library Associations and Institutions (IFLA) is a multinational library organization, and its Free Access to Information and Freedom of Expression Committee (FAIFE) advocates for the principles of intellectual freedom and privacy for people in all countries.

- According to Barbara Jones, director of ALA's Office for Intellectual Freedom and executive director of the Freedom to Read Foundation, the mission of libraries in developing countries is often linked to "social justice."

- Inside the United States intellectual freedom is based on the right of free speech in the First Amendment. Outside the United States, librarians in developing countries use the United Nations' "Declaration of Human Rights" to support their efforts for intellectual freedom and access to information. Relevant concepts are found in Articles 2 (equality in all rights), 12 (privacy), 19 (freedom of expression), and 26 (the right to a free education).

- School libraries are not available in many developing countries. The United Nations Educational Scientific and Cultural Organization (UNESCO) and IFLA created the "School Library Manifesto" to provide a guide for creating, staffing, funding, and managing library programs where they are not available.

Resource Roundup:
The Intellectual Freedom Community

- **American Library Association. 1991. "Universal Right to Free Expression: An Interpretation of the Library Bill of Rights." January 16, 1991. http://www.ifmanual.org/universalright**

This little-known interpretation of the *Library Bill of Rights* supports and endorses select principles of the United Nations' "Universal Declaration of Human Rights" that was approved in December 1948. Especially noted are Article 18 (freedom of thought and conscience), Article 19 (freedom of expression and opinion), and Article 20 (freedom of assembly and association). It also takes a strong stand against censorship in any form.

- **Free Expression Network (FEN). http://www.freeexpression.org**

FEN is a coalition of associations whose aim is to protect the First Amendment right of free expression and resist attempts by governmental units to silence free speech. Its members meet four times per year to discuss issues and plan strategies. The ALA Office for Intellectual Freedom is a member of FEN.

- **International Association of School Librarians (IASL). http://www.iasl-online.org/ index.htm**

IASL is an organization for school librarians, educators, and university instructors in library science programs interested in meeting those engaged in school librarianship internationally. Membership options include personal, student, retired, and association levels. Benefits include a newsletter, access to the website "School Libraries Online" (for articles, papers, minutes of meetings, etc.), and international and regional fellowship through association conferences. Intellectual freedom and censorship is a concern of the organization, and research abstracts, conference presentations, and articles in the association's journal, *School Libraries Worldwide* reflect this fact.

- **International Federation of Library Associations and Institutions (IFLA) School Libraries and Resources Centers Section. http://www.ifla.org/en/ school-libraries-resource-centers**

Members of this section within IFLA focus on improving school libraries worldwide and advocating for appropriate staffing and practice. The group serves as a global forum for sharing ideas, research, and practice. Its School-L electronic list disseminates information to members, and members present papers at IFLA conferences. It creates publications, including an annual report on the section's activities and a newsletter. One of the most interesting parts of the website is its "School Library Advocacy Kit" (http://www.ifla .org/en/publications/school-library-advocacy-kit) with links to many resources.

- **Media Coalition. http://www.mediacoalition.org**

The eight Coalition members include the American Booksellers Foundation for Free Expression, the Association of American Publishers, the Comic Book Defense League Fund, the Entertainment Merchants Association, the Entertainment Software Association, the Freedom to Read Foundation, the Motion Picture Association of America, and the Recording Industry Association of America. This alliance defends the First Amendment right of free expression in the creation, production, and sales of books, films, magazines, video games, and other forms of entertainment, as well as citizens' First Amendment rights to read, hear, and view these creative forms for learning and entertainment. Its "Legislative Tracker" outlines and gives the status of pending state legislation that would affect producers' and citizens' First Amendment rights; however, it also monitors federal bills, writes summaries highlighting concerns of members, and works with lobbyists to defend free speech.

- **National Coalition Against Censorship (NCAC). http://www.ncac.org**

This is a partnership of more than fifty non-profit groups who advocate for free expression and defend against censorship. NCAC's website lists member organizations, provides current news on censorship attempts and issues, and offers the "Blogging Censorship" blog. Visit the site for resources (including an online archive of the "NCAC Censorship News," a "First Amendment in Schools Toolkit," and a downloadable "Book Censorship Toolkit") and guidance on organizing or taking a personal stand against censorship.

Discussion Questions

- Describe your personal ideal "intellectual freedom community" (local, state, national, and international) and your plan (in steps) to achieve the assistance, skills, and information you need.

- Describe the actions you can take to create a local cadre of individuals who are 1) educated about First Amendment access to information and free expression rights and 2) willing to take action to defend against censorship in a school or public library.

- If you were facing a potentially serious intellectual freedom issue, to which two organizations highlighted in this chapter would you turn? Provide rationale for your choices.

- Given the current decline in support for school libraries and the subsequent cuts in library budgets and professional staffing, list three key points you would include in an American "School Library Manifesto." Offer reasoning for your answer.

- Barbara Jones, director of ALA's Office for Intellectual Freedom and executive director of the Freedom to Read Foundation, asserted that the mission in libraries in developing countries is often closely connected to "social justice." Give an example of when the mission of American public or school libraries have a connection to "social justice." In your opinion, is this a role American libraries should play? Provide rationale for your answer.

Chapter 8

Advocating for Intellectual Freedom

Including the Columns

"New Year's Resolutions and Resources"

"Advocating for Intellectual Freedom with Principals and Teachers"

"Reaching Out to Parents"

"Citizens in Training: Twelve Ways to Teach Students
about Intellectual Freedom"

"Protecting Students' Rights and Keeping Your Job"

"Banned Books Week: Just the Beginning"

"Choose Privacy Week: A New ALA Initiative"

"The Intellectual Freedom Calendar: Another Advocacy Plan
for the School Library"

Chapter 8

Advocating for Intellectual Freedom

INTRODUCTION

In this time of diminishing school library professional positions, there is a focus on advocating for a strong school library program led by a credentialed school librarian. There is, however, another type of advocacy. School librarians have an advocacy role in supporting and protecting students' First Amendment right to access information in a school library: the right to read, hear, and view library resources without monitoring and restrictions.

"A" is for Advocacy

Advocacy is a capital-letter word among school library professionals because library programs across the country are at risk of being marginalized and their positions eliminated. The expert advice found in professional literature, blogs, conference sessions, and webinars frequently ties the value of the school library program and its full-time professional staffing to success in student learning and achievement. In this chapter, advocacy has another purpose: to promote and protect students' First Amendment right to seek information in a school library and to ensure that their privacy will be respected. The eight columns in Chapter 8 describe unique aspects of advocacy focused on promoting intellectual freedom in a school library.

1. The first column, "New Year's Resolutions and Resources," applies the custom of making self-improvement resolutions at the beginning of each year to improving the intellectual freedom atmosphere in a school. Readers are provided with five "resolutions" for broad actions and offered selected resources to accomplish the goals.

2. "Advocating for Intellectual Freedom with Principals and Teachers" supplies strategies to target the principal, as the school's educational leader, for conversion to an intellectual freedom advocate if not already a supporter. The second column also furnishes ideas for creating allies among educational colleagues for students' First Amendment free speech rights.

3. Beginning with a real life "parent story," the third column details three examples of "sticky" circumstances where school librarians can find themselves in conflict with parents over school library resources. "Reaching Out to Parents," affirms parents' rights to guide their children's reading choices and lays out strategies for creating supportive allies among parents, grandparents, and guardians.

4. Students have little knowledge about their First Amendment free speech rights as they apply to using school library resources. The fourth column, "Citizens in Training: 12 Ways to Teach Students about Intellectual Freedom," gives school librarians a dozen ideas for educating students on this topic.

5. "Protecting Students' Rights and Keeping Your Job" asks whether a school librarian can defend students' First Amendment rights in a range of areas, such as speaking out against overly restrictive filtering, without risking job loss. One of the three strategies discussed in this fifth column is creating a network of intellectual freedom supporters.

6. The sixth column, "Banned Books Week: Just the Beginning," describes the annual September resistance-to-censorship observation. The column provides ideas for highlighting the week in school libraries and for ongoing anti-censorship awareness activities throughout the year.

7. Privacy of individuals and library users is accented in the seventh column, "Choose Privacy Week: A New ALA Initiative." It details ways that school librarians can educate students during the week and resources for planning activities.

8. The final column, "The Intellectual Freedom Calendar: Another Advocacy Plan for the School Library," lays out a school-year's worth of activities and celebrations that will enable a school librarian to emphasize students' intellectual freedom and privacy from August through June.

Although the purpose of advocacy in Chapter 8 differs from promoting the role of school libraries and librarians in students' academic achievement, the strategies and tools recommended by advocacy proponents can be adapted successfully for intellectual freedom advocacy.

Advocacy, Leadership, and Vision

Advocacy for any cause requires leadership. Although some school librarians seem as though they are "born leaders," in fact, they have developed skills and strategies over the years and have a passion for their vision of a school library program. When championing intellectual freedom, their vision is a library where students:

- enjoy the right to read and borrow resources free from scrutiny;
- select books and other materials, without constraints based on age, grade level, or reading level;
- find materials and information representing diverse points of view;
- are not required to request materials on "controversial topics" from a restricted area;
- ask reference questions without being cross-examined about why the information is needed;
- search Internet sites without encountering over-blocking of legal information;

- utilize social technologies (blogs, wikis, and others) to complete assignments and share creative expression;
- obtain materials through interlibrary loan services;
- find the facility, materials, and services that meet the needs of *all students* including those with physical, cognitive, and learning disabilities;
- are not barred from borrowing or using library materials because of overdue book fines, assessments for damaged materials, or replacement costs for lost materials;
- trust that their library use and records are kept confidential by staff;
- possess the information and technology literacy skills needed to be effective users of information; and
- learn about their First Amendment rights in the school library media center (Adams 2008, 1–2).

Moving from a vision for students' intellectual freedom to reality, however, requires the school librarian to exhibit leadership and skillfully employ advocacy skills that turn the stakeholders (students, teachers, parents, administrators, and the rest of the school community) into allies. This conversion demands continuous advocacy, and the columns in this chapter provide ideas on how it can be accomplished.

REFERENCE

Adams, Helen R. 2008. *Ensuring Intellectual Freedom and Access to Information in the School Library Media Program.* Westport, Connecticut: Libraries Unlimited.

IF Matters: Intellectual Freedom @ your library®

New Year's Resolutions and Resources

By Helen R. Adams

Originally published in the IF Matters: Intellectual Freedom @ your library® column, *School Library Media Activities Monthly*, XXV (5) (January 2009): 54.

It's the season for writing New Year's resolutions and popular choices include spending more time with family and friends, becoming fit, and getting organized. This month's IF Matters column reflects this January activity and offers resolutions to improve the intellectual freedom climate in a school with recommended resources to provide support. YOU supply the resolve! (Note: The following URLs were current in January 2013.)

Resolution #1: Be well-informed about local, regional, national, and global intellectual freedom issues.

Resources:

- **American Library Association. Intellectual Freedom Action News (IFACTION).** http://www.ala.org/offices/intellectual-freedom-email-lists
  The ALA Office for Intellectual freedom staff maintains IFACTION, a news-only, no discussion, electronic list with media reports relating to intellectual freedom. Sign up to receive daily news stories via email or use the digest feature to receive the bundled information in a single message. Instructions for subscribing are found on the website.

- **Library Law Blog.** http://blog.librarylaw.com
  Mary Minow, an attorney, consultant, and former public librarian, maintains a blog focusing on legal issues in all types of libraries. Privacy and First Amendment rights are often featured. Note: Mary Minow maintains the archive of her Library Law Blog; however, she has moved her active communications to Twitter where you can follow her @LibraryLaw (http://twitter.com/librarylaw).

Resolution #2: Confront intellectual freedom issues in your school and community using the knowledge and strategies of experienced advocates.

Resource:

- **Cooperative Children's Book Center (CCBC), University of Wisconsin-Madison. What If? Questions and Answers on Intellectual Freedom.** http://www.education.wisc.edu/ccbc/freedom/whatif/default.asp
  "What If?" is a Q & A forum for teachers, school and public librarians and others in the library and education fields. Visitors may submit a question confidentially, and CCBC staff will answer it in a thoughtful manner emphasizing how "the principles of intellectual freedom are carried out in practice" (CCBC). The answer archive can be sorted by relevancy to classroom, school and public library, self-censorship, and "other" issues. Seek answers to your intellectual freedom questions on topics such as what to do if a

principal directs a school librarian to remove a controversial book from the collection and whether it is ethical to suspend students' borrowing privileges if they have overdue, lost, or damaged library materials.

Resolution #3: Review your library's policies and practices to ensure they reflect the principles of the *Library Bill of Rights* and *The Code of Ethics of the American Library Association.*

Resources:

- **New York Library Association. Intellectual Freedom Committee. "Intellectual Freedom Self-Censorship Checklist."** http://www.nyla.org/images/nyla/files/Self-Censorship.pdf.
  Although aimed at public library staff, the eighteen question checklist will assist library media specialists in determining their level of preparedness to protect students' intellectual freedom in school library media centers.

- **American Library Association, Office for Intellectual Freedom website.** http://www.ala.org/oif
  This website has a wealth of information ranging from developing a material selection policy to dealing with the media to intellectual freedom toolkits on such topics as privacy, the Internet, and dealing with challenges to gay, lesbian, bisexual, and transgender resources. The full texts of the *Library Bill of Rights*, its interpretations, and the *Code of Ethics* also are available.

- **"Resources for School Librarians."** http://www.sldirectory.com/index.html#top
  Retired school librarian Linda Bertland maintains an extensive list of policy manuals and examples as well as many other types of resources for school library professionals.

- **American Library Association. 1998. "Workbook for Selection Policy Writing."** http://www.ala.org/Template.cfm?section=dealing&Template=/ContentManagement/ContentDisplay.cfm&ContentID=11173
  Aimed specifically at school library media specialists, the document includes the recommended sections and sample language for a school library materials selection policy with reconsideration procedures.

Resolution #4: Develop an advocacy plan to inculcate intellectual freedom concepts and advance support for minors' access to information in your school.

Resources:

- **New York Library Association. School Library Media Section. "Real Ideas from the Trenches."** http://web.archive.org/web/20060929152350/http://www.nyla.org/content/user_19/real%20ideas.pdf
  This short downloadable booklet in pdf format describes successful advocacy ideas practiced by New York school library media specialists that can be adapted for educating others about intellectual freedom. [No longer available.]

- **American Association of School Librarians. "School Library Program Health & Wellness Toolkit."** http://www.ala.org/aasl/aaslissues/toolkits/slmhealthandwellness#resources
  In addition to the lengthy list of advocacy resources, the toolkit lays out a plan of action that can be adapted for promoting intellectual freedom.

- **American Association of School Librarians. 2008. "What Is Intellectual Freedom?"** http://www.ala.org/aasl/sites/ala.org.aasl/files/content/aaslissues/intellectual_freedom_brochure1210.pdf

Created in 2008, the brochure describes why intellectual freedom is important in a school library media program and is available for download, duplication, and distribution. Although prepared for library media professionals, the brochure can also be used to educate teachers and administrators about intellectual freedom in schools.

Resolution #5: Become an active member of a state or national library association's intellectual freedom committee to provide collegial support to others.

Resources:

- **American Association of School Librarians. "Affiliate Assembly Organizations."** http://www.ala.org/aasl/aboutaasl/affils/regions
  You can easily locate the names of state school library media organizations and their current presidents and presidents-elect with their contact information at this website. Join and volunteer to serve on the intellectual freedom committee.

- **American Association of School Librarians. "Committee Volunteer Form."** http://www.ala.org/aasl/aboutaasl/aaslcommunity/volunteeropps/aaslvolunteeropportunities
  Submit this online form to become an AASL *regular committee member* [attending committee meetings in person] or a *virtual committee member* [participation by conference call, email, or other electronic means].

New Year's resolutions are made with the best intentions but frequently are abandoned by spring. Be determined to keep at least one resolution related to intellectual freedom and the protection of students' First Amendment right to access information.

REFERENCE

CCBC. "What IF . . . Questions and Answers on Intellectual Freedom." http://www.education.wisc.edu/ccbc/freedom/whatif/default.asp (accessed January 16, 2013).

IF Matters: Intellectual Freedom @ your library®

Advocating for Intellectual Freedom with Principals and Teachers

By Helen R. Adams

Originally published in the IF Matters: Intellectual Freedom @ your library® column, *School Library Media Activities Monthly*, XXV (6) (February 2009): 54.

Intellectual freedom is "the right of every individual to both seek and receive information from all points of view without restriction" (ALA http://www.ala.org/Template.cfm?Section=basics&Template=/ContentManagement/ContentDisplay.cfm&ContentID=164089). Unlike library media specialists, it is rare for principals and teachers to learn about intellectual freedom in their education classes. Nor is it likely that they are taught about First Amendment court decisions that affirm minors' rights to receive ideas and information in school library media centers. Therefore, if minors' intellectual freedom is to be protected, library media specialists must take responsibility for educating administrators and teachers. The concept of *intellectual freedom* can be advocated by library media specialists to other educators as providing *access* to a wide range of resources. Also, using stories or examples make intellectual freedom principles more concrete to colleagues.

Prior to beginning an advocacy campaign, the library media specialist should first check the status of intellectual freedom in schools locally, statewide, and nationally. The following strategies for promoting intellectual freedom for students are recommended by the American Library Association (ALA):

- Seek up-to-date information on censorship, privacy, and other intellectual freedom issues in library professional literature and other media sources and through attendance at conferences and workshops.

- Subscribe to intellectual freedom-related electronic lists such as ALA's IFAction (http://www.ala.org/offices/intellectual-freedom-email-lists).

- Become familiar with pro-First Amendment organizations and their advocacy efforts (ALA http://www.ala.org/Template.cfm?Section=basicrelatedlinks&Template=/ContentManagement/ContentDisplay.cfm&ContentID=11699). Note: Appendix B contains a list of pro–First Amendment and privacy advocacy organizations with a description of each and contact information.

Next the library media specialist can develop an advocacy plan to promote intellectual freedom concepts. The American Association of School Librarians (AASL) has defined advocacy as the "On-going process of building partnerships so that others will act for and with you, turning passive support into educated action for the library media program" (AASL). Although one resolute person can achieve a great deal, having administrators and teachers as allies can change a school's climate. AASL's online toolkits, including the "School Library Program Health & Wellness Toolkit" can be used to prepare a local plan for promoting intellectual freedom principles (http://www.ala.org/aasl/aaslissues/toolkits/toolkits).

As educational leaders, principals exert a great deal of influence; therefore, winning their support for students' intellectual freedom is critical. If the principal does not support a collection with materials reflecting a broad range of ideas on controversial issues, does not believe that students' library records should be confidential, or does not accept that minors have the right to research a variety of topics, it is difficult for the library media specialist to ensure students' access to information and guard their intellectual freedom. To help administrators understand the importance of protecting students' information needs, library media specialists can:

- Assist administrators in making the connection between intellectual freedom and "growing" future citizens. To ensure that today's students are educated for citizenship in a global society, students must be able to use resources on a wide range of subjects in print and electronic formats. Unrestricted access to information in the school library media center creates a positive academic atmosphere where students learn how to evaluate competing ideas, a skill needed by all citizens.
- Meet with the principal to review the materials selection policy, how materials are selected, and district reconsideration procedures, clarifying any steps that are unclear.
- Initiate a discussion when issues such as the confidentiality of students' library records arise (Adams 2008, 204).

Teachers also need to be educated about intellectual freedom. Although educators may understand that administrators and school boards have strict control over instructional resources used in classrooms as part of the approved school curriculum, there are limits on their ability to remove library resources that are intended for free inquiry by students (Adams 2008, 205). To nurture teachers' development as supporters of students' rights, the school librarian can use these strategies:

- Orient new staff members to library policies including those related to selection of library resources, reconsideration of challenged library materials, confidentiality of student library use records, reserves and interlibrary loan requests, and use of the Internet.
- Collaborate with teachers to create learning experiences that include the First Amendment and students' free speech rights.
- Plan staff development programs that include information about intellectual freedom.
- Add materials to the library's professional collection that will help staff understand intellectual freedom and censorship (Adams 2008, 206–207).

By reaching out to principals and teachers, the library media specialist has the potential to create allies who will support minors' access to information when a challenge occurs. The advocacy process is not quick, and it requires more than celebrating Banned Books Week each September. The library media specialist must model the principles of intellectual freedom in year-round, day-to-day actions. When advocacy is successful, however, it can change students' lives and impact their effectiveness as citizens.

REFERENCES

Adams, Helen R. 2008. *Ensuring Intellectual Freedom and Access to Information in the School Library Media Program.* Westport, Connecticut: Libraries Unlimited.

American Association of School Librarians. "Issues & Advocacy." http://www.ala.org/aasl/aasl issues/advocacy/definitions / (accessed January 16, 2013).

American Library Association. Office for Intellectual Freedom. "Intellectual Freedom and Censorship Q & A." http://www.ala.org/Template.cfm?Section=basics&Template=/Content Management/ContentDisplay.cfm&ContentID=164089 (accessed January 16, 2013).

American Library Association. Office for Intellectual Freedom. "What You Can Do to Oppose Censorship." http://www.ala.org/Template.cfm?Section=basics&Template=/Content Management/ContentDisplay.cfm&ContentID=24792/ (accessed January 16, 2013).

IF Matters: Intellectual Freedom @ your library®

Reaching Out to Parents

By Helen R. Adams

Originally published in the IF Matters: Intellectual Freedom @ your library® column, *School Library Monthly*, XXVII (8) (May/June 2011): 48–49.

Cheryl, a K–12 librarian in the Midwest, recounts the following true "parent story":

Last May at the end of my second year in the library, our superintendent received a call from an unhappy parent. Her eighth grade daughter brought home a book that she did not approve of—in her words it was "pornographic." She was disgusted and wanted to know how this book ended up in a school library. She wanted to know how many other middle school kids had been allowed to read this "trash." Additionally, the parent wanted a committee, including her, to select all library books. (Cheryl 2010)

Other "Sticky" Situations

Parents can be supportive allies for school librarians, but they can also cause complications as Cheryl learned. The concerns of some parents over specific library titles can lead them to ask the school librarian to take actions that clash with the *Library Bill of Rights* and the ALA *Code of Ethics*. For example, parents may request that their child(ren) not be allowed to check out books on such topics as Halloween, vampires, or sex education. Unfortunately, it may be nearly impossible for school library professionals to monitor what individual students are checking out. Automated circulation systems can "flag" a student's circulation record, but some libraries allow student self-checkout, creating the potential for a student to borrow books on the family's prohibited topics list. One solution that upholds intellectual freedom principles is to ask the parents to speak with their child(ren) about guidelines for personal reading choices that meet family values. The school librarian can emphasize that enforcement of family reading parameters is a matter between the parent and child, not the school librarian and student.

Another potential conflict can occur if a parent requests that an "inappropriate" book be removed from the collection. Some parents want only to be heard and have their viewpoints acknowledged, although others are serious about removing or restricting the book to protect *all children*. If the concern is not resolved informally, the school librarian should explain the reconsideration process to the complainant, who then has the option to challenge the book formally following district policy.

Given situations such as the three described, how can a school librarian become a positive partner with parents to create lifelong readers and encourage the use of the school library?

Parental Rights and Common Ground

Parents are legally and morally responsible for caring for and educating their children including overseeing their child(ren)'s reading. "Free Access to Libraries for Minors: An Interpretation of the Library Bill of Rights" confirms this right and explains the relationships among the parent, child, and school librarian:

> . . . We affirm the responsibility and the right of all parents and guardians to guide their own children's use of the library and its resources and services. Librarians and library governing bodies cannot assume the role of parents. . . . Parents and guardians who do not want their children to have access to specific library services, materials, or facilities should so advise their children. (ALA 2008a)

According to "Access to Resources and Services in the School Library Media Program: An Interpretation of the Library Bill of Rights," it is the responsibility of a school librarian to create a program where students have free access to information and can learn the twenty-first century information literacy skills needed to function in a global society. In addition, it is the responsibility of the school library professional to select resources students need to support their academic studies and to explore personal interests (ALA 2008b). With clearly defined roles and responsibilities, parents and the school librarian can be good partners because each wants students to be successful.

Putting Out the Welcome Mat

Parental interest in their children's development can be used proactively to educate them about quality children and young adults' literature as well as minors' use of a school library. Discussions between the librarian and parents can foster the concept of giving students personal choice in what they read, connecting "choice" to exploring new ideas and diverse viewpoints as well as developing literacy skills.

The Parent Advocate

Parents can be valuable advocates for school library programs. Do you know about the "Spokane Moms"? Three mothers from Spokane, Washington, began their advocacy campaign when they were concerned about the reduction of a local elementary librarian's hours. As their concern for the cutting of time for other school librarians grew, they reached out to parents and Washington School Library Association members and made a direct request to Washington state legislators for funding to restore school librarian positions in the 2008–2009 school year. Four million dollars was approved, but sadly, the funds were designated for only one year (Whelan, Deborah Lau. 2008. "Three Spokane Moms Save Their School Libraries." September 1, 2008. *School Library Journal*. http://www.schoollibraryjournal.com/article/CA6590045.html [accessed January 16, 2013]). Although the Spokane Moms were only partially successful,

The school librarian can employ these strategies to reach out and engage parents:

- Post the district's materials selection policy on the library's Web page.
- Introduce new library books to members of the school's parent organization during one of its meetings and explain how the materials are selected (Adams 2008, 72).
- Start a reading group for parents that will enable them to learn about new children's and YA books, help their children select books appropriate for their age and social, emotional, and cognitive development, and discuss books with their children (Adams 2008, 72).

- Write a library column for parents in the school's newsletter. Promote new books and tips for creating lifelong readers (Adams 2008, 72).

- Invite parents and students to a "Back to School" library program featuring an author, book discussions, and a book fair (Adams 2008, 72).

- Open the library to families for browsing and checkout during parent-teacher conferences (Adams 2008, 213).

During discussions with parents about what students are reading, the school librarian must strike a balance between promoting children and young adults' self-selection in reading choices and acknowledging the right of parents to guide their children's reading choices (Adams 2008, 72). The school librarian must also be cognizant that grandparents are raising many children, and these older adults may find it difficult to accept the "edgier" books. Reaffirming the parent's (or grandparent's) right to guide his/her child's (or grandchild's) reading may allay personal concerns over individual titles and begin to build the trust and respect necessary for a positive partnership (Adams 2008, 214).

REFERENCES

Adams, Helen R. 2008. *Ensuring Intellectual Freedom and Access to Information in the School Library Media Program.* Westport, Connecticut: Libraries Unlimited.

American Library Association. 2008a. "Free Access to Libraries for Minors: An Interpretation of the Library Bill of Rights." http://www.ala.org/ala/issues advocacy/intfreedom/librarybill/interpretations/freeaccesslibraries.cfm (accessed January 16, 2013).

their actions demonstrate what three dedicated individuals can do when they form coalitions and secure the backing of thousands for a popular cause.

There are countless news stories of parents speaking both for and against a particular library resource or advocating for the retention or removal of a classroom reading list book that has garnered concerns. Single-issue advocacy can also be successful. A group of parents in Belleville, Wisconsin, supported the retention of Chris Crutcher's *Staying Fat for Sarah Byrnes* on a ninth grade language arts reading list after seeking guidance from the Wisconsin American Civil Liberties Union. Using Facebook to organize support, the group was able to explain to the school board why this book was a good choice and articulate the reasons for its remaining in the curriculum. In the end, the board voted to retain the book as part of the ninth grade curriculum. For the parents and students involved on both sides, the situation was a learning experience. Read more about this story in the Chapter 7 column, "The American Civil Liberties Union: Another Ally for School Librarians."

Over the years AASL has developed an arsenal of advocacy tools. One such resource is the "Parent Advocate Toolkit" (http://www.ala.org/aasl/aaslissues/toolkits/parentoutreach) that provides rationale for why schools need school libraries and professionally trained staff: students require strong information literacy skills to compete in a global society and school librarians help empower student learners by providing diverse resources and instruction to meet AASL's "Standards for the 21st-Century Learner." The toolkit includes resources to teach parents the facts about today's school libraries, how libraries contribute to the academic success of students, and tips on advocating for school library programs (AASL. "Parent Advocate Toolkit." http://www.ala.org/aasl/aaslissues/toolkits/parentout reach [accessed January 16, 2013]). AASL created another resource for parents: "The School Library: What Parents Should Know" that provides parents with a list of questions to ask about their school's library program and ways in which to support their child(ren)'s education (http://www.ala.org/aasl/aaslissues/toolkits/whatparentsshould).

School library professional journals frequently have articles on advocacy such as *School Library Monthly's* "Creating a Parent Advocacy Plan" (February 2007, 23.6 and available online http://www.schoollibrarymonthly.com/articles/pdf/ParentAdvocacy.pdf). The article and AASL's advocacy resources can be used to advocate for intellectual freedom, increased library staffing, and budgets because the advocacy strategies remain the same.

American Library Association. 2008b. "Access to Resources and Services in the School Library Media Program: An Interpretation of the Library Bill of Rights." http://www.ala.org/advocacy/intfreedom/librarybill/interpretations/accessresources (accessed January 16, 2013).

Cheryl. Online discussion with author, October 1, 2010.

IF Matters: Intellectual Freedom @ your library®

Citizens in Training: Twelve Ways to Teach Students about Intellectual Freedom

By Helen R. Adams

Originally published in the IF Matters: Intellectual Freedom @ your library® column, *School Library Media Activities Monthly*, XXV (8) (April 2009): 55.

In the Knight Foundation's "Future of the First Amendment" survey of 100,000 high school students in 2004, researchers found that American students lack knowledge and understanding about the First Amendment with over 33 percent expressing the opinion that it "goes too far in the rights it guarantees" (http://www.mindfully .org/Reform/2005/First-Amendment -Knight31jan05.htm). Referring to the survey results, Knight Foundation President Hodding Carter III commented, "Ignorance about the basics of this free society is a danger to our nation's future" (http://www.mindfully .org/Reform/2005/First-Amendment -Knight31jan05.htm).

Young Americans do not automatically become knowledgeable about citizenship when they reach the age of eighteen; therefore, schools must teach students about their legal rights and corresponding responsibilities as citizens. School library media specialists can play a key role in educating "citizens in training" about their First Amendment rights as applied to school libraries and laws protecting the confidentiality of minors' library use— all integral aspects of their *intellectual freedom*. Here are twelve ways school library professionals can inform students about their intellectual freedom and encourage civic engagement:

Students and the First Amendment, Revisited

On behalf of the John S. and James L. Knight Foundation, Dr. Kenneth Dautrich, surveyed American students in 2004, 2006, 2007, and 2011 for its "Future of the First Amendment" project to provide a snapshot of what students know about the First Amendment and their attitudes toward their right of free expression. The 2004, 2006, and 2007 results were distressing, with students having little knowledge of or appreciation for their free speech rights. The 2011 survey had a slightly different focus, trying to determine how the use of digital communications and social media changes students' attitudes toward their right of free expression.

Since the original survey in 2004, digital communication and media have proliferated. The 2011 findings contrast earlier students' attitudes on whether the First Amendment right of free expression is too liberal. In 2004, 45 percent of students said First Amendment rights "went too far." In 2011, the opposite was true, with 53 percent of students saying the rights were not too extreme. What caused this shift in attitude? Although there is less instructional time spent on learning about the First Amendment in high schools, those who were taught about their guaranteed freedoms were 6–7 percent more likely to support freedom of the press and the prerogative of persons to vocalize unpopular opinions. The overall findings of the 2011 survey conclude: 1) students are becoming more supportive of First Amendment rights; 2) student use of the Internet (digital media) as a source of news and information is increasing exponentially; and 3) student use of social media appears to correlate with support of First Amendment rights (Dautrich, Kenneth. 2011. "Future of the First Amendment: 2011 Survey of High School Students and Teachers." John S. and James L. Knight Foundation: 6, 8. http://www.knightfoundation. org/publications/future-first-amendment-2011 [accessed January 16, 2013]). Between the 2004 and 2011 surveys, students' use of social media, their personal expression of ideas, and their creative media posted online appear to have made them more aware and supportive of their First Amendment rights.

- Appeal to students by using "kid friendly" language. Students may not be familiar with the term *intellectual freedom*, but they can likely identify with the concept of *access*. In this context, *access* means having a school library collection that provides them with information reflecting many points of view in a variety of formats.

- Teach information and digital literacy skills students can apply to their information seeking and evaluating throughout their adult lives, thus, enabling them to be well-informed, critical thinking citizens.

- Incorporate AASL's *Standards for the 21st-Century Learner*, Standard 3, Student Responsibility 3.37 "Respect the principles of intellectual freedom" into collaboratively planned lessons in social studies, English, journalism, science and other curricular areas (AASL 2007).

- Encourage students to participate in selecting and recommending new materials. Use selection policy criteria such as "reflect the pluralistic natural of a global society" or "free of bias and stereotyping" to teach students about the right of all members of a democratic society (including minors) to view, listen to, and read materials with diverse perspectives.

- Celebrate Banned Books Week in September. Attract students' attention by creating displays of books that have been challenged, providing information about the First Amendment and banned books via the school's public address system, giving away bookmarks promoting the freedom to read, presenting book talks on "banned" books, and encouraging teachers to incorporate the theme of banned books and censorship into their lessons (Doyle 2007, 210, 214).

- Create a book discussion group, and encourage students to read books that have been "banned" or those in which intellectual freedom is a central theme such as *Fahrenheit 451* or *The Giver*. Knowing a book is "controversial" may intrigue students and motivate them to read it. The First Amendment First Aid Kit provides tips for book discussion leaders (http://www.randomhouse.com/teens/firstamendment/talking.html).

- Display intellectual freedom documents prominently in the library including the Bill of Rights of the U.S. Constitution, the *Library Bill of Rights*, and the Universal Declaration of Human Rights (especially Article 19). Explain their connection to the library, and refer to them during library skills instruction. Post news articles, cartoons, and posters to provide daily reminders of intellectual freedom and its importance in our society.

- Collaborate with teachers to observe Constitution Day on September 17th. Recommend resources provided online by the National Constitution Center (http://constitution center.org/ConstitutionDay/Default.aspx) and the Illinois First Amendment Center (http://www.illinoisfirstamendmentcenter.com). Help students connect their First Amendment right to access information with their responsibilities as citizens to understand national issues.

- Encourage students to realize that citizens have privacy rights under the 4th and 5th Amendments, state, and federal laws.

- Turn ordinary library situations into teaching opportunities about privacy. For example, if a student is looking for a book not on the shelf and asks who has checked it out, library staff can explain that information about who has borrowed the item from the library is confidential, referencing the library program's privacy policy and their state's library record law (Adams 2008, 88).

- Use National Library Week to spotlight libraries as places where students have the freedom to read what they choose. Sponsor a library card sign-up campaign to encourage students to use their public library.
- Promote KidSPEAK, a website sponsored by nine national organizations. It offers ideas on how students can use their First Amendment rights to protest attempts at censoring of library and curricular materials (http://www.kidspeak-online.org).

REFERENCES

Adams, Helen R. 2008. *Ensuring Intellectual Freedom and Access to Information in the School Library Media Program.* Westport, Connecticut: Libraries Unlimited.

American Association of School Librarians. 2007. *Standards for the 21st-Century Learner.* American Library Association. http://www.ala.org/aasl/guidelines andstandards/learningstandards/standards (accessed January 16, 2013).

Doyle, Robert P. 2007. *Banned Books: 2007 Resource Guide.* Chicago, Illinois: American Library Association.

Knight Foundation. 2005. "Survey Finds First Amendment is Being Left Behind in U.S. High Schools." January 31, 2005. http://www.mindfully.org/Reform/2005/First-Amendment -Knight31jan05.htm (accessed January 16, 2013).

Position Statement on the Role of the School Library Program

AASL's "Position Statement on the Role of the School Library Program" describes the many ways in which the school library provides students with opportunities to learn. Most importantly from an intellectual freedom perspective, the final paragraph explains how the school library program supports students' First Amendment right of free speech, including the right to choose what they read, view, and hear. The school library also provides students with information from multiple points of view, giving them an opportunity to develop the critical thinking skills needed by citizens in a democratic society (AASL. 2012. "Position Statement on the Role of the School Library Program." http://www.ala.org/aasl/aasl issues/positionstatements/roleslp [accessed January 16, 2013]).

IF Matters @ your library

Protecting Students' Rights and Keeping Your Job

By Helen R. Adams

Originally published in the IF Matters column, *School Library Monthly*, XXVIII (6) (March 2012): 27–28.

How do you reply to a fellow school librarian who states, "If my principal tells me to remove a book from the shelves, I'm going to do it. I need this job." Or when discussing book selection, a librarian in a neighboring district comments, "I'll never buy those titles. There would be complaints, and my principal already thinks libraries can be run by aides." It is understandable that school librarians are feeling threatened as school districts across the United States cut library positions and replace certificated librarians with assistants. Will standing up for students' intellectual freedom put a school librarian's job at additional risk?

Finding the Balance

In today's economy, there are no guarantees for any position. Championing students' access to information reflecting diverse points of view, speaking against overly aggressive filtering practices, defending students' privacy when using library materials, advocating for students with special needs, and resisting censorship raises the visibility of the school librarian and may make some administrators uneasy, especially when scrutiny of schools is high. Does this mean that school librarians should step back from advocacy of minors' rights in school libraries? No, it is just the opposite; it is important to continue to consciously integrate the tenets of the ALA *Code of Ethics* and the *Library Bill of Rights* into daily practice. How can a school librarian find the balance between protecting students' First Amendment right to access information and risking job loss? Two common sense strategies strengthen the librarian's position: establishing a positive relationship with the principal and building a network of intellectual freedom supporters.

> **Essential Intellectual Freedom Documents for School Librarians**
>
> *Code of Ethics of the ALA* http://www.ifmanual.org/part4
>
> *Library Bill of Rights* http://www.ifmanual.org/lbor
>
> "Access to Resources & Services in the School Library Media Program: An Interpretation of the Library Bill of Rights" http://www.ifmanual.org/accessslmp
>
> "Free Access to Libraries for Minors: An Interpretation of the Library Bill of Rights" http://www.ifmanual.org/freeaccessminors

Target the Principal

The principal has huge responsibilities and will appreciate a library professional who takes time for regular communications about current library issues. Be proactive from your first day on the job. As a starting point, go through the district's selection policy with the principal; describe how selection is accomplished, outline areas of the collection that need strengthening, and explain your plan for the upcoming year. Review the reconsideration process together annually *before* an oral complaint or challenge occurs. Over time, teach the principal about students' First Amendment rights to read and research topics in the school library and how students' evaluation of unbiased information contributes to their education as "citizens in training." These actions and others will create a positive, collaborative relationship with the principal.

Building an Intellectual Freedom Network

Think strategically about creating a network of allies who oppose censorship and support the intellectual freedom principles and policies on which effective school library programs are based. Potential supporters who can help protect minors' intellectual freedom include:

Faculty: Be visible in your school, and make it a priority to communicate information about the library's services, resources, and policies to teachers, especially new staff. Create an open selection process by inviting teachers to recommend library materials for their curricular areas. Those who participate are likely to be supportive if concerns about library resources arise.

Students: Young adults can also be part of the intellectual freedom network that protects their right to read and receive information in a school library. They can be vocal and effective voices when a popular book is threatened with removal.

The Community: Reach out to parents, extended families, and community members through the library's website, a library newsletter, and special events such as Internet safety programs and book fairs. Give presentations to local groups, and solicit volunteers to work in the library. Make certain the community is aware of the school's selection policy, and help families understand the importance of students having choices in their library selections.

Public Librarians: Build a collegial relationship with youth services staff by planning jointly sponsored activities such as a public library card signup campaign. Public library staff can provide a sounding board and professional support in difficult times.

Final Thoughts

Despite a school librarian's best efforts, a principal may, for example, remove a book without following policy, causing intellectual freedom principles and minors' rights to be compromised. In those instances, you must be content knowing that you have done all that is possible. Realizing that there will be other advocacy opportunities and challenges ahead, regroup and continue to work with the principal and library allies.

IF Matters: Intellectual Freedom @ your library®

Banned Books Week: Just the Beginning

By Helen R. Adams

Originally published in the IF Matters: Intellectual Freedom @ your library® column, *School Library Monthly*, XXVI (1) (September 2009): 48–49.

---

30 Candles for Banned Books Week

In September 2012, intellectual freedom advocates celebrated the thirtieth anniversary of Banned Books Week (BBW) sponsored by many pro-First Amendment organizations including the American Library Association, the Freedom to Read Foundation, and the National Coalition Against Censorship. Since 2011, book lovers have been encouraged to participate in "virtual read-outs" during BWW and post videos of themselves reading sections of a banned book on BBW's YouTube channel (http://www.youtube .com/bannedbooksweek). Check out the Banned Books Week website for more information and upcoming activities (http://www.bannedbooks week.org).

Everything You Want to Know about Most Frequently Challenged Books

An announcement of the ten most challenged books in school, public, and academic libraries in the *previous year as reported to the ALA Office for Intellectual Freedom* (OIF) is made annually in April. As noted earlier in Chapter 3, it is estimated that only about 20 percent of all challenges are reported to the OIF. The OIF website lists the top ten (reported) challenged books by year beginning in 2001, frequently challenged authors, and challenges to classic literature (http://www .ala.org/advocacy/banned/frequentlychallenged/ 21stcenturychallenged). There is also a link to graphs that show the number of reported challenges per year, initiators of challenges, the

---

Founded in 1982, Banned Books Week is celebrated annually during the last week in September. The event acknowledges Americans' right to read the books of their choice regardless of whether the ideas, language, or images are controversial. This annual observance is a good opportunity to explore the difference between a book being *banned* and a book being *challenged*. A *challenge* questions the appropriateness of a book for inclusion in a library's collection and is an attempt to remove or restrict access to the book based on personal objections of an individual or group. If the challenge is successful, the book is *banned* [removed from the library's collection] or restricted in some manner [i.e., minors must have written parental permission to check out the book]. Most of the books highlighted during Banned Books Week have been challenged but not banned (ALA).

Challenges

Every year the ALA Office for Intellectual Freedom (OIF) website lists the ten most frequently challenged books in schools and libraries for the previous year as reported to OIF. The 2008 list includes *And Tango Makes Three* for the third consecutive year. The list is available at the ALA website (http://www .ala.org/advocacy/banned/frequentlychallenged/2 1stcenturychallenged). The majority of the titles on the 2008 list are books for children and young adults, and the reasons for the challenges include offensive language, positive portrayal of homosexuality, sexual explicitness, violence, portrayal of religious or political points of view, and/or being unsuited to the age of potential readers. Those who challenged the appropriateness of these books to be in school and public library collections requested their removal, thereby, making them inaccessible to *anyone.* Parents have the responsibility and right to guide their children's reading choices, but those who challenge books to "protect" all children take away the right of other parents to decide for themselves.

> reasons for challenges, and the types of libraries in which challenges occur. Schools and school libraries top the location of challenges (ALA OIF. "Frequently Challenged Books." http://www.ala.org/advocacy/banned/frequentlychallenged [accessed January 16, 2013]).

Recognizing Banned Books Week

During Banned Books Week, many school library media specialists create displays of books from their own collections that have been challenged and/or banned. Library staff can subtly inform patrons that while many books have been challenged, these books are still freely available in libraries due to the efforts of librarians, teachers, and organizations that support minors' First Amendment right to read. Other ideas for celebrating Banned Books Week from the 2007 *Banned Books Resource Guide* include:

> **ABFFE's Banned Books Week Handbook**
>
> The American Bookseller's Foundation for Free Expression (ABFFE) was introduced in Chapter 7 as a pro-First Amendment organization that defends against censorship. One of the sponsors of Banned Books Week, ABFFE has created an online "Banned Books Week Handbook" that describes the history of Banned Books Week (BBW), includes five ways to celebrate the week-long event, tells about challenges to many well-known books primarily in school libraries, makes available BBW posters for download or purchase, and publicizes books and films about free expression (http://www.abffe.org/?page=BBWHandbook). It also provides links to online resources such as "Banned Books Online" (http://digital.library.upenn.edu/books/banned-books.html) and sites such as "Parents Against Bad Books in Schools" (http://www.pabbis.com) that encourage restricting students' access to books the organization touts as inappropriate to be included in a school library (ABFFE. 2011. "Banned Books Week Handbook." http://www.abffe.org/?page=BBWHandbook [accessed January 16, 2013]).

- Collaborate with teachers to have students create Banned Book Week podcasts featuring challenged and banned books.
- Promote the right to read by placing table tent cards in study halls, the cafeteria, and the library.
- Purchase Banned Book Week promotional materials including posters, bookmarks, buttons, and t-shirts from the American Library Association Store (http://www.alastore.ala.org/, search for Banned Books Week).
- Plan collaborative activities with the local public library related to Banned Books Week.
- Use public address system announcements to promote awareness of the right to read and the negative effects of censorship.
- Create a quiz for students to complete related to books that have been challenged or removed from libraries and award prizes (Doyle 2007, 208–216).

Ongoing Awareness

After celebrating Banned Books Week, school library professionals may think that they have done enough to support intellectual freedom. Exposing students to the idea of censorship during one week, however, is not adequate to meet Standard 3 of AASL's *Standards for the 21st-Century Learner* that asks students to:

"Share knowledge and participate ethically and productively as members of our democratic society" and lists a corresponding Student Responsibility 3.37: "Respect the principles of intellectual freedom." (AASL 2007)

Students will not be able to understand and respect the principles of intellectual freedom unless they are taught about them. Banned Books Week is a good time to kick off a year's worth of activities to teach students about their First Amendment right to read and access information available in the school library media center. The school library media specialist has a responsibility to educate students about intellectual freedom not just during Banned Books Week but throughout the school year.

How can the school library professional promote the right to read and access information beyond this one week in September? In 2009, those observing Banned Books Week are urged to:

- **KNOW the First Amendment**
- **SPEAK your mind**
- **READ banned books** (ALA 2009).

Library media specialists can use these three key ideas to promote intellectual freedom throughout the academic year. **(Note: These ideas are as valid today as when they were recommended in 2009.)**

The First Amendment First Aid Kit

Most publishers of literature aimed at children and young adults are First Amendment proponents. Random House, for example, sponsors the "First Amendment First Aid Kit" website that includes resources for school librarians, teachers, and students (http://www.randomhouse.com/teens/firstamendment/index.html). A quick review shows that the website includes what to do if a book challenge occurs, poignant comments from authors whose books have been challenged, guidelines for conducting a discussion of banned books, and a list of discussion questions (Random House. "First Amendment First Aid Kit." http://www.randomhouse.com/teens/firstamendment/index.html [accessed January 16, 2013]).

Student Rights

To help students *know the First Amendment* and their rights as minors, consider the following:

- Collaborate with social studies teachers to use information, lesson plans, and promotional materials found on these websites:
  ○ First Amendment Center. http://www.firstamendmentcenter.org
  ○ First Amendment Schools. http://www.firstamendmentschools.org
  ○ Illinois First Amendment Center. http://www.illinoisfirstamendmentcenter.com
- Sponsor an essay contest asking students to reflect on the meaning of the freedom to read or their First Amendment rights (Doyle 2007, 210).
- Set up a cooperative project between social studies and art teachers to create posters on the First Amendment concept of free speech/free expression. Display them in the library.

Speaking Up

If citizens remain silent or uninvolved when books are banned, access to those materials is lost to all library users. Ideas for helping students *speak their minds* to protect the right to read include:

- Recommend language arts teachers plan an assignment having students write letters to the editor of a newspaper in response to one of its articles or in support of/or opposition to a local issue.
- Ask speech teachers to include censorship and minors' First Amendment rights as topics for classroom speeches.
- Request that the school newspaper commit one issue of the paper to censorship in its many forms (Doyle 2007, 210).

The Role of the Library Media Specialist

AASL's "Position Statement on the School Librarian's Role in Reading" emphasizes the importance of selecting materials for academic as well as recreational reading as one facet of developing lifelong readers (AASL 2009). School library professionals can encourage students to *read banned books* (and new library acquisitions) by doing such activities as the following:

- Feature books from ALA's 100 Most Challenged Books for 2000–2007 list on the library's blog and ask students to write reviews (http://www.ala.org/advocacy/banned/frequently challenged/challengedbydecade/2000_2009). [Note: The list now includes titles from 2000–2009.]
- Collaborate with teachers to present monthly book talks in their classes using a "theme of the month" approach.
- Initiate a student book discussion club.
- Work with the public library staff to plan and promote a summer reading program.

Celebrating the freedom to read during Banned Books Week is only the beginning. As the primary defenders of intellectual freedom in schools, library media specialists must help students recognize and learn to protect their precious right to read throughout the school year. As the 2008 Banned Books Week's posters and bookmarks warned: "Closing books shuts out ideas . . . limits understanding . . . and closes possibilities" (ALA 2008).

The 100 Most Challenged Books

In addition to publicizing each year's ten most frequently challenged books, in 1990, the ALA Office for Intellectual Freedom began keeping a list *by decade* of the top 100 challenged books. The longer list is valuable to provide context and show trends in challenges (http://www.ala.org/advocacy/banned/frequentlychallenged/challengedbydecade).

REFERENCES

American Association of School Librarians. 2007. *Standards for the 21st-Century Learner.* http://www.ala.org/aasl/guidelinesandstandards/learningstandards/standards (accessed January 16, 2013).

American Association of School Librarians. 2009. "Position Statement on the Library Media Specialist's Role in Reading." http://www.ala.org/aasl/aaslissues/positionstatements/role inreading (accessed January 16, 2013).

American Library Association. 2008. "Banned Books Week Bookmark and Poster Slogans." http:// www.alastore.ala.org/detail.aspx?ID=2447 (accessed July 8, 2012) [no longer available].

American Library Association. 2009. "Banned Books Week Button Slogans." http://www.ala store.ala.org/detail.aspx?ID=2710 (accessed July 8, 2012) [no longer available].

American Library Association. Office for Intellectual Freedom. "Banned Books Week Basics." http://web.archive.org/web/20090516213610/http://www.ala.org/ala/issuesadvocacy/ banned/bannedbooksweek/basics/index.cfm (accessed January 16, 2013).

Doyle, Robert P. 2007. *Banned Books: 2007 Resource Guide.* Chicago, Illinois: American Library Association.

 **Privacy Matters**

Choose Privacy Week: A New ALA Initiative

By Helen R. Adams

Originally published in the Privacy Matters column, *School Library Monthly*, XXVI (8) (April 2010): 48–49.

There has been much written about the lessening of Americans' privacy with the causes being everything from the widespread use of social networking sites to the provisions of the USA PATRIOT Act. To raise awareness among U.S. citizens about privacy issues, in 2006, the American Library Association (ALA) Council directed the ALA Intellectual Freedom Committee and other groups within the association to work on a national campaign to heighten consciousness about the fragility of individuals' privacy.

Why Are Libraries Involved with Privacy?

It is not surprising that a national professional library association like ALA would promote a privacy initiative. Consider the following:

- Privacy/confidentiality is one of the core values of the library profession (ALA 2004).
- Article III of the *Code of Ethics of the ALA* states: "We protect each library user's right to privacy and confidentiality with respect to information sought or received and resources consulted, borrowed, acquired, or transmitted" (ALA 2008).
- "Privacy: An Interpretation of the Library Bill of Rights" declares that patron privacy and protecting the confidentiality of library users has been embedded in the mission of libraries throughout recent history (ALA 2002).
- "Minors and Internet Interactivity: An Interpretation of the Library Bill of Rights" acknowledges the need to protect minors' privacy online, not through prohibiting the use of social networking but rather through educating students how to be responsible, ethical, and safe. The interpretation underlines the key role librarians and teachers play in instructing students about online actions (ALA 2009).

The Rationale for Choose Privacy Week

According to Angela Maycock, assistant director of the ALA's Office for Intellectual Freedom (OIF), "One part of the (national) conversation about privacy is having libraries across the country participate in Choose Privacy Week, May 2–8, 2010. Much like Banned Books Week, Choose Privacy Week will raise awareness about privacy issues and get library users talking and thinking about what privacy means to them" (Maycock 2009).

Choose Privacy Week

Celebrated Annually

First Week in May

www.privacyrevolution.org

Privacyrevolution.org, the website associated with ALA's new privacy initiative, provides a succinct rationale for Choose Privacy Week. In a nutshell, it explains that technology provides the means to collect and analyze personal information from many sources that would have been impossible in a paper-only society. In exchange for the ability to use the Internet, individuals give up personal information through their online information seeking and purchasing, and their actions create records making them vulnerable to tracking by the government and others (ALA http://www.privacyrevolution.org/index.php/our-story/the_situation).

How Can School Libraries Participate in Choose Privacy Week?

To help observe Choose Privacy Week with students and staff, ALA has created posters, bookmarks, and buttons. They are available for purchase online through the ALA Store (http://www.alastore.ala.org). Additionally, ALA has published a *Choose Privacy Week Resource Guide* with basic information on privacy to enable school librarians to maintain student privacy and teach K–12 students about protecting their privacy in a digital age. The guide includes four lesson

The School Library Program Privacy Checklist

The privacy checklist has been renamed to acknowledge AASL's change from using the term "school library media center" to "school library." A revised version of the 2009 checklist is located in Chapter 6 of this book.

plans involving privacy instruction divided by grade level: K–2, 3–5, 6–8, and 9–12; the instructional plans were developed by members of the American Association of School Librarians Intellectual Freedom Committee. The "10 Steps to Privacy" discussion starter game is another instructional tool included in the guide; and although it is aimed at teens, it can be adapted for use in a middle school classroom. Throughout the guide, there are recommended resources that can be used to support classroom instruction on privacy. A "School Library Program Privacy Checklist," will help determine the status of students' privacy in the school library. The guide costs fifteen dollars and can be ordered from the ALA Store. Some districts are nearing the end of their instructional year in May; however, like Banned Books Week, Choose Privacy Week can be celebrated at any time during a school year. School librarians can be among the first to celebrate Choose Privacy Week in its inaugural year (2010).

ALA's Privacy Initiative Website

Librarians can read more about ALA's initiative at the website sponsored by ALA (http://www.privacyrevolution.org). It has a wealth of information including:

- A privacy myth buster list suitable for sharing with high school students and faculty
- Video clips on privacy issues such as "Know What's Posted about You Online," "Business and Consumer Perspectives on Privacy," and "2009 Internet Privacy: Are You in Control?"

There are also links to content on websites maintained by some of ALA's allies in the initiative such as the Privacy Rights Clearinghouse (http://www.privacyrights.org). It has a multitude of resources providing information on privacy basics, medical privacy, banking and finance privacy, online privacy, protecting privacy while shopping online, and privacy protections for social security numbers. This information can be used to prepare staff development programs.

The ALA website also encourages persons interested in reclaiming and retaining their personal privacy to complete a brief form to let their national legislators know their desire for policies and legislation to protect privacy. In May 2010, ALA will present to members of Congress the total number of persons who participated in the signature drive indicating that they want legal protection from the continuing assault on their personal privacy by surveillance, data mining, and other intrusive practices (ALA http://www.privacyrevolution.org/index.php/take_action/join_the_revolution).

> **Update on ALA's Privacy Initiative**
>
> Since the first Choose Privacy Week in 2010, the goal of the initiative has not changed. Libraries and librarians are still in the forefront of the battle to protect the privacy rights of Americans in their personal day-to-day online and non-cyber lives. The privacyrevolution.org website was redesigned in early 2013, and its content has expanded. A companion website (http://chooseprivacyweek.org) dedicated specifically to celebrating Choose Privacy Week was also launched in spring 2013 (American Library Association. privacyrevolution.org http://privacyrevolution.org [accessed January 16, 2013]).
>
> ALA's "@ your library" campaign also supports Choose Privacy Week and the general theme of protecting individuals' privacy. Promoting the privacy of children online has not been overlooked, as evidenced by the inclusion of "What Parents Should Know about Privacy Online" (http://atyourlibrary.org/connectwithyourkids/its-digital-world/what-parents-should-know-about-privacy-online) as part of the "Connect with your kids @ your library" section of the website.

Seeking Assistance for School Library Privacy Issues

As mentioned in a previous IF Matters column, the ALA Office for Intellectual Freedom encourages school librarians to call them for advice on matters relating to student privacy in school libraries. Deborah Caldwell-Stone, Deputy Director of the OIF, is an attorney and has particular expertise in the area of privacy. Telephone queries can be directed to the OIF staff at 1-800-545-2433, Ext. 4220, from 8:30–4:30 pm CST, Monday–Friday, or via email to oif@ala.org. *ALA/AASL membership is not required.*

REFERENCES

American Library Association. 2008. "*Code of Ethics of the American Library Association.*" http://www.ala.org/advocacy/proethics/codeofethics/codeethics (accessed January 16, 2013).

American Library Association. 2004. "Core Values of Librarianship." http://www.ala.org/ala/aboutala/offices/oif/statementspols/corevaluesstatement/corevalues.cfm (accessed January 16, 2013).

American Library Association. 2009. "Minors and Internet Interactivity: An Interpretation of the Library Bill of Rights." http://www.ala.org/advocacy/intfreedom/librarybill/interpretations/minorsinternetinteractivity (accessed January 16, 2013).

American Library Association. 2002. "Privacy: An Interpretation of the Library Bill of Rights." http://www.ala.org/advocacy/intfreedom/librarybill/interpretations/privacy (accessed January 16, 2013).

American Library Association. "Join the Revolution." privacyrevolution.org. http://www.privacy revolution.org/index.php/take_action/join_the_revolution (accessed February 22, 2013).

American Library Association. "The Situation." privacyrevolution.org. http://www.privacy revolution.org/index.php/our-story/the_situation (accessed February 22, 2013).

Maycock, Angela. Interview with author, October 22, 2009.

IF Matters: Intellectual Freedom @ your library®

The Intellectual Freedom Calendar: Another Advocacy Plan for the School Library

By Helen R. Adams

Originally published in the IF Matters: Intellectual Freedom @ your library® column, *School Library Monthly*, XXVIII (7) (April 2011): 52–53.

When school begins, many school librarians look forward to celebrating Banned Books Week in September. It is certainly a good starting point, but advocating for intellectual freedom should not be confined to that single week. Ways to celebrate intellectual freedom throughout the entire school year are suggested in a month by month calendar in this column. Ideas and resources are included to highlight intellectual freedom and educate administrators, teachers and other school staff, students, and parents about students' First Amendment right to use library resources and the confidentiality of students' library records.

August

Get the year off to a good start by focusing on the principal. S/he is the educational leader of the school and sets the tone. Make an appointment with the principal to:

- review the materials selection policy and reconsideration procedures and
- describe the areas of the collection on which you will focus selections this school year.

A principal who is knowledgeable about the selection of library resources and the reconsideration process will not easily yield to a demand to remove an "inappropriate" book or other resources from the school library without following the district's reconsideration process.

Arrange with the principal for an opportunity to speak to teachers about how library materials are selected, to solicit suggestions for library resources, and to review reconsideration procedures. Ensure transparency in materials selection by posting the materials selection policy and reconsideration procedures on the library's website.

September

Train library staff, volunteers, and student assistants to keep student library records confidential. Discuss students' privacy when using the library and library record confidentiality with the principal, and schedule an after-school privacy information session for teachers. Model protecting the confidentiality of student library records when students, teachers, or the principal asks who has a library resource checked out.

Two Additional September Events

Banned Websites Awareness Day (BWAD) was created in 2011 by the AASL Board of Directors and is celebrated annually during Banned Books Week. The day focuses attention on the overly aggressive Internet filtering practices that impede teachers and students from using legitimate educational websites. The AASL website has more information about BWAD and resources for recognizing the day (http://www.ala.org/aasl/bwad). Revised in 2012, ALA's "Libraries and the Internet Toolkit" is another valuable resource for observing BWAD. The Toolkit explains the requirements of the Children's Internet Protection Act, recommends guidelines for items to include in acceptable use policies for schools, and connects teaching about digital citizenship to AASL's *Standards for the 21st-Century Learner* (http://www.ifmanual.org/litoolkit).

Constitution Day and Citizenship Day (dual observances on a single day) were created by federal law in 2004 and are celebrated annually on September 17. The day has double significance in that it recognizes the signing of the U.S. Constitution in 1787 and the status of being a U.S. citizen, natural (native born) and naturalized (Cornell University Law School Legal Information Institute. 2004. 36 USC § 106—Constitution Day and Citizenship Day. http://www.law.cornell.edu/uscode/text/36/106 [accessed January 16, 2013]). In 2005, the Department of Education (DOE) announced the requirement that all educational institutions that receive federal funding from the DOE must acknowledge the day with an educational program (U.S. Federal Register. 2005. "Department of Education Notice of Implementation of Constitution and Citizenship Day." May 24, 2005. 70 no. 99. http://www2.ed.gov/legislation/FedRegister/other/2005-2/052405b.html [accessed January 16, 2013]).

Celebrate **Banned Books Week** during the last week in September. Provide teachers with information for downloading the "Censorship Creates Blindness—Read" poster from the First Amendment First-Aid Kit website. Share the Association for Library Services to Children (ALSC) brochure, "Kids Know Your Rights," with students. The American Library Association (ALA) website includes ideas for activities and displays. Where there is administrative resistance to the phrase "banned books," refocus the topic as promoting the "right to read." Create a display using the Freedom to Read Foundation's (FTRF) tag line "Free People Read Freely" (FTRF).

October

Focus on parents! Establish regular communication with parents and community members through a "library column" in the school newsletter or on the library's blog. Provide information on such topics as checkout policies, online library resources accessible remotely by students at home, new books added to the collection, and upcoming special events such as a book fair.

Sponsor a library open house during parent/teacher conferences. Create bookmarks with the library's website address and information about grade appropriate online resources students can access from home. Demonstrate the resources, and emphasize that the library provides information on many topics from varying points of view to teach students to critically evaluate information and reach their own conclusions.

November

If overly restrictive filtering is limiting access to educationally useful websites for instruction and student research, share your concerns with the principal. Describe the educationally appropriate sites blocked by faculty and students and suggest establishing a faculty committee to study the issue and make recommendations.

Request five minutes during faculty meetings to introduce a topic related to intellectual freedom. For example, highlight library resources and services to support students with physical, cognitive, and learning disabilities; or make a case for *not* restricting students' library reading choices to only those books on Accelerated Reader or other reading management program lists.

December

Help students understand the First Amendment and their right to freedom of speech and expression. Collaborate with social studies teachers to observe the **Bill of Rights Day** on December 15, the date the first ten amendments to the U.S. Constitution were ratified. Make the connection between democracy and the need for citizens to be well-informed and have access to information from many perspectives. Check out resources at the National Archives, the Library of Congress, and the National Constitution Center with its interactive Bill of Rights Game.

Using holiday treats, lure teachers and the principal to peruse new books. Discuss with staff additional resources to support their curricula.

January

Get better acquainted with families by initiating a book club for parents. Introduce some of the best new contemporary children's and YA literature and candidly discuss the portrayal of youth, family, and societal issues. Emphasize how students learn to question and think more critically through their encounters with new ideas in books.

February

Post the *Library Bill of Rights* and the *Code of Ethics of the ALA* in the library, and be prepared for questions and "teachable moment" conversations with students, faculty, and the principal!

March

Share "Minors and Internet Interactivity: An Interpretation of the Library Bill of Rights" with the principal and offer to introduce faculty to selected Web 2.0 tools aimed at increasing student 21st-century technology literacy skills and personal expression online.

Advocacy Resources for Intellectual Freedom

Banned Books Week

- **ALA Resources:** http://www.ala.org/ala/issues advocacy/banned/bannedbooksweek/index.cfm

- **Banned Books Week:** http://www.bannedbooks week.org

- **Censorship Creates Blindness (downloadable poster):** http://www.randomhouse.com/teens/ firstamendment

- **ALSC Kids Know Your Rights (4 page flyer):** http://www.ala.org/ala/mgrps/divs/alsc/issuesadv/ intellectualfreedom/kidsknowyourrights.pdf

Banned Websites Awareness Day

- **AASL BWAD:** http://www.ala.org/aasl/bwad

Constitution Day and Citizenship Day

- **Constitution Day:** http://www.constitutionday.com

- **Center for Civic Education (lesson plans):** http://www.constitutionday.us/link_frameset.asp?url =http://www.civiced.org/byrd

- **National Archives:** http://www.constitutionday .us/link_frameset.asp?url=http://www.archives.gov/ education/lessons/constitution-day

Bill of Rights Day

- **National Archives:** http://www.archives.gov/ exhibits/charters/charters.html

- **Library of Congress:** http://memory.loc.gov/ ammem/today/dec15.html

- **National Constitution Center (Bill of Rights game):** http://constitutioncenter.org/billofrightsgame

School Library Month: http://www.ala.org/aasl/slm

Choose Privacy Week

- **ALA Store:** http://www.alastore.ala.org/ (Search: Choose Privacy Week)

- **ALA Privacy Website:** http://privacyrevolution.org

- **Privacy Lesson Plans:** http://www.privacy revolution.org/images/uploads/SchoolLibraryLessons .pdf (paste url into browser)

Showcase the creations during spring parent/teacher conferences and gain support for the use of Web 2.0 technology for instruction.

More Information about School Library Month

AASL has been celebrating School Library Month since 1985. Each year the theme changes, and school librarians are given online resources to showcase the school library program to principals, teachers, parents, local officials, and legislators. The materials often include a proclamation, a poster and graphics for the library's website, prerecorded public service announcements, and ideas for special activities for the month (AASL. 2013. "School Library Month." http://www.ala.org/aasl/aaslissues/slm/schoollibrary [accessed January 16, 2013]).

Update on Choose Privacy Week

In May 2013, a new website dedicated to celebrating Choose Privacy Week was launched at http://www.chooseprivacyweek.org/. Like School Library Month, the theme for Choose Privacy Week changes annually. The 2012 theme was "Freedom from Surveillance," spotlighting how government surveillance impacts Americans' civil liberties (ALA. 2012. "Voices for Privacy" (blog). http://www.privacyrevolution.org [accessed January 16, 2013]). The 2013 theme is "Who's Tracking You" and promotes the idea that Americans need to be aware of the ways in which their personal data is collected, allowing their online actions to be monitored (ALA. "2013 Choose Privacy Week Set." ALA Store. http://www.alastore.ala.org/SearchResult.aspx?KeyWords=cpw [accessed January 18, 2013]).

School Library Summer Book Checkout Program

Because many of her students are unable to go to the public library, Catherine Beyers, an elementary librarian in Wisconsin, increased her students' access to books in the summer by starting a school library summer book checkout program. According to Catherine:

Summer library book checkout began about six years ago at Southern Bluffs Elementary. This is how it works. I send a permission

April

April is **School Library Month.** Use the 2011 theme, "create your own story@ your library," and resources on the AASL website to plan activities. Tie the theme to intellectual freedom by sponsoring a contest for students to tell their stories of why the school library is important to them and how it supports their learning as "citizens in training." Share ideas and events with colleagues by posting them on the AASL Blog, the School Library Month Facebook Fan Page, or Twitter.

May

Spotlight students' right to privacy during ALA's **Choose Privacy Week** during the first week in May annually or at another time during the school year. Use the ALA *Choose Privacy Week Resource Guide*, available from the ALA Store, to gain knowledge about minors' privacy in school libraries. Teach students to protect their privacy using four online lesson plans developed by AASL's Intellectual Freedom Committee and aimed at grades K–2, 3–5, 6–8, and 9–12.

June

Extend students' reading choices and information access during the summer. Team with the public library youth services librarian(s) to initiate a public library card signup for students and help kick-off the **summer reading program** for children and teens.

Schedule a final meeting with the principal to report on library program accomplishments, including advocacy for intellectual freedom and privacy, and confer about program goals for next year.

Encouraging Thoughts

School librarians are a major force in protecting intellectual freedom in their libraries and having allies who support students' access to information can make the school climate friendly to intellectual freedom. It may take years, but progress in educating about students' First Amendment and privacy rights in school libraries can be made one teacher, principal, parent, and student at a time.

REFERENCE

Freedom to Read Foundation. "Free People Read Freely (tagline)." http://www.ftrf.org (accessed February 22, 2013).

letter home to families in mid-May to allow parents to decide whether they want their children to borrow between 10 and 20 books for summer reading. Parents are notified in the letter that they are responsible for the books and that they must be returned promptly in the fall. I provide the bag (donated by friends and colleagues and supplemented with conference bags) to transport the books and a list of the titles their child has selected.

In past years students in grades one through four participated, and we usually have about 90–100 children check out books. *I've never lost a book or had one damaged during the summer book checkout project.* We circulated approximately 1,800 books during the 2011 summer. Each student receives a free paperback book of his or her choice when their books are returned. The free books are from various sources: extra books received as book club premiums, gently used books donated by families, free copies from conference vendors, and some purchased for the purpose

(Beyers, Catherine, email messages to the author, May 2 and 4, 2012).

Key Ideas Summary

Readings in this chapter discuss advocacy for school libraries and describe specific celebrations, activities, and strategies that school librarians can use to promote students' intellectual freedom and privacy. Major ideas include:

- There are five steps that school librarians can take to improve the climate of intellectual freedom in their schools:

    1. Be knowledgeable about current and historical intellectual freedom issues.

    2. Address local intellectual freedom issues rather than ignoring them or appeasing those who would limit students' access to information.

    3. Review and revise library program policies to align them with the ALA *Code of Ethics* and the *Library Bill of Rights*.

    4. Create an advocacy plan to educate the school community about intellectual freedom.

    5. Join library, educational technology, and/or pro–First Amendment organizations and work to promote intellectual freedom issues and the battle against censorship.

- School librarians have been educated about intellectual freedom and have knowledge of how the First Amendment right of free speech and major First Amendment court decisions impact students' use of resources in the school library. Administrators and teachers, on the other hand, rarely learn this information in their college courses.

- As a local intellectual freedom "expert," a school librarian has the responsibility to educate teaching colleagues and the principal about intellectual freedom through a formal advocacy campaign to promote and protect minors' access to information in the school library.

- Parents can be allies and support school library programs, but, out of concern and possibly because of their personal perspectives and biases, they may also ask school librarians to remove an "inappropriate" book that concerns them or prohibit their child(ren) from checking out selected book titles, series, or genres. These requests are counter to the ALA *Library Bill of Rights* and the *Code of Ethics* that direct school librarians' practice.

- Parents are legally responsible for guiding the education of their children, including their choices of reading materials. Parents who desire to restrict their child's access to specific library materials should convey that message directly to their child.

The librarian should not be involved in enforcing a family's values and thereby limiting a student's access to library materials.

- There are many strategies a school librarian can use to help parents understand how library materials are selected, how "choice" impacts students' reading selections, how to assist their child(ren) in selecting books that fit their social, emotional and cognitive development, and why books should not be removed from the library collection without following district reconsideration process.

- To be productive adult citizens, students must first learn about their rights, especially their First Amendment right to free speech. The school librarian should be an integral part of teaching this information.

- Court decisions, including the *Right to Read Defense Committee v. School Committee of the City of Chelsea* (1978), *Case v. Unified School District* (1995), and *Counts v. Cedarville School District* (2003), have given minors the right to receive information through free inquiry and to make personal reading choices in a school library. The ALA Office for Intellectual Freedom website includes an explanation of First Amendment court cases relevant to library users' rights including the three highlighted cases (http://www.ala.org/offices/oif/firstamendment/courtcases/courtcases).

- Consider two strategies to protect students' intellectual freedom and retain your school library position: educate the principal and develop a network of supporters.

- Begin by discussing with the principal the district's selection policy and the reconsideration process and explaining how you use the policy to select materials for the school library collection. Gradually educate the principal about students' First Amendment right to read, view, and listen to library resources.

- In addition to working with the principal, develop an intellectual freedom network of allies that could include teachers, students, parents, community members, and public library staff.

- Banned Books Week is an annual celebration during the last week in September to acknowledge Americans' right to read books they choose regardless of whether the ideas, language, or images are controversial or offend others.

- Because of personal bias and fear of parental objections, some principals are concerned about or disapprove of having displays and library programs related to banned or frequently challenged books.

- Pointing out censorship of books only once during the school year is insufficient to help students understand their First Amendment rights in the school library. Promoting the personal right to read, view, and hear the expression of others should be an ongoing advocacy campaign throughout the year.

- Choose Privacy Week is an ALA initiative begun in 2010 to highlight the erosion of privacy among Americans in their physical world and online lives. Activities and resources associated with the annual event are located on the chooseprivacyweek.org website.

- The ALA Office for Intellectual Freedom staff provides guidance on library privacy issues and encourages school librarians to call for assistance about concerns related to student privacy. Membership in AASL or ALA is not required for those seeking help.

- Advocating for intellectual freedom requires regular, intentional planning along with formal and informal programming aimed at the school community (the principal, teachers, support staff, students, school board, parents, and extended family members) throughout the school year.

- There are numerous "special" events throughout the year that naturally promote the principles of intellectual freedom, library privacy, and minors' First Amendment free speech rights in libraries. These include, but are not limited to, Banned Books Week, Banned Websites Awareness Day, Constitution Day and Citizenship Day, Bill of Rights Day, School Library Month, and Choose Privacy Week.

Resource Roundup:
Intellectual Freedom Advocacy

- **@ your library (The Campaign for America's Libraries). http://www.atyourlibrary.org**

School librarians cannot carry the banner for intellectual freedom alone; they must have allies among administrators, teachers, students, parents, and community members. ALA's @ your library campaign reaches out virtually to library users through its website and spotlights the value of libraries and librarians. Subtle messages to parents promoting privacy, access, and online safety are woven into its web pages, especially in the "Connect with Your Kids," "Teen Spotlight," and "It's a Digital World" sections of the website.

- **AASL. School Libraries Count! http://www.ala.org/aasl/researchandstatistics/ slcsurvey/slcsurvey**

Since 2007, AASL has been sponsoring an annual "School Libraries Count!" survey to gather information about the status of America's school libraries. The majority of the questions are repeated, but each year a special topic is examined. The 2009 survey asked supplementary questions about services to English language learners. The 2010 extra questions centered on moving from print to digital content in the school library. The 2011 survey questions focused on filtering Internet resources. Each school that participates has access to personalized reports that compare a local school's data to those programs of similar size and grade level both in the school's state and nationwide. The information can be used by the school librarian to advocate for students' intellectual freedom in areas of budgets, resources, staffing, hours of operation, and other measures.

- **Coatney, Sharon, ed. 2010. *The Many Faces of School Library Leadership*. Santa Barbara, California: Libraries Unlimited.**

Former elementary librarian Sharon Coatney collected ten essays on leadership covering various aspects of school library professional practice, including intellectual freedom, inquiry, curriculum, technology, advocacy, and literacy. Ken Haycock's essay explains the concept of informal power, or "leading from the middle," and David Loertscher considers how leadership is integral to moving from more traditional school libraries to the new vision of a learning commons.

- **Hartzell, Gary N. 2003.** *Building Influence for the School Librarian: Tenets, Targets, and Tactics* **(2nd ed.). Worthington, Ohio: Linworth Publishing.**

Although older, this book maintains value from the experiences and perspectives of the author (a former principal, superintendent, and retired university instructor preparing school administrators) who gives advice to school librarians from an administrator's perspective.

- **Levitov, Deborah D., editor. 2012.** *Activism and the School Librarian: Tools for Advocacy and Survival.* **Santa Barbara, California: Libraries Unlimited.**

Comprised of carefully selected articles originally published in *School Library Monthly*, this book describes various types of advocacy and activism including legislative advocacy aimed at influencing legislation and funding, and local advocacy in support of district and school programs. It includes realistic experience-tested advice from expert practitioners and useful tools to meet advocacy goals.

- **Library Research Services. "School Library Impact Studies." http://www.lrs.org/impact.php**

Staff at Library Research Services (LRS), a part of the Colorado State Library and linked to the Colorado Department of Education, began studying the effect of school libraries on student achievement in Colorado in 1993 and continued in twenty other states from 2000 through 2010. The school library impact studies repeatedly report that student learning and scores on state tests are better when there is a full-time state certified school librarian, when the library has sufficient funding to provide a well-stocked collection, and when access to technology is connected to library resources. Another important indicator is the presence of school librarians taking leadership roles: meeting regularly with the principal, serving on school committees, collaborating with teachers, and providing staff development. School librarians can use the LRS information to advocate for full-time professionals in each library, which anecdotally improves the opportunity for a more positive intellectual freedom climate in the school.

- *School Library Monthly.* **http://www.schoollibrarymonthly.com**

Each issue of *School Library Monthly* includes an article on advocacy written by successful school library advocates. An article in the May/June 2012 issue focused on creating a school library advocacy plan and using an annual report with graphs, photos, and links to showcase how the school library program contributes to student learning. Selected articles are online at the magazine's website (http://www.schoollibrarymonthly.com/articles/index.html).

Discussion Questions

- The word "censorship" is often used indiscriminately. Define, in your own terms, the difference between a "challenge" and "censorship."

- How is advocacy for students' intellectual freedom similar to, yet different from, advocacy for school library programs? Consider such factors as the First Amendment and professional ethics.

- In the column "New Year's Resolutions and Resources," with which resolution (numbered 1–5) would you begin, and what would be your initial three steps?

- If the principal is hesitant about having displays of "banned" books in the library during Banned Books Week, what alternate strategy could you use to help students understand censorship?

- Describe two ways that you, as a school librarian, can help your principal understand intellectual freedom and its importance for students using the school library.

- Discuss how you would manage a situation in which the parent of an elementary child asks you to restrict her child from checking out books on (you select the topic). Include in your answer the impact of such factors as 1) the parents' responsibility for guiding their child's education; 2) the principles found in the *Library Bill of Rights* and the *Code of Ethics*; 3) whether your library's circulation records are automated; and 4) the difficulties of limiting student checkout to a selected title or series.

- Selecting an elementary, middle school, or high school setting, describe two ways in which you could teach students about how the First Amendment impacts their right to read and seek information in a school library and, subsequently, become more informed citizens.

Chapter 9

The Future of Intellectual Freedom in School Libraries

Including

"Fewer School Librarians: The Effect on Students' Intellectual Freedom"

"Solo Librarians and Intellectual Freedom: Perspectives from the Field"

Chapter 9

The Future of Intellectual Freedom in School Libraries

INTRODUCTION

Students' intellectual freedom is tightly bound to having full-time knowledgeable school librarians who support minors' First Amendment rights. Amid evidence of the decrease in full-time school librarians across the United States, this chapter focuses on the future of intellectual freedom in school libraries and whether it can continue to exist and thrive without the active advocacy and leadership of a school library professional.

What's in This Chapter?

The first reading, "Fewer School Librarians: The Effect on Students' Intellectual Freedom," asks an important question: What will happen to students' intellectual freedom if there is no school librarian to champion minors' access to library resources? One answer is provided by a former Arizona school librarian who shares a true story of what happened when (with no librarian serving the school) an untrained library clerk made a purchasing error and caused a ripple effect in the library collections of other schools. Another answer is found in the column's lengthy list of actions that school librarians regularly take to protect (and educate about) intellectual freedom and privacy; these actions will cease and diminish students' intellectual freedom.

The second article, "Solo Librarians and Intellectual Freedom: Perspectives from the Field," was originally published in the American Association of School Librarians' (AASL) journal *Knowledge Quest*. It focuses on whether intellectual freedom can remain a high priority if there is a single librarian for an entire school district. Three solo school librarians in the Midwest speak from experience about their intellectual freedom goals and being realistic in what they can accomplish. They answer the question "What can one person accomplish?"

Reflections on the Future of Intellectual Freedom

School librarians may take intellectual freedom for granted, not considering its very recent history in the United States. The core intellectual freedom documents of the American Library Association (ALA) were all written in the past seventy-five years: The *Library Bill of Rights* (1939), the *Code of Ethics* (1938), and the *Freedom to Read* statement (1953) (ALA 2010, 49, 305, 206). The ALA Office for Intellectual Freedom (OIF) was founded on December 1, 1967 (ALA http://www.ala.org/offices/oif), and the Freedom to Read Foundation (FTRF) was established in 1969 (ALA http://www.ala.org/groups/affiliates/relatedgroups/freedomtoreadfoundation/ aboutftrf/aboutftrf). The first *Intellectual Freedom Manual* was published in 1974 in a three-ring notebook format (ALA 2010, xii), and the LeRoy C. Merritt Humanitarian Fund, described in Chapter 3, was created in 1970 (ALA http://www.ala.org/groups/affiliates/relatedgroups/ merrittfund/merritthumanitarian). Judith Krug was the first executive director of both the OIF and FTRF from their inception to her death in 2009. The more than forty years of Krug's leadership can be considered as the "golden age" of intellectual freedom at ALA and established the basis for the important work currently being undertaken.

The future of intellectual freedom in school libraries is likely to be similar to its past. Some individuals will want to protect children from "bad books" and ideas that (from their perspective) might corrupt them or destroy their innocence. To books, librarians can add all the other forms of expression found in libraries—resources such as magazines, e-books, audio books, DVDs, web pages and others. The format does not change the need to defend students' right to read, view, and hear the expression (a.k.a. free speech right under the First Amendment) of others. The emphasis on technology and use of Web tools in many schools and libraries does not diminish the need for intellectual freedom. Instead, it increases its importance because of the continually increasing means of human expression afforded by technology.

In the 2010 edition of *Banned Books: Challenging Our Freedom to Read*, Robert P. Doyle compiled an extensive list of banned and challenged books reaching back in history to 1121 (*Introduction to Theology* by Pierre Abelard) and ending in 2010 with examples such as *Anne Frank: The Diary of a Young Girl* among the titles challenged that year (Doyle 2010, 130, 199). It appears that censors have been present throughout history and continue trying to restrict library users from freely choosing what they want to read. In Doyle's compilation of censorship attempts, Judy Blume holds the record for a single author's books being questioned with twelve children's and young adult books being repeatedly challenged, restricted, and/or removed, including *Forever, It's Not the End of the World*, and *Blubber* (Doyle 2010, 151–154).

> **Censorship: An Unusual Beginning**
>
> In 443 BC, the Roman government created the office of censor with the goal of molding its citizens' character. Censorship was considered in a positive light as part of governance. Over time, however, the positive nature of being a censor to guide the moral strength of citizens and members of a religious faith has turned the word "censor" into a pejorative term (Beacon of Free Expression. "On Censorship" http://www.beaconforfreedom .org/liste.html?tid=415 [accessed January 16, 2013]).

On balance, however, ardent individuals, groups, and organizations continue supporting minors' intellectual freedom. The ALA remains strong in its defense of intellectual freedom as one of the profession's core values, and the OIF staff work tirelessly to meet the requests for help and to monitor for new threats to intellectual freedom. The members of ALA's Intellectual Freedom Committee diligently review and update ALA's intellectual freedom documents; within two years (2009–2010), four new interpretations of the *Library Bill of Rights* were added ("Services to Persons with Disabilities," "Minors and Internet Interactivity," the "Importance of Education to Intellectual Freedom," and "Prisoners' Right to Read").

The FTRF Board of Trustees continues to approve legal actions and financial grants to assist pro-First Amendment litigants with their legal expenses. In January 2012, the FTRF Board voted to approve its new strategic plan that will guide its future actions, including 1) creating a plan to become more proactive in litigation as a plaintiff (originator of a lawsuit) rather than filing an *amicus curiae* brief (a "friend of the court" statement to support the argument of one side in a lawsuit [Free Dictionary]); 2) increasing educational programming for lawyers, librarians, and library and information technologies students; and 3) mentoring new (and younger) intellectual freedom advocates (FTRF). The latter is of special importance to help young adults understand that intellectual freedom encompasses the right to read and access information in print and any electronic format and that technology has created a new set of issues that affect them.

Outside of the ALA and the FTRF, trustees of the LeRoy C. Merritt Humanitarian Fund meet annually to provide financial assistance to librarians defending intellectual freedom. State library organizations also foster and support librarians who face intellectual freedom issues. Undergraduate and graduate library programs instill in pre-service librarians the principles of intellectual freedom and their role in protecting patrons' First Amendment right to free speech as interpreted from court decisions. Finally, those organizations recognized in Chapter 7 as part of the "community of the book" (Association of American Publishers, American Booksellers Foundation for Free Expression, and others) also follow their missions of protecting First Amendment free expression for library users.

Chapter 1 began with a recipe for intellectual freedom, and through nine chapters, the ingredients and instructions remained the same. Maintaining the essence of intellectual freedom still requires a dedicated school librarian with supportive allies. As a quote from the second reading in this chapter states, "One person can accomplish a lot, but recruiting allies increases the likelihood of protecting students' First Amendment right to access library resources" (Adams 2011, 33). Whatever format school library resources take in the future, the framework of individual supporters, professional library associations, and other pro-First Amendment organizations is in place to support intellectual freedom in all types of libraries.

There are, however, two overarching questions: 1) Will there be professionally trained school librarians employed in schools to protect students' First Amendment and privacy rights? and 2) Will those school librarians stand up to protect their students' intellectual freedom in school libraries, even at the risk of their jobs? The answer to the first question is in debate in many districts as school budgets and state finances worsen. In some places, the value of school librarians is unquestioned; in other places, however, school librarians are quickly sacrificed. Advocacy campaigns for school librarians and their programs are occurring across the country, but the outcomes are uncertain.

The response to the second question is very personal and lies in the inner strength of each school librarian. It depends on how much an individual is willing—or financially able—to jeopardize for an ethical principle. Some will have the passion and freedom to do so. Others (those who are the sole support a family or do not want children or other family members exposed to an adversarial atmosphere, for example) may concede that they have done all they can do by bringing an intellectual freedom issue to a principal's attention, advocating for following district policy (such as the reconsideration process in a library resource challenge), or supporting less restrictive local filtering practices (Adams 2008, 133). These are very private, agonizing choices with both rewards and consequences. The answers to both questions will influence the future of intellectual freedom in a school library.

REFERENCES

Adams, Helen R. 2008. *Ensuring Intellectual Freedom and Access to Information in the School Library Media Program*. Westport, Connecticut: Libraries Unlimited.

Adams, Helen R. 2011. "Solo Librarians and Intellectual Freedom: Perspectives from the Field." *Knowledge Quest* 40, no. 2 (2011): 30–35.

American Library Association. "About the Freedom to Read Foundation." http://www.ala.org/groups/affiliates/relatedgroups/freedomtoreadfoundation/aboutftrf/aboutftrf (accessed July 9, 2012). (Note: In August 2012, the Freedom to Read Foundation moved to a new website: http://www.ftrf.org/.)

American Library Association. 2010. *Intellectual Freedom Manual*. 8th ed. Chicago, Illinois: American Library Association.

American Library Association. "LeRoy C. Merritt Humanitarian Fund." "In Memorium." http://www.ala.org/groups/affiliates/relatedgroups/merrittfund/merritthumanitarian (accessed January 16, 2013).

American Library Association. Office for Intellectual Freedom. "Office for Intellectual Freedom: Mission." http://www.ala.org/offices/oif (accessed January 16, 2013).

Free Dictionary. "Friend of the Court." http://legal-dictionary.thefreedictionary.com/friend+of+the+court (accessed January 16, 2013).

Freedom to Read Foundation. 2012. "FTRF Report to ALA Council. Strategic Plan: Securing the Future, Renewing Our Commitment." March 1, 2012. *Newsletter on Intellectual Freedom* 61, no. 2: 53.

Q & A about Job Loss

The online "What IF?" collection of questions and answers about intellectual freedom in practice, managed at the Cooperative Children's Book Center (CCBC) at the School of Education, University of Wisconsin-Madison, includes several questions on the threat of job loss for school librarians related to the defense of minors' First Amendment right to receive information in school libraries.

The Question: Could I someday lose my job as a school librarian because someone challenges a book in the library?

The Answer: http://www.education.wisc.edu/ccbc/freedom/whatif/archiveDetails.asp?idIFQuestions=42 (accessed January 16, 2013).

The Question: How do you balance censorship and selection if you have an administrator who has implied that if there are complaints received about library materials, then the materials budget, or even your position, is in jeopardy?

The Answer: http://www.education.wisc.edu/ccbc/freedom/whatif/archiveDetails.asp?idIFQuestions=66 (accessed January 16, 2013).

IF Matters: Intellectual Freedom @ your library®

Fewer School Librarians: The Effect on Students' Intellectual Freedom

By Helen R. Adams

Originally published in the IF Matters: Intellectual Freedom @ your library® column, *School Library Monthly*, XXVII (6) (March 2011): 52–53.

In recent years, school districts have been eliminating or reducing school librarian positions, and giving those remaining on the job more responsibilities in multiple schools. In some schools, library assistants and volunteers, who once worked under the direction of a school library professional, are now operating libraries.

A Map with Consequences

In March 2010, Shonda Brisco, assistant professor and curriculum materials librarian at Oklahoma State University, posted a Google map titled "A Nation without School Librarians" (http://tinyurl.com/253ehp3). Red and blue flags on the map represent communities that have either cut certified school librarian positions (blue flag) or are requiring those professionals remaining to work in two or more school library programs (red flag) (http://tinyurl.com/253ehp3). The map tells a story; and behind every flag, there are hundreds, sometimes thousands, of students with diminished access to the resources, instruction, and the services that school librarians provide. Elementary school library professional staffing is especially threatened. The graphical representation is disheartening to those who understand the positive impact school librarians have on student academic achievement as evidenced by state school library impact studies (http://www.lrs.org/impact.php).

> **School Library Impact Studies**
>
> Learn more about school library impact studies conducted by the Colorado-based Library Research Service (http://www.lrs.org) in the Resource Roundup near the end of Chapter 8.

The map reveals that in spring 2010, the Fullerton Joint Union High School District (California) eliminated four teacher librarian positions saving approximately $440,000, but *leaving only two school library professionals to serve six high schools* with assistance from one library technician per building (http://tinyurl.com/253ehp3). Local media reported, ". . . these libraries lost their greatest resource, the person who makes all that the library has to offer come alive. . . . these teacher librarians offer cyber-safety lessons, teach students how to cite reputable sources, how to integrate video with class assignments, . . ." (http://www.ocregister.com/articles/school -271735-teacher-students.html). Students at Troy High School notice the difference with one library user stating, "No one knows as much as Ms. Slim [teacher librarian Marie Slim] did. Students would come in and she'd help them with essays and projects. There's just no one to do that anymore" (http://www.ocregister.com/articles/school-271735-teacher-students.html).

What Will Happen If . . .?

The "Nation without School Librarians" map is alarming to those who value students' intellectual freedom and the role school librarians have in protecting minors' First Amendment right to access information. According to the American Library Association, between 2001 and 2009, 4,312 challenges were reported to the ALA Office for Intellectual Freedom (http://www.ala .org/ala/issuesadvocacy/banned/frequently challenged/21stcenturychallenged/index.cfm). Intellectual freedom is fragile if it is not nurtured and defended vigorously.

What will happen to students' intellectual freedom if there is no school librarian to:

- ensure the existence of library policies related to materials selection, reconsideration of a resource, circulation of resources, confidentiality of library records, interlibrary loan, and Internet use,

- model best practices in selection of library resources by resisting outside pressures to avoid selecting materials considered by some to be controversial,

- demonstrate leadership when there is a formal challenge to a library resource,

- educate administrators and teachers proactively about materials selection, reconsideration of library materials, and how to respond to a complaint about a library resource,

- protect the First Amendment right of children and young adults to receive information in a school library,

- speak out against restricting students' choice of library books based on computerized reading management programs title lists and assigned reading levels,

- advocate for the reduction of overly restrictive filtering that limits students' access to constitutionally protected information online,

- champion the rights of students with special needs and provide access to library resources and services for students with physical, cognitive, and learning disabilities,

---

Update on Challenges: The Numbers and What They Could Mean

Annually in early spring, the ALA Office for Intellectual Freedom (OIF) reports on the top ten most frequently challenged books of the prior year as *reported* to that office. Since this column was published in March 2011, new book challenge totals reported to OIF are available for 2010 (348 challenges) and 2011 (326 challenges). Between 2001 and 2011, there were 4,986 challenges to library and classroom resources, with generally more than 400 to more than 500 in all years except for 2010 and 2011 (American Library Association Office for Intellectual Freedom. 2011. "Frequently Challenged Books of the 21st Century." http://www.ala.org/advocacy/banned/ frequentlychallenged/21stcenturychallenged#2010 [accessed January 16, 2013]).

Is there any significance to the reduction in the number of reported challenges in 2010 and 2011? Are there:

- fewer concerned persons formally challenging library and classroom resources?

- fewer individuals reporting challenges to the OIF?

- library materials being removed by the principal, the librarian, or volunteers without due process occurring?

- a smaller number of school librarians to ensure that their district-approved reconsideration processes occur and who later report the result to OIF?

Or does the answer lie in a combination of the four?

As noted in Chapter 3 of this book, in 2011 ALA OIF began a "Defend the Right to Read" campaign to encourage librarians to report all challenges to OIF. OIF staff estimate that only 20 to 25 percent of formal challenges are communicated to ALA (American Library Association Office for Intellectual Freedom. 2011. "It's Everybody's Job to Report Challenges." October 26, 2011. OIF Blog. http://www.oif .ala.org/oif/?p=2879 [accessed January 16, 2013]).

- welcome and provide resources and support for English language learners,
- reflect on ways in which the library staff can support the learning needs of homeless children and young adults,
- create flexible solutions for children from low-income families to overcome economic barriers such as fines for overdue materials,
- maintain the confidentiality of students' library records,
- guard the privacy of students using library resources,
- teach students to "Respect the principles of intellectual freedom," a student responsibility within Standard 3 of AASL's *Standards for the 21st-Century Learner* (AASL 2007), and
- build support for students' access to information with the principal, school staff, students, parents, and community members.

Former school librarian Ann Dutton Ewbank supplies one answer to the question what will happen if there is no school library professional.

In December 2005, I was the President-elect of the Arizona Library Association. Our state Superintendent of Instruction, Tom Horne, sent a letter to all Arizona K–12 principals warning them about "morally objectionable" materials in school libraries. The book in question was *The Perks of Being a Wallflower* by Stephen Chbosky. While Horne did not have authority to remove the book from school libraries, he strongly encouraged principals to review the book. The source of the complaint was the grandmother of a 6th grade student who had obtained the book from her K–6 school library. After some investigation, I discovered that the clerk who operated the library ordered the book because it was designated "4th grade reading level" in the Accelerated Reader program, and therefore, inappropriately selected the book for this elementary school population.

Horne's remarks prompted the removal of the book from several middle school and high school libraries across Arizona who didn't want to invite controversy. This unfortunate situation could have been prevented if a certified school librarian, with appropriate training and an understanding of the difference between "reading level" and "interest level," had been responsible for materials selection. (Ewbank 2010)

Act for Intellectual Freedom

There's an app for protecting intellectual freedom in school libraries; it is a school librarian! Students will not learn about the principles of intellectual freedom unless a full-time school librarian is in place. If students' full access to library resources and patron privacy are to survive, remaining school librarians and professional associations must take action. The American Association of School Librarians provides a wide range of advocacy tools on its website (http://www.ala.org/aasl/aasl issues/toolkits/toolkits), especially the "School Library Program Health and Wellness Toolkit."

Act for School Libraries and Student Learning (Act4SL) is an independent advocacy group supporting legislation at the federal level to require a full-time certified school librarian in all publicly funded schools (http://act4sl.wikispaces.com). Its wiki hosts a grass roots plan and resources to persuade legislators. *All school librarians must Act4IF* (Act for Intellectual Freedom). Strategies to promote intellectual freedom throughout the school year can be found in Chapter 8, "Advocating for Intellectual Freedom."

REFERENCES

Act4SL. http://act4sl.wikispaces.com/ (accessed January 16, 2013).

American Library Association. "Frequently Challenged Books of the 21st Century." http://www.ala.org/ala/issues advocacy/banned/frequentlychallenged/21stcenturychallenged/index.cfm (accessed January 16, 2013).

American Association of School Librarians. 2007. *Standards for the 21st-Century Learner.* American Library Association. http://www.ala.org/aasl/standards (accessed January 16, 2013).

Brisco, Shonda. 2010. "A Nation without School Librarians." http://tinyurl.com/253ehp3 (accessed January 16, 2013).

Cabrera, Yvette. 2010. "Fullterton Teacher Librarian is Last One Standing." October 18, 2010. Orange County Register. http://www.ocregister.com/articles/school-271735-teacher-students.html (accessed January 16, 2013).

Ewbank, Ann Dutton, email message to author, November 28, 2010.

More about Act4SL

Act4SL began in 2009 when Dr. Christie Kaaland, a school library program director for Antioch University in Seattle, Washington; Alice Yucht, a retired New Jersey school librarian and author, speaker, and school library consultant; Deb Logan, a school librarian and active school library advocate in Ohio; and Deb Kachel, a former Pennsylvania school librarian and current online instructor for the Mansfield University (Pennsylvania) School Library & Information Technologies program, began to see school library job losses across the U.S. According to Deb Kachel,

At the time, we knew that NCLB (No Child Left Behind federal legislation) was ending and that Congress would be examining new language to reauthorize ESEA (the federal Elementary and Secondary Education Act), replacing NCLB. This along with two other key factors played into the birth of Act4SL: 1) federal legislation could have a huge impact on state legislatures in the regulations for school librarian positions and programs, and 2) the model established by the Spokane Moms grassroots advocacy worked. [Author's note: See Chapter 8 of this book for more information on the "Spokane Moms" in reading three, "Reaching Out to Parents."]

As a result, Act for School Libraries and Act for Student Learning was born. Our concept was to provide librarians with the tools and talking points to contact their federal legislators. Thus, the foldable wallet card (http://act4sl.wikispaces.com/Action+Card) was developed with a video on how to contact a legislator (http://www.youtube.com/watch?v=9P2nFWoMrJ8).

Since the Congress has still not reauthorized ESEA, we continue working on the initiative. Our email list of over 250 key librarians across the nation helps us get the word out quickly when communication with members of Congress is needed. (Kachel, Debra, email message to author, March 9, 2012)

In some districts, school library positions are still being eliminated, and Congress has not acted. Deb Kachel likes to say, however, "Advocacy is a marriage, not a kiss. You are in it for the long haul, and you have to work hard at it. However, the results are all worth it!" (Kachel, Debra, email message to author, March 9, 2012).

Knowledge Quest Themed Issue: The Solo Librarian

Solo Librarians and Intellectual Freedom: Perspectives from the Field

By Helen R. Adams

Originally published as an article in *Knowledge Quest* 40 no. 2 (2011): 30–35. Reprinted with permission from the American Association of School Librarians, a division of the American Library Association.

As schools across the country face increasing fiscal restraints, school library professional positions are being eliminated at an alarming rate. As a result, many school librarians are becoming the only certified library professional in a district, serving multiple schools and grade levels. Suddenly, each is a solo librarian.

If you are the sole school librarian in a school district, where does intellectual freedom rank in your list of priorities? With so many responsibilities, how will you protect and advocate for students' First Amendment rights and privacy of their library usage records when YOU cannot be in all school libraries all the time? What can *one person* accomplish?

Three K–12 librarians—Marcia, Elaine, and Cheryl—all working in rural communities in the Midwest were queried by the author on the facets of intellectual freedom on which they focus. Although their priorities vary, their enthusiasm and passion for students' access to school library resources is evident.

Marcia's Intellectual Freedom Priorities

As a solo school librarian responsible for school libraries in two buildings, Marcia focuses on student privacy, collection development, and assistant training and expectations. She shares, "In a smaller educational community, rumors travel quickly. I guarantee students' confidentiality about the materials they check out. Additionally the kids feel free to ask me for information about anything and trust that I won't ask why they want to know and won't share their inquiry with others" (Marcia 2011).

Marcia spends considerable effort on collection development and is aware of the potential for concern about books perceived by some as including controversial topics. In her experience, "Small communities can pose challenges that can quickly become causes 'for the good of the children.' One person or a group of adults should not make choices for what all students in the community can read or research" (Marcia 2011).

Marcia depends on library assistants to manage two school libraries in her absence. From her perspective, "Library programs often require using paid or volunteer assistants. Anyone that works in these programs must be adequately trained not in just library maintenance jobs such as checking out or shelving, but in the fundamental beliefs of intellectual freedom and privacy. It must then be conveyed that these translate into expectations that hold true for *every* student or adult patron" (Marcia 2011).

Elaine's Perspective on Intellectual Freedom

Elaine places a high priority on selection of resources, especially those that provide students with diverse viewpoints. "In rural districts with a particularly homogeneous population," she states, "students need more information about the world beyond the county line or State Fair, and to know they have choices and options regardless of their situation or circumstance. We do not have a lot of cultural diversity among our student population, so I think it is essential that students have access to more than stories and magazines about farmers and small towns. I make it a point to include fiction from a variety of perspectives, including stories about inner-city urban students and people from other countries. I talk book titles like *Parvana's Journey, Absolutely True Diary of a Part-Time Indian,* and quality fiction from the perspective of African American, Hispanic, and Asian American characters or writers. I also include *The Economist* and *Foreign Policy* magazine on the rack with *Seventeen* and *Thrasher*" (Elaine 2011).

Elaine works in three different schools each with its own challenges. She explains, "When I came to the district, I found *And Tango Makes Three* hidden in a book closet. The elementary library associate [aide] said the former librarian was concerned about the themes expressed in the book. I put it on the shelf and said, 'Let's see what happens.' So far, nothing has come of it despite the book being prominently featured in many challenges statewide. At the middle school, I battle with an associate who hides books in her desk rather than put them on the shelves. At the high school, I have been aggressively weeding the entire collection, particularly all the books that have been 'donated' by people in the community and that a kid wouldn't touch with a ten-foot pole" (Elaine 2011).

In many schools, excessive filtering beyond the requirements of the Children's Internet Protection Act (CIPA) blocks much constitutionally protected online content for students. Elaine says, "I fight a constant battle with the technology coordinator and the filtering system over access. Students cannot get information on Babe Ruth, and teachers cannot contact anyone in the Essex Community School District because the filter has targeted the words 'babe' and 'sex' as automatic blocks. Related to this are social media. I recognize that Facebook and Twitter are huge time-wasters for many students, but they are a fact of life. We ought to be advocating for appropriate use and best practices for protecting user privacy, but I cannot demonstrate the value of social media because all of it is filtered. YouTube access is also blocked, despite there being a vast amount of legitimate educational material that our teachers would like to use. I spend a lot of time teaching them [teachers] how to download videos to MP4 files at home to play on their [classroom] computers later" (Elaine 2011).

Cheryl's Choices

Cheryl works in a single K–12 facility with four-year-old pre-kindergarten students on one side of the school library and seventeen- and eighteen-year-old seniors on the other, but her intellectual freedom priorities do not differ substantially from those of Marcia or Elaine. She is focusing her efforts on collection development and the need to update library policies. She states, "In a small rural community, I know that exposing our readers to a vast variety of reading materials, genres, and topics is extremely important, and I am working on adding even more variety to the fiction collections for the middle and high school readers. Since many of our students are not exposed to different lifestyles and choices, I am taking on that responsibility of providing richer reading experiences. I ask for suggestions from students, and I encourage every teacher to request topics and materials to accompany their curriculum. As their teaching changes, I want the collections in the library to accommodate student needs" (Cheryl 2011).

One means of protecting students' intellectual freedom is through formally approved policies in such areas as materials selection, reconsideration of a library resource, circulation of resources, confidentiality of library records, interlibrary loan, and Internet use. "Our current library policies," Cheryl declares, "need updating and clarification, and this is one area I plan to tackle this fall. If books are challenged, we need to be ready and have everybody (administration, school board, and library staff) in agreement about the [reconsideration] procedure. Being proactive will assure that any challenges will be handled fairly, respectfully, and in a timely manner" (Cheryl 2011).

The intellectual freedom issues that Marcia, Elaine, and Cheryl face are common to all librarians, but the responsibility seems even greater for the solo school librarian. The protection of students' First Amendment right to access information and the confidentiality of their library use records rest with one person. Yet in practice, a library assistant or volunteer, who may not have sufficient knowledge, may be making decisions on how these critical rights are accorded. As Marcia pointed out, all school library workers must be educated to understand intellectual freedom principles and legal requirements.

Setting Priorities

Marcia, Elaine, and Cheryl highlighted their priority areas, but there are other components of students' intellectual freedom to consider. School librarians are champions of providing equitable access to library resources and services to *all students* including those with physical and learning disabilities. School library professionals welcome and provide resources and encouragement for English Language Learners and find ways to support the learning of homeless children and young adults. As teachers, school librarians educate students to "Respect the principles of intellectual freedom," a student responsibility within Standard 3 of AASL's *Standards for the 21st-Century Learner* (AASL 2007). Through the school librarian's proactive advocacy efforts, principals, teachers, and parents may begin to understand the various facets of intellectual freedom and support students' rights.

Intellectual Freedom Resources for the Solo Librarian

ALA Office for Intellectual Freedom (OIF)

The ALA OIF provides assistance for school librarians facing challenges, local filtering issues, and privacy concerns. ALA/AASL membership *is not required* for assistance.

Phone: 800-545-2433, Ext. 4220 Hours: 8:30 a.m. to 4:30 p.m., Central Time, Monday-Friday
Email: oil@ala.org

ALA Office for Intellectual Freedom website www.ala.org/oif

The OIF website includes a wide range of resources on such issues as challenges in schools, CIPA and Internet filtering, and privacy in libraries. Banned Books Week information and toolkits such as the Gay, Lesbian, Bisexual, and Transgender Toolkit are available. Visitors can also

A solo librarian has many competing interests, and priorities must be established in all areas of practice. Elaine notes, "As the lone teacher-librarian, I have to pick my battles" (Elaine 2011). Which is more important for protecting students' rights to access materials in school libraries—working toward a board-approved selection and reconsideration policy or advocating against over-zealous filtering beyond CIPA's requirements? Should a school library professional begin to educate the principal in one building or work with all administrations as a group? With limited time, what is the most critical need, and which strategy is best? Because every school situation is different, the most practical answer is "it depends." The solution lies in analyzing local circumstances and making the best choice possible.

Finding Allies

One person can accomplish a lot, but recruiting allies increases the likelihood of protecting students' First Amendment right to access library resources. Marcia facilitates her focus on collection development, by making certain teachers and administrators know what resources are being added to the library. She sends targeted email about new materials of interest to specific faculty and hosts "breakfasts" to allow teachers and administrators to peruse the new materials (Marcia 2011).

Elaine uses another approach. "I spend time getting to know people. When I am in a building, I often check with my associate and then make my rounds visiting teachers with whom I have worked in the past and those whom I am trying to convince that working with me on a collaborative assignment would be an excellent idea" (Elaine 2011). While developing collegial relationships, Elaine also has the opportunity to assess which faculty members may become allies in case of a challenge or who may actively support her efforts to lessen the level of filtering.

Marcia works closely with administrators. "I take care to never be a complainer," she says. "If I have a problem, I talk to the administrator involved, lay out the issue, and list my suggestion(s) for dealing with it." As a result, Marcia notes, "If there is a complaint, the principals have always come to me first, even before talking to parents. I can give background information, and the principal feels confident rather than being put on the spot" (Marcia 2011). Marcia's proactive approach is creating strong relationships that are useful if a challenge to a library resource occurs.

sign up for the IFAction news-only e-list, report a challenge, or read the OIF Blog.

ALA Intellectual Freedom Manual. www.ifmanual .org

Complementing the eighth print edition of the ALA *Intellectual Freedom Manual*, this site features a growing collection of resources such as retired school librarian Pat Scales' essay "School Library Media Centers and Intellectual Freedom" and ALA policy statements including the *Library Bill of Rights*, its interpretations, the ALA *Code of Ethics*, and other related documents.

Privacyrevolution.org. privacyrevolution.org

At ALA's one-stop website on privacy, school librarians will find multiple short videos, including the 2011 "Choose Privacy Week" video with a downloadable video study guide www.privacyrevolution.org/images/uploads/VideoLibrarianGuide.pdf, lessons plans for teaching students about privacy, and information about the May 2012 Choose Privacy Week.

What IF? Questions and Answers on Intellectual Freedom. www.education.wisc.edu/ccbc/free dom/whatif/default.asp

Maintained by the Cooperative Children's Book Center at the University of Wisconsin-Madison, "What IF?" is an online question-and-answer service for teachers as well as school and public librarians. Visitors may submit questions confidentially, and staff will answer them by blending principles of intellectual freedom with practical advice. The archive of questions can be sorted by relevancy to classroom, school and public library, self-censorship, and "other" issues.

The three school librarians all experience the need to connect with other school librarians. Marcia is actively involved in her state's school library and technology association and chairs its intellectual freedom special interest group. Elaine uses Twitter to follow the ideas of others, is exploring personal learning networks, and relies on her state's teacher-librarian e-list to exchange thoughts with fellow library professionals. Cheryl, too, has reached out, participating as a reading team member for a state book award and learning about the latest in YA literature.

Taking the First Step

No solo school librarian can focus on all intellectual freedom issues in a single year, but as evidenced by the comments of Marcia, Elaine, and Cheryl, it is clear that solo school librarians

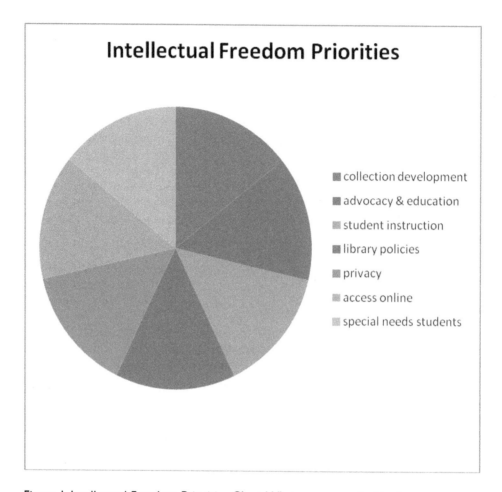

Figure 1. Intellectual Freedom Priorities Chart. What are your priorities?

can take positive and substantive actions to promote students' rights in a school library. To avoid being stuck in a reactive mode, consider Cheryl's strategy of focusing on the most critical issue (in her case policies) for the upcoming school year. Uncertain about the breadth of intellectual freedom issues? Check the Intellectual Freedom Priorities chart Figure 1; and use the resources accompanying this article for quick assistance and for educating yourself about best practices that affect students' use of a school library.

REFERENCES

American Association of School Librarians. *Standards for the 21st-Century Learner,* 2007. http://www.ala.org/ala/mgrps/divs/aasl/guidelinesandstandards/learningstandards/standards.cfm (accessed January 16, 2013).

Cheryl (K–12 librarian). 2011. Personal email correspondence. July 6 and 8.

Elaine (pseudonym for a K–12 librarian) 2011. Personal email correspondence. July 6 and 7.

Marcia (K–12 librarian). 2011. Personal email communication. June 17 and July 7.

Key Ideas Summary

Readings in this chapter concentrate on the future of intellectual freedom in school libraries. Major ideas include:

- Shonda Brisco's map, "A Nation without School Librarians" (http://tinyurl .com/253ehp3) documents the termination of school library positions or the reduction of positions with the remaining school librarian(s) responsible for two or more school libraries.

- Fifteen facets of students' intellectual freedom (listed in the first reading) will be in jeopardy if no full-time school librarian is present to ensure careful selection of library resources, protect students' First Amendment rights to receive information in a school library, and defend students' privacy when borrowing library materials.

- Act for School Libraries and Student Learning (Act4SL) is a grassroots advocacy organization that advocates for federal legislation requiring a full-time certified library in all public K–12 schools.

- As school library positions are eliminated, some school library professionals are finding themselves becoming a "solo librarian," defined as a single school librarian serving all K–12 students in multiple school buildings.

- A major concern of solo librarians is protecting students' First Amendment right to receive information and their privacy because they cannot be present full time in each school library.

- Solo librarians must ensure that support staff are well-trained in library management practices and understand the principles of intellectual freedom and privacy.

- A single librarian serving all K–12 students must set priorities for intellectual freedom responsibilities, including collection development, accessibility to information in all formats (including online), student instruction, library policies, service to students with special needs, privacy and confidentiality of students' library records, and education and advocacy.

- Although one energetic, confident, and knowledgeable person can accomplish a great deal, recruiting allies for support of students' intellectual freedom is an effective strategy.

- Busy administrators appreciate the school librarian who explains a problem, lays out the issues, and suggests solutions.

- With many competing interests and responsibilities, solo librarians must pick their battles and prioritize because they cannot attack all issues simultaneously.

Resource Roundup:
The Future of Intellectual Freedom

- **American Association of School Librarians. 2007.** *Standards for the 21st-Century Learner.* **http://www.ala.org/aasl/guidelinesandstandards/learningstandards/standards**

As noted throughout this book, AASL's *Standards for the 21st-Century Learner* include as one of students' responsibilities to "Respect the principles of intellectual freedom." The future of intellectual freedom depends on librarians to teach students about their responsibility as citizens to locate information with diverse perspectives, evaluate the information, synthesize it, and use it ethically in their formative and adult years. Other complementing resources for school librarians include *Standards for the 21st-Century Learner in Action* and *Empowering Learners: Guidelines for School Library Programs*; all are available from the ALA Store (http://www.alastore.ala.org/).

- **Future Librarians for Intellectual Freedom Blog. http://flifblog.blogspot.com**

Canadian library and information students at the University of Alberta's School of Library and Information Studies have been blogging about intellectual freedom and social responsibility since 2007. The posts provide insights into their thoughts about and reactions to current issues and news in the areas of intellectual freedom and social responsibility.

- **Lankes, David R. 2011.** *Atlas of New Librarianship.* **Chicago: MIT Press.**

Lankes looks at librarianship through a different lens and states that one of the purposes of libraries is to *improve society,* especially by facilitating conversations leading to new knowledge in their communities. In the "Improve Society" section of the book, he posits that librarians are activists, not liberal or conservative, but professionals who seek to improve the overall quality of life. He looks at intellectual freedom as a core value of the profession, but decries the ability of librarians to be unbiased in offering service. The book also explores the issue of social justice as a means of improving society.

- **Valenza, Joyce. 2010. "Manifesto for 21st Century Librarians." October 2010. http://www.voya.com/2010/09/15/tag-team-tech-october-2010/**

Joyce's essay focuses on the full-spectrum skills, knowledge, attitudes, and activities of a 21st-century school librarian. Under the heading "Access, Equity, and Advocacy," she highlights the need for school librarians (in any age) to be aware of continuing equity issues (digital divide and the technology have and have-nots) and access issues (providing resources in the formats required by students with varying disabilities). Joyce's essay is especially worthwhile because of her emphatic support for intellectual freedom beyond concern for book censorship: "You don't stop at 'no.' You fight for the rights of students to have and use the tools they need. This is an equity issue. Access to the new tools in an intellectual freedom issue."

Discussion Questions

- Considering that some districts are eliminating professionally trained school librarians and replacing them with aides or volunteers, what are *your* concerns for students' intellectual freedom in those circumstances?

- Articulate two actions you (as a teacher, parent, community member, and/or pre-service school librarian) can take to advocate for school libraries and the services of a full-time school librarian with support staff.

- In the second reading, Elaine realistically declares that she has to choose her battles. Although each school district is unique, list your top three intellectual freedom priorities and the first steps you would take as a solo librarian.

- No job is ever totally secure, but there are ways to build support before a crisis occurs. Discuss your perspective on defending students' intellectual freedom and strategies for retaining your position as a school librarian.

- This chapter centers on the future of intellectual freedom in a time of shrinking professional staff and financial resources. In the introduction, the history of intellectual freedom associated with the ALA over the past seventy-five years was described, including the establishing of the Office for Intellectual Freedom, the Freedom to Read Foundation, and the LeRoy C. Merritt Humanitarian Fund. Describe your vision of the prospects for intellectual freedom during the next twenty-five years. What will be the next new big issue(s), or will the same issues of access, privacy, and censorship simply evolve in different resource formats?

Appendix A

Core Intellectual Freedom Documents from the American Library Association

Library Bill of Rights

The American Library Association affirms that all libraries are forums for information and ideas, and that the following basic policies should guide their services.

I. Books and other library resources should be provided for the interest, information, and enlightenment of all people of the community the library serves. Materials should not be excluded because of the origin, background, or views of those contributing to their creation.

II. Libraries should provide materials and information presenting all points of view on current and historical issues. Materials should not be proscribed or removed because of partisan or doctrinal disapproval.

III. Libraries should challenge censorship in the fulfillment of their responsibility to provide information and enlightenment.

IV. Libraries should cooperate with all persons and groups concerned with resisting abridgment of free expression and free access to ideas.

V. A person's right to use a library should not be denied or abridged because of origin, age, background, or views.

VI. Libraries which make exhibit spaces and meeting rooms available to the public they serve should make such facilities available on an equitable basis, regardless of the beliefs or affiliations of individuals or groups requesting their use.

Adopted June 19, 1939, by the ALA Council; amended June 18, 1948; February 2, 1961; June 27, 1967; and January 23, 1980; inclusion of "age" was reaffirmed January 23, 1996.

Code of Ethics of the American Library Association

As members of the American Library Association, we recognize the importance of codifying and making known to the profession and to the general public the ethical principles that guide the work of librarians, other professionals providing information services, library trustees and library staffs.

Ethical dilemmas occur when values are in conflict. The American Library Association Code of Ethics states the values to which we are committed, and embodies the ethical responsibilities of the profession in this changing information environment.

We significantly influence or control the selection, organization, preservation, and dissemination of information. In a political system grounded in an informed citizenry, we are members of a profession explicitly committed to intellectual freedom and the freedom of access to information. We have a special obligation to ensure the free flow of information and ideas to present and future generations.

The principles of this Code are expressed in broad statements to guide ethical decision making. These statements provide a framework; they cannot and do not dictate conduct to cover particular situations.

I.   We provide the highest level of service to all library users through appropriate and usefully organized resources; equitable service policies; equitable access; and accurate, unbiased, and courteous responses to all requests.

II.   We uphold the principles of intellectual freedom and resist all efforts to censor library resources.

III. We protect each library user's right to privacy and confidentiality with respect to information sought or received and resources consulted, borrowed, acquired or transmitted.

IV.   We respect intellectual property rights and advocate balance between the interests of information users and rights holders.

V.   We treat co-workers and other colleagues with respect, fairness, and good faith, and advocate conditions of employment that safeguard the rights and welfare of all employees of our institutions.

VI.   We do not advance private interests at the expense of library users, colleagues, or our employing institutions.

VII. We distinguish between our personal convictions and professional duties and do not allow our personal beliefs to interfere with fair representation of the aims of our institutions or the provision of access to their information resources.

VIII. We strive for excellence in the profession by maintaining and enhancing our own knowledge and skills, by encouraging the professional development of co-workers, and by fostering the aspirations of potential members of the profession.

Adopted at the 1939 Midwinter Meeting by the ALA Council; amended June 30, 1981; June 28, 1995; and January 22, 2008.

Reprinted with permission from the Office for Intellectual Freedom, the American Library Association.

Appendix B

Pro–First Amendment
and Privacy Organizations

This list of sixteen organizations has two purposes: 1) it provides descriptions and contact information for selected advocacy groups that provide assistance with intellectual freedom and privacy threats; and 2) it offers references as a starting point to learn about the most current intellectual freedom and privacy issues nationally.

American Library Association Office of Intellectual Freedom (OIF)
www.ala.org/offices/oif
800-545-2433, ext. 4220 or 312-280-4220
Email: oif@ala.org

The ALA OIF staff provide assistance with challenges to library and classroom materials, filtering issues, and library privacy matters. Report a challenge to OIF using the official online form at http://www.ala.org/advocacy/sites/ala.org.advocacy/files/content/banned/challengeslibrary materials/challengereporting/challengedatabaseform_2003.pdf. Staff field questions and provide support by telephone and email. Individuals seeking assistance need not be members of the ALA or AASL. The OIF website includes extensive information on all aspects of intellectual freedom and privacy. The companion website for the 8th edition of the *Intellectual Freedom Manual* (http://ifmanual.org) is easy to navigate and can be used to quickly locate *Library Bill of Rights* interpretations and additional resources. ALA's privacy-related website is http://privacy recolution.org/.

American Booksellers Foundation for Freedom of Expression (ABFFE)
www.abffe.com
24 hour hotline: 212-587-4025
To report book censorship: info@abffe.org

ABFFE represents booksellers in the fight against censorship. Founded in 1990 by the American Booksellers Association, the Foundation promotes freedom of expression through statements to the media on free speech issues and controversies, education of the public, and participation in First Amendment legal challenges. ABFFE and the National Coalition Against Censorship together sponsor the "Kids' Right to Read Project" that supports persons fighting book censorship by providing advice, advocacy, and a "clearinghouse" for documenting book censorships.

American Civil Liberties Union (ACLU)
www.aclu.org
212-549-2500

The ACLU is a fierce civil rights advocacy organization and an influential ally for school librarians. The organization opposes censorship of all types and most recently has been involved in successful legal challenges to the Internet filtering practices of a number of school districts. Online privacy is another of its issues. In addition to the national umbrella organization, the ACLU has affiliates in fifty states, where staff and volunteers monitor the lawmaking of legislatures and take legal action as appropriate. School librarians can contact their state's ACLU affiliate for direct assistance via the state affiliates list at http://www.aclu.org/affiliates/.

Association of American Publishers (AAP)
publishers.org
Washington, DC: 202-347-3375
New York City: 212-255-0200

The AAP is the trade association for book publishers, and its Freedom to Read Committee monitors First Amendment free speech issues. The Committee works as a partner with other organizations such as the ALA to promote intellectual freedom. Its interests coincide with school librarians and teachers in the areas of Internet censorship, challenges to books, and privacy of library patrons. It frequently is a plaintiff or files "friend of the court" documents in cases involving First Amendment free speech rights.

Center for Democracy and Technology (CDT)
www.cdt.org

CDT is a public policy non-profit organization of interest to school librarians because of its watchdog attitude, advocacy, and legal activities to ensure that the Internet remains free and accessible to users. The staff work on issues related to national security and government surveillance, Internet neutrality, minors' safety online, and digital copyright. The organization hosts a blog covering comments on its current issues, publishes the bi-monthly newsletter "Tech Policy," and emails in-depth policy analyses and announcements to subscribers.

Comic Book Legal Defense Fund (CBLDF)
cbldf.org
212-679-7151

The purpose of the CBLDF is to support creators of comic books and graphic novels, retailers, and librarians in legal battles or formal challenges stemming from these works. This advocacy group promotes graphic novels as legitimate literary works that are worthy of shelf-space in school libraries. Membership dues support litigation as well as the Kids' Rights to Read Project and Banned Books Week activities. The "Resources" section of the CBLDF website contains links to case files of CBLDF legal battles.

Electronic Frontier Foundation (EFF)
www.eff.org
San Francisco: 415-396-9333
Washington, DC: 202-797-9009
Email: action@eff.org

Founded in 1990, the EFF defends Americans' digital rights and carries out legal battles against the policies of government agencies and corporations on issues within the broad categories of First Amendment free speech, privacy, fair use of intellectual property, and consumer rights. EFF mobilizes members to contact legislators and is involved in multiple projects listed on its website. For example, its "Teaching Copyright" project and curriculum helps teachers and students learn about copyright law and fair use of materials online. Its "Deeplinks Blog" provides frequent updates on the issues and court cases in which the EFF is involved.

Electronic Privacy Information Center (EPIC)
epic.org
202-483-114

Established in 1992, EPIC is an organization with diverse issues under the umbrella of civil liberties, privacy, and free speech. Current privacy issues include but are not limited to search engine privacy, Facebook facial recognition technology, "locational privacy" (cell phone and GPS tracking), children's online privacy, and the USA PATRIOT Act. The organization publishes a newsletter, the "Epic Alert" (http://epic.org/alert/).

Free Expression Network (FEN)
www.freeexpression.org

The FEN is a project of the National Coalition Against Censorship and is comprised of more than thirty pro-First Amendment free expression organizations, including many that appear in this list. FEN's mission is to defend First Amendment free expression and resist censorship. FEN's website includes an "archive" of recent news about its advocacy, First Amendment free speech litigation, and topics within its scope of interest. Another interesting facet of the site is a description of each member organization, its services, and main area of interest.

Freedom to Read Foundation (FTRF)
www.ftrf.org
800-545-2433, ext. 4226
Email: ftrf@ala.org

Although an independent organization, the FTRF backs up ALA's support for free expression guaranteed by the First Amendment with direct participation in litigation and/or financial grants to litigants. It has participated in legal battles that affected access to school library materials for students including *Board of Education, Island Trees Union Free School District v. Pico* (1982), *Counts v. Cedarville School District* (2003), and the *ACLU of Florida v. Miami Dade School District* (2009). Member-based, its dues plus donations support its legal advocacy.

International Reading Association (IRA)
www.reading.org
800-336-7323 or 302-731-1600

The IRA is a global professional organization whose members (individual and institutional) promote reading, literacy, and access to books, newspapers, and magazines. Of particular importance to school librarians is the association's "Providing Books and Other Print Materials for Classroom and School Libraries" position statement (approved in 1999 and revised in 2010) supporting the funding of school libraries. The full text of the statement is available as a PDF at http://www.reading.org/General/AboutIRA/PositionStatements/LibrariesPosition.aspx .

Media Coalition
www.mediacoalition.org
212-587-4025

The Coalition is a group of eight organizations (including the American Booksellers Foundation for Free Expression, the Association of American Publishers, the Comic Book Defense Fund, the Freedom to Read Foundation, the Entertainment Merchants Association, the Entertainment Software Association, the Motion Picture Association of America, and the Recording Industry Association of America) that have banded together to protect the free expression and commercial sale of all forms of media: everything from books to films to audio recording to video games. In addition, the Coalition supports the First Amendment right to access all forms of media, regardless of point of view. The group tracks state and federal legislation relating to media engaging in litigation to protect First Amendment free expression and access to that expression. Of particular interest is the lengthy list and descriptions of current and past litigation in which the Media Coalition has been involved. It posts annual reports of its activities.

National Coalition Against Censorship (NCAC)
www.ncac.org
212-807-6222
To report book censorship: ncac@ncac.org

The NCAC is a coalition of more than fifty organizations dedicated to protecting and promoting free speech (a.k.a. free expression). Organization members include the International Reading Association, the National Council of Teachers of English, the National Council for the Social Studies, the ACLU, the PEN American Center, and American Association of Publishers (to name a few).

Its website includes the "Book Censorship Toolkit" for students, parents, and teachers (http://www.ncac.org/literature/bookcensorshiptoolkit.cfm) and a form to report censorship including book challenges in schools (http://ncac.org/Report-Censorship-Form). Other website resources include a "First Amendment in Schools Toolkit" (http://www.ncac.org/First-Amendment-in-Schools-Teachers); "The File Room," an interactive online art project; and the Free Expression Policy Project (http://www.ncac.org/free_expression_policy_project), an exhaustive online source of information on censorship of youth, the Internet, and other free speech topics. NCAC operates the Youth Free Expression Project (http://ncac.org/yfep) to advocate for the free speech rights of minors and to educate them about censorship. The site also includes a timely blog titled "Blogging Censorship."

National Council of Teachers of English (NCTE)

www.ncte.org

Report a challenge: 800-369-62283, extension 3634

The NCTE is a professional association for K–12 and college language arts teachers. Because fewer language arts anthologies are used in K–12 schools, literary works (including contemporary novels) included on required or optional reading lists are often challenged. Of interest to school librarians and English/language arts teachers, its "Anti-Censorship Center" at http://www.ncte .org/action/anti-censorship provides advice and support for teachers facing challenges to works of literature, films, plays, or teaching strategies. Center resources include the "Students' Right to Read" statement and "Rationale for Teaching Challenged Books." The site also includes an on-line form to report a censorship challenge at https://secure.ncte.org/forms/reportcensorship.

PEN American Center

www.pen.org

PEN American Center is the U.S. wing of PEN International, a global literary and human rights organization dedicated to protecting authors and working against censorship. Its membership is comprised of professional authors. The organization operates many programs aimed at free expression, including the "Freedom to Write," assisting persecuted or imprisoned authors; the "Prison Writing Program," providing mentors and encouragement to inmates to express themselves; and the "Open Book" Program, encouraging authorship of multi-cultural American literature. The organization publishes a free newsletter that is distributed by email list.

People for the American Way (PFAW)

www.pfaw.org

PFAW is a membership-based organization formed in 1981 to defend and advocate for the continuation of tolerance, pluralism, and civil liberties (including freedom of expression). The organization is concerned with such issues as freedom of religion, the right to vote, legal justice, and equality. The site includes three blogs: "People for Blog," "Right Wing Watch Blog" (news about the religious right), and "Young People For Blog."

REFERENCES

American Booksellers Foundation for Freedom of Expression. "About ABFFE." http://www .abffe.org/?page=AboutUs (accessed January 18, 2013).

American Booksellers Foundation for Freedom of Expression. "About the Kids Right to Read Project." http://www.abffe.org/?page=KRRP (accessed January 18, 2013).

American Library Association. Office for Intellectual Freedom. "Notable First Amendment Court Cases." http://www.ala.org/offices/oif/firstamendment/courtcases/courtcases (accessed January 18, 2013).

Association of American Publishers. "Freedom to Read Committee." http://publishers.org/ committees/5/ (accessed January 18, 2013).

Center for Democracy and Technology. "About CDT." https://www.cdt.org/about (accessed January 18, 2013).

Comic Book Defense League Fund. "Membership." http://cbldf.org/contribute/membership (accessed February 23, 2013).

Electronic Freedom Foundation. "About EFF." https://www.eff.org/about (accessed January 18, 2013).

Electronic Privacy Information Center. "About EPIC." http://epic.org/epic/about.html (accessed January 18, 2013).

Free Expression Network. "Background." http://www.freeexpression.org/?page_id=6 (accessed January 18, 2013).

Free Expression Network. "People for the American Way (PFAW)." http://www.freeexpression.org/?p=68 (accessed January 18, 2013).

International Reading Association. "About IRA." http://www.reading.org/General/AboutIRA.aspx (accessed January 18, 2013).

Media Coalition. "About." http://72.52.64.193/About (accessed June 30, 2012) [no longer available].

National Coalition Against Censorship. "Who We Are." http://www.ncac.org/who-we-are (accessed January 18, 2013).

National Council of Teachers of English. "Anti-Censorship Center." http://www.ncte.org/action/anti-censorship (accessed January 18, 2013).

PEN American Center. "About PEN." http://www.pen.org/about (accessed January 18, 2013).

People for the American Way. "Issues." http://www.pfaw.org/issues (accessed January 18, 2013).

Index

About the Author

HELEN R. ADAMS, a former school librarian and technology coordinator in Wisconsin, is an online instructor in the School Library and Information Technologies Program at Mansfield University, Mansfield, PA. She is a regular columnist for *School Library Monthly*, and her published works include *Ensuring Intellectual Freedom and Access to Information in the School Library Media Program* (Libraries Unlimited 2008), *Privacy in the 21st Century: Issues for Public, School, and Academic Libraries* (co-author, Libraries Unlimited 2005), and a contributor to *The Many Faces in School Library Leadership* (Libraries Unlimited 2010). She holds a Master's Degree in Library Science from Western Michigan University and a Master's Degree in Media Technology from the University of Wisconsin-Stout. A dedicated intellectual freedom and privacy advocate, she is a trustee of the Freedom to Read Foundation and has served on numerous American Library Association and American Association of School Librarians committees that work to protect and promote First Amendment speech in libraries. A dedicated intellectual freedom and privacy advocate, she is a trustee of the Freedom to Read Foundation and has served on numerous American Library Association and American Association of School Librarians committees that work to protect and promote First Amendment speech in libraries.

CPSIA information can be obtained
at www.ICGtesting.com
Printed in the USA
BVHW012018120722
641613BV00005B/3